Suicide Tourism

Suicide Tourism

DANIEL SPERLING

OXFORD
UNIVERSITY PRESS

OXFORD
UNIVERSITY PRESS

Great Clarendon Street, Oxford, OX2 6DP,
United Kingdom

Oxford University Press is a department of the University of Oxford.
It furthers the University's objective of excellence in research, scholarship,
and education by publishing worldwide. Oxford is a registered trade mark of
Oxford University Press in the UK and in certain other countries

© Daniel Sperling 2019

The moral rights of the author have been asserted

First Edition published in 2019

Impression: 1

Published in the United States of America by Oxford University Press
198 Madison Avenue, New York, NY 10016, United States of America

British Library Cataloguing in Publication Data
Data available

Library of Congress Control Number: 2019941571

ISBN 978-0-19-882545-6

Printed and bound by
CPI Group (UK) Ltd, Croydon, CR0 4YY

To Aryeh, Galia, Noam, and Elad: The light and hope in my life

Acknowledgements

The understanding and conceptualization of the main issues presented in this book took more than 4 years and was supported by the help of many people and organizations to whom and to which I owe many thanks and much appreciation. My initial travel to Switzerland and the research I did there was supported by the Nordmann Fellowship. While in Switzerland I had the opportunity to present my work in progress and reflect on my arguments with the help of many colleagues—most of whom I also interviewed, but other people at the Universities of Fribourg, Lucern, Zurich, Geneva, and many others as well. Other institutions that provided the means to work on parts of my research to which I am also grateful are MOFET Institute, Minerva Center for Interdisciplinary Studies of the End of Life, and Yezreel Valley Academic College.

I would like to acknowledge the help and information I received from all of my interviewees listed in this book and for the academic support which facilitated parts of my research in Europe received especially from Markus Zimmermann, Margot Braizer, Charles Foster, Richard Huxtable, and Jonathan Ives. In addition, I have had extensive communication with various scholars and colleagues on my project whom I would like to thank. These include Raphael Cohen-Almagor, Roberto Andorno, Joachim Cohen, Luc Deliens, Mirko D. Garasic, Simona Giordano, David A. Jones, Shai Lavi, Johan Legemaate, Alexandra Mullock, Agnes van der Heide, Mary Shariff, Silke Schicktanz, and Gila Yakov.

Finally, and as always, I am indebted mostly to my family which shows endless love and support and provided time and emotional and cognitive availability to deal with the issues raised in this book. Special thanks are reserved to my partner Aryeh who not only encouraged me to pursue the writing of this book in times of crisis and personal difficulties but also helped to facilitate this; to my beloved parents, Rina and Adrian, for whom I wish good ageing and prolonged quality of life; and to my beloved children Galia, Noam, and Elad who are the continual light in my life.

Contents

Introduction

What would it take for a child to accompany a terminally ill parent to another country to receive aid in dying? What would it mean for the partner of a motor neurone disease sufferer to travel with them to Dignitas? How would a couple suffering from chronic illnesses explain their decision to end their life to their children?

This book examines the phenomenon of 'suicide tourism'. It is about strong wishes to die and people who are ready to leave their home country in order to receive aid in dying. For this final journey they may pay great sums of money and inadvertently expose their loved ones to risk of criminal charges in order to die legally in unfamiliar surroundings.

There has been a noticeable rise in the number of people seeking aid in dying in recent years, including through suicide tourism. A search on YouTube reveals that there are dozens of documentary films on suicide tourism and on good death—some of which have already attracted more than a million views each. Here and there, you read news stories of more or less familiar people taking the plane, train, or car to meet a stranger who will be with them during their last precious moments. The travel for assisted suicide has become a global practice involving citizens of many Western democracies who, due to local laws prohibiting assisted suicide, are unable to pursue their perhaps most intimate and meaningful goal in their homeland.

The current state of affairs in international politics—with its relatively new trend towards globalization—has strengthened the connection between biomedical ethics and political philosophy, international relations, and global justice. Among some of the most challenging and controversial cases are those concerning euthanasia and assisted suicide.[1] Academic papers, as well as general media coverage, have

---

[1] Dan W. Brock, 'Voluntary active euthanasia' (2002) 22 *The Hastings Center Report* 10–22; Kumar Amarasekara and Mirko Bagaric, 'Moving from Voluntary Euthanasia to Nonvoluntary Euthanasia: Equality and Compassion' (2004) 17 *Ratio Juris* 398–423; H.C. Muller-Busch, F.S. Oduncu, S. Woskanjan, and E. Klaschik, 'Attitudes on Euthanasia, Physician-Assisted Suicide

Suicide Tourism. First Edition. Daniel Sperling. © Daniel Sperling 2019. Published 2019 by Oxford University Press.

followed the topic extensively but, somehow, some of the problems related to this debate have been either given insufficient consideration or left to one side altogether.

In this book, I wanted to bring forward a comprehensive analysis that would engage directly with the recent practice of suicide tourism at times also called 'death tourism'. The analysis is based on intensive and extended research conducted between 2013 and 2018. It includes theoretical discussion of suicide tourism from varied contexts and disciplinary perspectives as well as an exploration of the major findings of my visits and in-depth interviews in Europe. This introduction provides the initial framework necessary for the understanding of this recent trend. Part I begins with an overview of the current state of affairs in the handful of countries that allow assisted suicide and contains a discussion of the recent trends and developments. It then goes on to explain in more detail the specific role that Switzerland—the country to which most people seeking assisted suicide travel to die, when unable to pursue their goal in their country of residence—has within that reality. The investigation gradually moves on to the core problem related to the globalized era in which we live: the freedom of movement that the international community grants to most people between most countries these days (at least theoretically), and its harsh clash with geographically contingent policies and laws. Part I continues with an analysis of the legality of suicide tourism before Part II opens with a consideration of its moral standing. This analysis is complemented with a discussion of the political-philosophical justifications for state intervention in the practice of suicide tourism. Part III sets out the major empirical findings obtained from, mostly, forty-five interviews conducted across Switzerland, France, Germany, the UK, Italy, and Israel to explore more closely the attitudes towards such practices and their effect on public policy and law, especially within countries of origin. By highlighting these considerations and debates, the book will provide an original basis—both useful and necessary—for further discussion on this developing issue.[2]

---

and Terminal Sedation: A Survey of the Members of the German Association for Palliative Medicine' (2004) 7 *Medicine, Health Care and Philosophy* 333.

---

[2] I am aware that global justice and freedom of movement carry with them many important debates that require in-depth analysis. With this book, I do not expect to find a satisfactory answer for all cases, but I hope at least to contribute to shaping a more coherent account of the

What is suicide tourism?

There are quite a few, relatively recent, forms of tourism that have occurred mainly as a result of the economic disparities between the original and the hosting country or because of their differing respective legal systems.[3] Among the more established (though not equally accepted in moral and legal terms) forms—'medical tourism',[4] 'sex tourism',[5] 'abortion tourism',[6] and 'reproductive tourism'[7]—there is the more gloomy form of 'death tourism',[8] [9] which encompasses

---

application of liberal values. For further analysis on the issue, see, for example, Rainer Bauböck, 'Global Justice: Freedom of Movement and Democratic Citizenship' (2009) 50(1) *European Journal of Sociology* 1.

---

[3] I do not want to oversimplify the debate by claiming that all these forms of tourism deserve the same kind of treatment: it is obvious that travelling abroad for the sexual exploitation of children is clearly wrong and can be condemned without much debate. However, it must be noted that the dynamics behind such a 'market' are similar in many respects to other forms of tourism considered here. The interconnection between globalization, bodies, the economic gap between regions, and freedom of movement are central issues in 'sex tourism' too, and for that reason it is included in the list of modern forms of tourism.

[4] Glenn Cohen presents a recent investigation of the main problems related to medical tourism that are equally applicable to this work. Glenn I. Cohen, *Patients with Passports: Medical Tourism, Law and Ethics* (Oxford University Press, 2015).

[5] Nancy Wonders and Raymond Michalowski provide an interesting parallel analysis of 'sex tourism', its definition, and its impact in two very distinct contexts. Nancy Wonders and Raymond Michalowski, 'Bodies, Borders, and Sex Tourism in a Globalized World: A Tale of Two Cities—Amsterdam and Havana' (November 2001) 48(4) *Social Problems* 545–71.

[6] Seth F. Kreimer, ' "But Whoever Treasures Freedom ...".': The Right to Travel and Extraterritorial Abortions' (1993) 91(5) *Michigan L. Rev.* 907–38.

[7] Reproductive tourism is probably the one that has more directly considered issues of global justice in relation to its existence and justification. This work can certainly benefit from some of the progress that the discussion has made in the past few years. See among others: Anne Donchin, 'Reproductive Tourism and the Quest for Global Gender Justice' (2010) 24(7) *Bioethics* 323–32; Guido Pennings, 'Reproductive Tourism as Moral Pluralism in Motion' (2002) 28(6) *JME* 337; Lauren Jade Martin, *Reproductive Tourism in the United States: Creating Family in the Mother Country* (Routledge, 2014).

[8] It should be noted that, of all the terms created to describe this phenomenon, 'death tourism' is the one that—although extremely accurate—suffers the most from a 'definition overlap' with other areas of research, particularly that concerning the kind of tourism related to visiting macabre places such as Auschwitz and Hiroshima. See for example: Brigitte Sion, *Death Tourism: Disaster Sites as Recreational Landscape* (Seagull Books, 2013).

[9] As a definitive terminology has not been agreed upon, other definitions are possible and commonly in use. For example, in his insightful article, Richard Huxtable opted for the definition 'suicide tourism'. This book follows this definition and discusses it in more detail in the next few chapters. Clearly each definition carries with it some unique undertones, but for reason of space they cannot all be included here. Most notably, however, Huxtable's work is interesting for taking into account the role of the only individuals who might pay some personal price in cases of 'death tourism', namely those accompanying the person into the country. Richard Huxtable, 'The Suicide Tourist Trap: Compromise Across Boundaries' (2009) 6 *Journal of Bioethical Inquiry* 327 (hereafter: 'Huxtable, Suicide Tourism').

'dark tourism', referring to the act of visiting sites associated with death.[10]

Since ancient times people have travelled to die outside their country. The idea of the pilgrim or Hajj meeting their end or preparing for their death while engaging in sacred journeys is well documented.[11] Modernity has brought about other scenarios, in which people travel to another country to commit suicide. One such example involves people who live outside the city of New York but who travel to the city to make use of, for example, the George Washington Bridge or Empire State Building to commit suicide.[12] To use Richard Huxtable's definition more generally, suicide tourism involves 'travel by a suicidal individual from one jurisdiction to another, in which s/he will (or is expected to) be assisted in their suicide by some other person/s'.[13]

Miller and Gonzalez offer four characteristics for death tourism more generally that explain why people seek such services. These characteristics also apply to suicide tourism: (1) the procedures may be illegal in their home countries;[14] (2) they wish to take care of unfinished business in their personal life or the business of ending their lives; (3) they seek an ultimate solution—not a medical fix to prolong or improve the quality of life; or (4) they seek the ideal of the 'death with dignity', where the deathbed is a notion of a death free from pain and suffering.[15]

---

[10] Julie S. Tinson, Michael A.J. Saren, and Bridget E. Roth, 'Exploring the Role of Dark Tourism in the Creation of National Identity of Young Americans' (2015) 31(7-8) *Journal of Marketing Management* 856.

[11] ERASMUS, 'Death and Pilgrimage: The Spectre of Death Has Always Loomed over Sacred Journeys', *The Economist* (25 September 2015) https://www.economist.com/erasmus/2015/09/25/the-spectre-of-death-has-always-loomed-over-sacred-journeys, accessed on 7 June 2018.

[12] Sewell Chan, 'Study Examines "Suicide Tourism" in New York City' (1 November, 2007) https://cityroom.blogs.nytimes.com/2007/11/01/study-examines-suicide-tourism-in-new-york-city/, accessed on 28 May 2018.

[13] Huxtable, Suicide Tourism (n 9) at 328. A complementary definition of 'assisted suicide tourism' refers to helping the suicidal individual to travel from one jurisdiction to another in order for them to be assisted in their suicide.

[14] More generally, travel for services that are illegal in the patient's home country is called 'circumvention tourism' by Glenn Cohen because the person is circumventing the prohibition on accessing that service in her own country. See Glenn Cohen, 'Circumvention Tourism' (2012) 97 *Cornell L. Rev.* 1309.

[15] Shondell Miller and Christopher Gonzalez, 'When Death is the Destination: The Business of Death Tourism Despite Legal and Social Implication' (2013) 7(3) *International Journal of Culture, Tourism, and Hospitality Research* 293 at 295. As for the fourth characteristic, the commercial tagline of the Swiss assisted-suicide organization, Dignitas, is 'Live with Dignity, Die with Dignity'. There also exists a practice of 'reverse suicide tourism' by which physicians travel outside their own country to provide aid in dying in countries where assisted suicide is legal when local doctors are unable to provide such aid. The Netherlands was once such a destination.

Moreover, Suzanne Ost highlights three major psycho-emotional needs that suicide tourism corresponds to. First, it makes the assisted death feel less medicalized and less clinical, thereby making it a less tense affair; second, it may reassure the traveller that her relatives approve of her decision, or at least that they are at peace with it; third, it provides the emotional support that relatives provide to the traveller.[16] It follows that suicide tourism offers a 'better death' for the person involved by having accompanying persons close to the experience of death as much as possible.

As can be deduced from its name, suicide tourism has a unique characteristic: the tourist does not come back home to describe their visit to the country. In fact, the 'tourist' does not come back at all. Indeed, the prevailing response of people who participated in the research for this book is repulsion at its title. Following this line of thought, it is argued that travelling to end one's own life does not constitute a form of medical tourism—or other form of tourism—since that involves selling 'luxury' and wellness along with surgery, promoted not only by the healthcare industry but also by the business development and tourism councils.[17] Another similar argument holds that travelling for assisted suicide is instead the antithesis of medical and health tourism, offering, as it does, physical and psychological escape without any perceptible rewards, thereby departing from the true recreational and leisure aspects of tourism.[18] It also seems that the title 'suicide tourism' was first introduced in the media, referring to stories of individuals who travelled to Switzerland for assisted suicide, and was later incorporated in the academic literature review. So why would we be tempted to define this journey as tourism in the first place?

One can argue that there are a few characteristics that make the travel to another country to receive aid in dying, resulting in an act

---

Rohith Srinivas, 'Exploring the Potential for American Death Tourism' (2009) 91 *Mich St. J. Med & Law* 91 at 104.

[16] Suzanne Ost, 'The De-Medicalization of Assisted Dying: Is a Less Medicalized Model the Way Forward?' (unpublished paper) http://eprints.lancs.ac.uk/34628/1/Ost_Demedicalisation_of_Assisted_Death_FINAL.pdf.

[17] Glenn Cohen, *Patients with Passports* (Oxford University Press, 2015), pp. 315–18.

[18] Gregory Higginbotham, 'Assisted-Suicide Tourism: Is It Tourism? (2011) 6(2) *Turismos: An International Multidisciplinary Journal of Tourism* 177.

of suicide, a form of tourism. First, like other forms of tourism, death tourism or suicide tourism is a practice that is limited in time and usually does not repeat itself. Second, such a practice involves and is shaped by market forces. It creates its own demand and supply and is usually associated with monetary exchange. Third, the travel for aid in dying consists of a dimension of exploitation of some kind; one can argue that modern travel from one place to another is a form of exploitation from an environmental perspective as, with its related carbon emissions, it is a threat and represents an 'unnatural' exploitation of the territory.[19]

There are, however, more specific elements of exploitation in suicide tourism. While in medical tourism the tourist exploits the health resources of another country, and in sex tourism the exploitation of women and children is at stake,[20] in suicide tourism, the visitor exploits the permissive law of country X as a way of escaping pain and suffering or promoting a wish to die,[21] and the companies running the business related to assisted suicide exploit the tourist's need and desire to accomplish such a goal. There may be other reasons for travel; a shortage of participating physicians who could prescribe the lethal drug even in places where assisted suicide is legal[22] or a personal wish to end one's life at a distance can also serve as motivations for suicide tourism.

A necessary but, in and of itself, insufficient condition for suicide tourism to take place is that assisted suicide be legal within the country to which the death tourist travels. Yet, suicide tourism can also take place within a federal country in which only some of the states or provinces include permissive laws on assisted suicide. The American case is a useful example here.

[19] Simon Caney, 'Cosmopolitan Justice, Rights and Global Climate Change' (July 2006) XIX(2) *Canadian Journal of Law and Jurisprudence* 255–78.
[20] Karen D. Breckenridge, 'Justice beyond Borders: A Comparison between Australian and U.S. Child-Sex Tourism' (2004) 13(2) *Pacific Rim Law & Policy Journal* 405–38.
[21] Although, as argued by Richard Huxtable, tourism could occur between two permissive jurisdictions, or between prohibitive jurisdictions. It is anticipated that such scenarios are less likely in the case of suicide tourism. Huxtable, Suicide Tourism (n 9) at 328.
[22] Paula Span, 'Physician Aid in Dying Gains Acceptance in the US', *New York Times* (16 January 2017) https://www.nytimes.com/2017/01/16/health/physician-aid-in-dying.html?smid=pl-share, accessed on 7 June 2018.

Domestic suicide tourism in the United States

As will be discussed in the following chapters, the states in the US that have a legal option for physician-assisted suicide, even if not as internationally oriented as Switzerland, do represent one form of suicide tourism, that is, intra-state suicide tourism. While allowing, in principle, assisted suicide only to residents of the given states, US citizens from other states can relatively easy overcome this restriction. For example, in Oregon, in little more than 6 months a person can become eligible for residency status by leasing a property.[23] In Washington State, the procedure seems even less problematic for those able to afford to buy a property in the state, as this would suffice to ensure residency.[24] In Vermont, the definition of 'Vermont resident' leaves room even for an international audience, as a driving licence[25] could be considered enough to fulfil the requirements of the legislation dealing with the issue.[26]

Indeed, media reports refer to some stories where terminally ill patients travelled from one US state to one of these other states to receive a prescription for a lethal drug. For example, Brittany Maynard, a 29-year-old who suffered from glioblastoma, a deadly form of brain cancer, travelled from San Francisco, California to Oregon to take advantage of Oregon's Death with Dignity Law. Maynard chose her date of death in advance and died on 1 November 2014 at the home she rented in Portland, surrounded by her friends and family.[27] It is believed that her

---

[23] The Oregon Death with Dignity Act, Oregon Revised Statutes, 127.860 §3.10. p.6. Available at: http://public.health.oregon.gov/ProviderPartnerResources/EvaluationResearch/DeathwithDignityAct/Documents/statute.pdf.

[24] Washington State Department of Health, 'Death with Dignity Act: Frequently Asked Questions' https://www.doh.wa.gov/YouandYourFamily/IllnessandDisease/DeathwithDignityAct/FrequentlyAskedQuestions, accessed on 28 November 2018.

[25] It is important to note that the Department of Motor Vehicles in fact states: 'In order to apply for a Vermont Driver's License you will need proof that you are ... a *Visiting Citizen of a Foreign Country with an authorized duration of stay with at least 30 days remaining*' (emphasis added). Available at: http://dmv.vermont.gov/licenses/drivers/newresidents.

[26] No. 39. An act relating to patient choice and control at end of life. Available at: http://www.procon.org/sourcefiles/ACT039_Vermont_Death_with_dignity.pdf.

[27] The Brittany Maynard Fund. Available at: http://thebrittanyfund.org/about/; Ashley Collman and Sophie J. Evans, 'She Was Asleep in Five Minutes and Died in 30: Brittany Maynard's Widower Describes Cancer-Stricken Wife's "Peaceful" Final Minutes after Taking Drug to End Her Life' (*MailOnline*, 14 January 2015) http://www.dailymail.co.uk/news/article-2910111/It-peaceful-experience-Brittany-Maynard-s-widower-describes-cancer-stricken-wife-s-final-moments-taking-drug-end-life.html.

case promoted public debate which led, more recently, to legalization of assisted suicide in California.

There is no doubt that this kind of internal suicide tourism underlines the problems of restricting such a practice to a specific group of people based on their geographical location or residency. After all, if we allow a citizen from the state of New York to move freely, start a business, buy a property, and take vacations in any of the other forty-nine states (enjoying the specific advantages—be it the climate or the taxation system—of that state), why should we place restrictions on one's choice of place to die?

Notably, the fear of intra-state suicide tourism is also present in other contexts, such as Australia and Canada where new assisted-suicide laws have been proposed or passed.[28] This worry might be legitimate only if we assume assisted suicide is a negative and unacceptable practice that should be totally prohibited. However, as many polls have started to suggest, public opinion in Europe, for example, is far from having such a straightforward view of the possibility to autonomously decide how and when to put an end to our lives.[29] On the contrary, and as the next chapter demonstrates, there appears to be a gradual understanding that the medical advances that can keep us alive for longer do not necessarily represent a standard choice to be made under *any* circumstances. The principle of being able to make decisions about one's own life (for good or bad) according to one's preferences is so much in line with the liberal values of Western democracies that the argument for allowing all citizens of the world to be granted that option sits at the very core of the moral arguments for suicide tourism, as elaborated in Chapter 3 and as exercised,

---

[28] After a period in which the Northern Territory allowed the performance of physician-assisted suicide, Tasmania looked at the option for a long time, but eventually in October 2013 the Bill did not pass with 13 votes against and 11 in favour. The proposal encountered a number of criticisms, with one of the fiercest ones based on the internal migration of elderly people that such a change would bring within Australia. See for example: http://www.lifesitenews.com/news/tasmanian-euthanasia-and-assisted-suicide-bill-to-be-debated-this-week and http://www.news.com.au/national/tasmania-bill-to-make-euthanasia-legal-could-lead-to-8216death-tourism8217/story-fncynjr2-1226729824901. For Canada see Parliament of Canada, *Medical Assistance in Dying: A Patient-Centered Approach—Report of the Special Joint Committee on Physician-Assisted Dying (Chairs: Kelvin Kenneth Ogilvie and Robert Oliphant)* (Parliament of Canada, 2016) p. 24 and the discussion in Chapter 5.

[29] Joachim Cohen, Paul Van Landeghem, Nico Carpentier, and Luc Deliens, 'Different Trends in Euthanasia Acceptance across Europe: A Study of 13 Western and 10 Central and Eastern European Countries' (2013) 23(3) *European Journal of Public Health* 378; Joachim Cohen, PaulVan Landeghem, Nico Carpentier, and Luc Deliens, 'Public Acceptance of Euthanasia in Europe: A Survey Study in 47 Countries' (2014) 59(1) *International Journal of Public Health* 143.

for example, by the Swiss right-to-die organizations discussed in the next chapter.

Suicide tourism and vulnerability

The freedom of movement of people who seek assisted suicide in another federal state or another country, supported by their rights to die with dignity and to promote quality of life, is a crucial element of the relationship between suicide tourism and global justice. As the next chapter observes, some critics argue that organizations such as Dignitas (which offer aid in dying to foreigners) draw in clients in ways that justify moral condemnation and perhaps also some legal restrictions. Others, however, may view their activities and the existence of the opportunity to use their services as a ray of light for all those individuals wishing to choose their life's path—including its ending.

The political and moral charge made about the distinction between assisted suicide—a practice by which the person ends her own life autonomously and voluntary—and non-voluntary euthanasia—where a person's life is taken from her whether in action or omission by another, usually a physician—is certainly worthy of attention. The same applies to the challenge that such a distinction has received from various other angles, underlining the intrinsic complexity of establishing the existence of such a counter-intuitive choice in individualistic terms.[30]

However, it is necessary to point out that certain countries have created several scenarios that need to be addressed by the global community if a convincing policy on the topic is to come about. In 2008, a few reports[31] sparked by *The Peaceful Pill Handbook* by Philip Nitschke[32]—the founder of Exit International, an Australian organization that aims to help people terminate their lives, and principal supporter of the brief period of legal

---

[30] Byron J. Stoyles and Sorin Costreie, 'Rethinking Voluntary Euthanasia' (2013) 38 *Journal of Medicine and Philosophy* 674.

[31] See, for example, Marc Lacey, 'In Tijuana, a Market for Death in a Bottle', *New York Times* (21 July 2008) http://www.nytimes.com/2008/07/21/world/americas/21tijuana.html?pagewanted=all&_r=1&, accessed on 7 June 2018 (hereafter: 'Lacey, In Tijuana').

[32] Phillip Nitschke and Fiona Stewart, *The Peaceful Pill Handbook* (Exit International Publishing Ltd, 2007).

physician-assisted suicide in the Northern Territory—investigated the ease with which citizens from anglophone countries (mainly Australia, but also New Zealand and the US) were able to purchase barbiturates in pet shops in Mexico. These cases involved substances that could cause death within seconds and yet were obtainable without any paperwork to complete or any monitoring system to report to.[33] Cases in other parts of the world also raise similar concerns. As discussed in the next chapter, although it would be difficult to receive assisted suicide in Belgium or the Netherlands by travelling to these countries, suicide tourism in these destinations cannot be excluded since there is no formal requirement of residency, and reporting requirements in cases of assisted suicide, at least in Belgium, is believed to be more lenient.[34]

Interestingly then, it seems that the main distinction between the selling of barbiturates in Mexico and offering aid in dying to foreigners in Switzerland is to be found in the absence or not of clinics and personnel, such as those of Dignitas or LifeCircle in the latter context, namely in the institutionalization of suicide tourism in Switzerland.

However, one important aspect that is always raised with regard to euthanasia and assisted suicide should be considered: the potential discrimination against and possible abuse of disabled or particularly vulnerable people. As mentioned, the cocktail of barbiturates available in Mexico does not differ much (if at all) from the services provided through right-to-die organizations in Switzerland. Being part of a recognized—albeit, as this book explores, imperfect—system of assisted suicide, the right-to-die organizations in Switzerland have the power both to alleviate and to exploit the condition of the people requesting assistance with suicide. When the person is a non-resident and has no other alternative to fulfil her wish to die, her dependence on these (few) organizations may be high. This may lead, under some perhaps exceptional circumstances, to more cases of exploitation and in any event it must raise concerns at the policy and legal levels.

---

[33] Susan D. James, 'Tourists Trek to Mexico for "Death in a Bottle"' (*ABC News*, 31 July 2008) http://abcnews.go.com/Health/MindMoodNews/story?id=5481482, accessed on 7 June 2018; Lacey, In Tijuana (n 31).

[34] Cecilia Rodriguez, 'Holland Targets Its Drugs-and-Death Tourism', *Forbes* (4 April 2012) https://www.forbes.com/sites/ceciliarodriguez/2012/04/04/holland-targets-its-drugs-and-death-tourism/#876977b620d3.

In addressing the current global health situation, Salomon Benatar noted in a symposium on global health and the law that,

> The most common response to the challenge of protecting health through law is to focus on protecting the rights of vulnerable individuals and to enhance their access to health care. Each one of us is vulnerable or potentially vulnerable because of the fragile, existential nature of the human condition.[35]

Undeniably, suicide tourism represents a particularly complicated issue to address, as it presents a tension between the two parts of the statement. On the one hand, there are no doubts that potential death tourists are especially vulnerable people, be it for physical, psychological, or social reasons, or a combination of these. On the other hand, however, it is not to be forgotten that it is part of our nature to be fragile, that is vulnerable, limited, mortal. To force upon us a longer life through artificial (i.e. iron lung) or semi-artificial (i.e. medicinal) devices, does not necessarily constitute a more humane and natural way of facing death. While the law attempts to represent the moral views of the majority and in many situations is the result of a political compromise, a legal and just system cannot be justified in its efforts to struggle with one's wish to die. The respect of such a wish is beyond national borders, civil status, and political affiliation. It requires constant reflection and discussions within and among nations. Analysing the global practice of suicide tourism creates the path to establishing this.

---

[35] Solomon R. Benatar, 'Global Health, Vulnerable Populations, and Law' (April 2013) 41(1) *Journal of Law, Medicine and Ethics* 42.

PART I
LEGAL ASPECTS OF SUICIDE TOURISM

1

The Status of Assisted Suicide

This book discusses the practice of suicide tourism, whereby people travel to countries or states to take advantage of permissive laws on assisted suicide that do not exist in their home countries or states. Assisted suicide is defined as an act where one or more persons, usually a physician, provides knowledge and/or material assistance to another person—most notably by providing instruction about lethal doses of drugs or prescribing such lethal doses—to enable that person to bring about her own death.[1]

Background

Assisted suicide should be distinguished from euthanasia, by which a person's death is brought about *directly* by the actions or omissions of another person. Euthanasia can be passive, for example where life-saving support is withheld from a terminal patient (in terms of it not being renewed), or it can be active, where such support is withdrawn from her (and is deliberately stopped). In either case, there is a causal relationship between the action for which the medical profession is usually responsible and the death of the person; it is the direct killing of the euthanized patient either by the fulfilment of, or by refraining to fulfil, professional obligations to the patient. Whereas assisted suicide requires the actual self-killing of the person herself and so must always be voluntary,

---

[1] The involvement of a physician in this act is usually referred to as physician-assisted suicide. In the literature there exists a debate as to whether the term 'physician-assisted suicide' is appropriate for such a practice. Other suggestions include 'physician-assisted death' or 'physician aid in dying'. Ezekiel J. Emanuel, Bregje D. Onwuteaka-Phillipsen, John W. Urwin, and Joachim Cohen, 'Attitudes and Practices of Euthanasia and Physician-Assisted Suicide in the United States, Canada, and Europe' (2016) 316(1) *JAMA* 79 (hereafter: 'Emanuel et al., Attitudes and Practices'). Some physicians who merely prescribe a lethal drug to a patient do not feel they assist in their dying. Rather, they view themselves as facilitators. See Browne C. Lewis, 'A Graceful Exit: Redefining Terminal to Expand the Availability of Physician-Facilitated Suicide' (2012) 91 *Oregon L. Rev.* 457–94 at 460 (hereafter: 'Lewis, Graceful Exit').

Suicide Tourism. First Edition. Daniel Sperling. © Daniel Sperling 2019. Published 2019 by Oxford University Press.

euthanasia, although usually involving voluntary patients, may apply—albeit in rare and severe cases—to involuntary patients as well.[2]

Of course, the alternatives to legally permitted physician-assisted suicide or euthanasia in one's homeland may be unsafe or cruel and may involve intolerable suffering. They may include acts of premature suicide, often by violent or dangerous means, or a long wait to die from natural causes.[3] Another alternative concerns purchasing lethal drugs through the Internet (usually from China) and taking them in one's own country.[4] As this book will show, travelling to another country to receive aid in dying is one possible solution to avoiding such alternatives when faced with a legal void.

Assisted suicide is considered a rare practice in the Western world though its publicity is on the rise. In most of the countries where assisted suicide is legal, data reveals an increase both in the requests made in this direction and in actual deaths, although this may have more to do with improved reporting and monitoring and may not represent a significant rise.[5]

Over recent decades, a limited number of Western countries have adopted laws permitting—to varying degrees—competent persons to put an end to their own suffering by terminating their lives with the help of another person.[6] The legal regulation of assisted suicide follows broad political and public debates that involve concerns over the sincerity and

---

[2] A machine invented recently by an Australian doctor, Philip Nitschke, can replace the physician's act of terminating the patient's life when the patient is unable to take the lethal drug herself. The machine is loaded with the drug and is set up to be digitally activated by the patient using a pass phrase via an eye blink computer. *R (on the application of Nicklinson and another) v. Ministry of Justice; R (on the application of AM) v. Director of Public Prosecutions* [2014] UKSC 38 (hereafter: '*Nicklinson*') § 4.

[3] *Carter v. Canada (Attorney General)* [2015] 1 S.C.R. 331 (hereafter: '*Carter v. Canada*') § 1.

[4] CBS/AP, 'Buying Deadly Drugs Online from China Takes Just Minutes' (*CBS*, 3 November 2016) https://www.cbsnews.com/news/buying-deadly-drugs-online-from-china-takes-just-minutes/, accessed on 23 January 2018.

[5] Bernard Dan, Christine Fonteyne, and Stéphan Clément de Clèty, 'Self-Requested Euthanasia for Children in Belgium' (2014) 383(9918) *Lancet* 671.

[6] It should be noted that competence is a fundamental a priori condition in death tourism as well. The very definition entails that the tourist is freely and competently choosing to undergo the trip abroad. Otherwise, we would be talking about an 'execution journey' or, to use a more standard definition that does not take into account the specific travelling aspect, 'involuntary euthanasia'. Historical experiences of such practices, such as Nazi actions carried out without compassion against 'inferior' lives, should lead any analysis of the issue to be completed with extreme caution. The competency aspect will be analysed in detail in the description of the various associations that deal with the procedure of assisted suicide in Switzerland.

firmness of one's wish to die, on the one hand, and the right to end one's own life with the aid of another person (be it a relative, friend, physician, or an organization), on the other, especially when suffering from a terminal illness (typically accompanied by much pain and a decrease in quality of life). While euthanasia and physician-assisted suicide remain relatively rare, comprising between 0.3 and 4.6 per cent of all deaths,[7] the public discourse and legal frameworks that surround them receive much attention.

The continuing legalization and social acceptance of assisted suicide in various places in recent years may correspond to an increasing phenomenon of medicalization of death. Under this phenomenon, physicians (and the medical profession more generally) manifest greater control over pain and death, and the act of suicide itself is transformed from a sin/crime into a decriminalized, secular solution to the problem of human suffering.[8] It represents a development of the concept of a person's right to control her dying and to end her life when, where, and in the form she finds appropriate. Within this bundle of rights also fall one's right to respect for private life,[9] the right to refuse life-saving medical treatment,[10] the right to choose cessation of food and fluids,[11] the right to be prescribed with high doses of pain relievers, most notably opioids, which could hasten death,[12] and one's right to receive palliative sedation to minimize awareness of pain (which can also be followed by death with high doses).[13] This group of rights can be defended by ideas of poor or diminished quality of life, extensive suffering and pain, loss of independence,

---

[7] Emanuel et al., Attitudes and Practices (n 1).

[8] Giza Lopes, *Dying with Dignity: A Legal Approach to Assisted Death* (Praeger, 2015).

[9] It was ruled that such an interpretation applies to Article 8 of the European Convention of Human rights. *Haas v. Switzerland* [2011] ECHR 2422 (hereafter: '*Haas*') at § 51.

[10] Alan Meisel and Kathy L. Cerminara, *The Right to Die: The Law of End-of-Life Decisionmaking* (3rd edn, Aspen, 2004). In some jurisdictions, such a right amounts to constitutional protection. See e.g. *Cruzan v. Dir., Mo. Dep't of Health* (1990) 497 U.S. 261; *Washington v. Glucksberg* (1997) 521 U.S. 702 (hereafter: '*Glucksberg*'); *Vacco v. Quill* (1997) 521 U.S. 793 (hereafter: '*Vacco*').

[11] Thaddeus M. Pope and Lindsey E. Anderson, 'Symposium: Health Law and the Elderly: Managing Risk at End of Life: Article: Voluntarily Stopping Eating and Drinking: A Legal Treatment Option at the End of Life' (2011) 11 *Widener L. Rev.* 363.

[12] *Vacco* (n 10) at 808; *Glucksberg* (n 10) at 737–8; Timothy E. Quill, 'Physician-Assisted Death in the United States: Are the Existing "Last Resorts" Enough?' (2008) 38(5) *Hastings Ctr. Rep.* 17 at 18–19.

[13] Augustin Boulanger et al., 'Opinions About the New Law on End-of-Life Issues in a Sample of French Patients Receiving Palliative Care' (2017) 16(7) *BMC Palliative Care*. doi: 10.1186/s12904-016-0174-8.

loss of control over one's life, and loss of autonomy with regard to end-of-life decision-making.

From a legal perspective, courts have refused to find an analogy between one's right to make abortion decisions and a person's right to make physician-assisted suicide choices. If accepted, such an analogy would have resulted in the finding that these choices should be regarded as central to major constitutional rights such as the person's dignity, autonomy, and liberty.[14] Moreover, the European Court of Human Rights has ruled that a person does not have a right to require a state to permit or facilitate her death, despite its centrality to and association with a person's right to respect for private life and self-determination. Signatories to the European Convention on Human Rights are under no obligation to decriminalize assisted suicide as they enjoy a degree of discretion in implementing its provisions under the doctrine of the margin of appreciation.[15]

Under the American jurisprudence, for example, the right to receive aid in dying was not considered a fundamental liberty under the Due Process Clause.[16] The very long resistance of Anglo-American common law to suicide and to assisted suicide was justified by the state interest in the preservation of human life, the state obligation to protect the integrity and ethics of the medical profession, and the state interest in protecting vulnerable groups of people from abuse, as well as by the fear that applying these actions to less severe cases—such as non-terminal, mentally incapacitated, or aged patients—would be a move towards euthanasia and potential abuse.[17]

Indeed, most legal cases that discuss the legality and constitutionality of assisted suicide laws attempt to balance a person's right to autonomy, human dignity, protection of privacy, or security with protection of the sanctity of life and the public interest in formulating safeguards against abuse and so-called 'slippery slope' cases that can follow from ideas of fundamental justice and a state's discretion to legalize and regulate these issues.[18]

---

[14] *Glucksberg* (n 10) at 725.
[15] *Pretty v. UK* (2002) 35 EHRR at § 54 (hereafter: '*Pretty*'); Emily Wada, 'A Pretty Picture: The Margin of Appreciation and the Right to Assisted Suicide' (2005) 27 *Loy. L.A. Int'l & Comp. L. Rev.* 275.
[16] *Glucksberg* (n 10) at 728.
[17] *Glucksberg* (n 10) at 728–33.
[18] *Rodriguez v. Attorney General of Canada* [1993] 3 S.C.R. 519 (hereafter: *Rodriguez*).

Practically, legalization of assisted suicide (and euthanasia more generally) may decrease the number of incidents where life-ending acts are offered to patients who have not explicitly requested it in the absence of open communication between physician and patient. In this respect it may play a protective role with regard to these patients.[19] In addition, it has been argued in recent years that legalization of physician-assisted suicide could result in substantial savings to the healthcare system. It is expected that these savings will exceed the costs associated with offering aid in dying.[20]

Legalization of assisted suicide attracts much criticism and opposition from people with disabilities and organizations promoting their rights. These groups of people argue that assisted suicide implicitly devalues their lives, thereby increasing the social discrimination against them and rendering them more vulnerable.[21] Moreover, it is argued that legalizing premature death as a 'treatment' option will sow the seed of doubt about their right to demand help and proper accommodation—not to die, but to live with dignity.[22] It is therefore argued that focus should be given to challenging assumptions that disabled people do not have a good quality of life, rather than reinforcing them.[23] However, other people within these communities hold that legalization of assisted suicide permits more control over certain aspects of their deaths, thereby protecting them by creating stronger safeguards for end-of-life care. This argument may gather strength as evidence suggests that while legalization of assisted suicide may have put some people with disabilities at risk of harm, improvement in end-of-life care has been spurred as a result.[24]

---

[19] Ilana R. Levene, 'Legislation Protects the Vulnerable?' (2010) 182(12) *CMAJ* 1330.

[20] Aaron J. Trachtenberg and Braden Manns, 'Cost Analysis of Medical Assistance in Dying in Canada' (2017) 189(3) *CMAJ* E 101; Wade M. Smith, 'The Ethical and Economic Concerns of Physician Assisted Suicide' (2017) Augustana Center for the Study of Ethics Essay Contest http://digitalcommons.augustana.edu/ethicscontest/11, accessed on 1 February 2018.

[21] Ashton D. Ellis, *'Measuring the Disability Rights Framing Effects on Public Opinions About Assisted Suicide: Elite Interviews and an Experimental Survey'*, Doctoral Dissertation (The Claremont Graduate University, 2016).

[22] Jane Campbell, 'It's My Life—It's My Decision? Assisted Dying Versus Assisted Living' in Luke Clements and Janet Read (eds), *Disabled People and the Right to Life: The Protection of Disabled People's Most Basic Human Rights* (Routledge, 2008) 85.

[23] Scope, *Why Scope Is Against Legalising Assisted Suicide* (2017) https://www.scope.org.uk/media/scope-against-legalising-assisted-suicide, accessed on 31 January 2018.

[24] Kathryn L. Tucker, 'Building Bridges between the Civil Rights Movements of People with Disabilities and Those with Terminal Illness' (2017) 78 *U. Pitt. L. Rev.* 329.

It is also argued in the literature that assisted-death cases are not fully reported and that the practice extends from terminal patients to newborns, children, old people who are tired of living, and people with dementia. In particular, the legalization of euthanasia and assisted suicide is said to place many people at risk, providing ineffective safeguards and controls.[25] Moreover, data recently collected in the US suggests that legalizing assisted suicide coincided with an increase in the total number of suicides, suggesting that there was no consequent reduction in rates of non-assisted suicide.[26]

From the perspective of much of the medical profession, physician-assisted suicide is simply wrong. According to the latest version of the American Medical Association Code of Ethics, for example, physician-assisted suicide ultimately causes more harm than good. It is incompatible with the physician's role as healer, would be impossible to control, and would pose serious societal risks. The code suggests that instead of offering assistance in dying to such patients, physicians should not abandon them; they should respect their autonomy, and should provide good communication, emotional support, appropriate comfort and care, and adequate pain control.[27]

The current position of the British Medical Association (BMA) on physician-assisted suicide is also non-supportive.[28] The BMA opposes all forms of assisted suicide and instead supports the current legal

---

[25] Jose Pereira, 'Legalizing Euthanasia or Assisted Suicide: The Illusion of Safeguards and Controls' (2011) 18(2) *Current Oncology* 38.

[26] Controlling for state and year fixed effects, research found that physician-assisted suicide was associated with an 8.9 per cent increase in total suicide rates. When controlled for a range of demographic and socio-economic factors, such an increase is 11.8 per cent. David Albert Jones and David Paton, 'How Does Legalization of Physician-Assisted Suicide Affect Rates of Suicide?' (2015) 108(10) *Southern Medical Journal* 599.

[27] American Medical Association, *Code of Medical Ethics: I, IV* (2016) § 5.7 https://www.ama-assn.org/sites/default/files/media-browser/code-of-medical-ethics-chapter-5.pdf, accessed on 23 January 2018. Recently, the AMA responded to claims in the media, especially by the *New York Times*, that it was considering revising its position towards physician-assisted suicide from opposition to neutral. The AMA stated that it had no plans to make any changes to its policy. Editorial, 'The AMA Claims It Is Not Studying Their Position on Physician-Assisted Suicide' (*National News Today*, 31 January 2017) http://www.nationalrighttolifenews.org/news/2017/01/the-ama-is-not-studying-their-position-on-physician-assisted-suicide/#.WUJ-iE0UlMs, accessed on 23 January 2018.

[28] Moreover, the BMA recently initiated a large project on this issue which explored the public's and physicians' attitudes (BMA End of Life Care and Physician Assisted Dying Project). During this project it re-examined its own position on physician-assisted suicide, specifically whether to move from opposition to a more neutral stance. A discussion on this was held during the Annual Representative Meeting in June 2016. After insightful discussion it was decided to uphold the BMA's existing opposition. BMA, 'End-of-Life Care and Physician-Assisted Dying'

framework, which allows compassionate and ethical care for the dying, and the establishment of a comprehensive, high-quality palliative care service available to all that will allow patients to die with dignity. The BMA acknowledges the broad spectrum of physicians' opinions on the issue of assisted dying, but ultimately refers to the long-held consensus that the law should not be changed to permit assisted suicide.

According to its policy, the BMA insists that physician-assisted suicide (as well as euthanasia) should not be made legal in the UK and believes that ongoing improvement in palliative care allows patients to die with dignity.[29] It is argued that, in its opinion, permitting assisted dying could put vulnerable people at risk and could weaken society's prohibition on killing which may result in undesirable consequences. In addition, it is claimed that only a minority of people wish to die and the rules for the majority should not be changed to accommodate such a small group. Above all, permitting physician-assisted suicide would be contrary to medical ethics, since the main purpose of clinical practice is to improve a patient's quality of life and not to shorten it.[30]

A somewhat different approach is reflected by the Canadian Medical Association (CMA) policy on physician participation in assisted suicide, where the CMA acknowledges that it is the prerogative of society to decide whether the laws on euthanasia and assisted suicide should be changed. A survey of 5,000 members of CMA conducted in 2014 indicated that 45 per cent of respondents supported legalization of assisted dying while only 27 per cent of them said they would participate in such a practice.[31] Nonetheless, the policy supports the right of all physicians, within the bounds of existing legislation, to follow their conscience when deciding whether to provide their patients with aid in dying.[32]

(BMA, 21 April 2017) https://www.bma.org.uk/collective-voice/policy-and-research/ethics/end-of-life-care, accessed on 23 January 2018.

---

[29] BMA, 'Physician-Assisted Dying: BMA Policy' (BMA, 9 May 2017) https://www.bma.org.uk/advice/employment/ethics/ethics-a-to-z/physician-assisted-dying, accessed on 23 January 2018. The policy also emphasizes that if euthanasia were legalized there should be a clear demarcation between physicians who are involved in it and those who are not.

[30] Ibid.

[31] CMA, 'A Canadian Approach to Assisted Dying: CMA Member Dialogue' https://www.cma.ca/Assets/assets-library/document/en/advocacy/canadian-approach-assisted-dying_e.pdf#search=assisted%20dying, accessed on 23 January 2018.

[32] CMA, 'Euthanasia and Assisted Death' (Update 2014) https://www.cma.ca/Assets/assets-library/document/en/advocacy/policy-research/cma-policy-euthanasia-and-assisted-death-update2014-pd15-02-e.pdf, accessed on 18 June 2017.

The next section considers various legal solutions to the issues raised by this debate, to understand the differences between them, and to better conceptualize the framework for suicide tourism. This includes a discussion of the major legal regulations that already exist, especially in Europe and North America, to help form an international perspective of the global phenomenon of suicide tourism.

Europe

A recent survey of public opinion across forty-seven European countries on euthanasia and its acceptance in Europe reveals a polarization by which most of Western Europe is becoming more permissive and most of Eastern Europe is becoming less permissive. Belgium, the Netherlands, and Luxemburg, which—as will be discussed below—have legalized euthanasia and assisted suicide, were among the countries for which the highest scores were found.[33]

Religiosity, as well as age and education, is an important factor to explain people's attitudes towards euthanasia and assisted suicide. One of the major explanations for the divide concerns the rapid and dramatic secularization in Western Europe along with the revival of religion in most parts of post-communist Europe. It may also be explained by the relative opposition towards democracy as a political system in Eastern countries compared to advanced beliefs regarding individual autonomy and freedom of choice in Western countries.[34]

From a legal perspective, while extensively protecting the right to life of every human being (especially through Article 2),[35] the European Convention on Human Rights does not have a clear statement concerning euthanasia or assisted suicide as such. Most cases

---

[33] Other countries with high scores were Denmark, France, and Sweden. Joachim Cohen, Paul van Landeghem, Nico Carpentier, and Luc Deliens, 'Public Acceptance of Euthanasia in Europe: A Survey Study in 47 Countries' (2014) 59(1) *Int J. Public Health* 143.

[34] Ibid.

[35] European Convention on Human Rights, Art. 2(1) states:

Everyone's right to life shall be protected by law. No one shall be deprived of his life intentionally save in the execution of a sentence of a court following his conviction of a crime for which this penalty is provided by law.

Available at: http://www.echr.coe.int/Documents/Convention_ENG.pdf.

discussing assisted suicide refer mainly to Article 8 of the Convention (the right to respect for private life and family life) and Article 5 (the right to liberty and security). Yet, as mentioned above, signatories to the Convention enjoy a margin of appreciation in their application of it and so in their regulation of assisted suicide are in no way under a duty to decriminalize such a practice to promote the values set out in the Convention.[36]

Switzerland

Currently, the only country that provides the opportunity for a full-scale form of suicide tourism is Switzerland. Although it is not the only country to have decriminalized assisted suicide, Switzerland is the exception in the way the practice takes place in law and by professional institutes, most notably for allowing non-residents to be eligible.

However, although the media focus on and public awareness of suicide tourism tend to involve cases of individuals travelling to Switzerland for assisted suicide, it is becoming a widespread phenomenon that goes beyond Switzerland and, in fact, beyond Europe.[37] The current divergence in laws concerning end-of-life issues has led to a proliferation of associations focussed on this exponentially growing practice. Why, then, is Switzerland such an attractive location for those seeking death?

In 1942, Switzerland became the first country in the world to decriminalize assisted suicide. Article 115 of the Swiss Penal Code states: 'Any person who for selfish motives, incites or assists another to commit suicide is, if that other person thereafter commits or attempts to commit suicide, liable to a custodial sentence not exceeding five years or to a monetary penalty'.[38] It will be argued that it is the (rather vague) definition of

---

[36] *Pretty* (n 15).

[37] DeMond S. Miller and Christopher Gonzalez, 'When Death Is the Destination: The Business of Death Tourism—despite Legal and Social Implications' (2013) 7(3) *International Journal of Culture, Tourism and Hospitality Research* 293 (hereafter: 'Miller and Gonzalez, When Death Is the Destination').

[38] Criminal Law and Assisted Suicide in Switzerland. Available at: https://www.admin.ch/opc/en/classified-compilation/19370083/201803010000/311.0.pdf, accessed on 23 January 2018.

selfish motives that creates the conditions for a very permissive approach towards those assisting a suicide.

It is interesting to note that historically the law did not refer to the phenomenon of assisted suicide in medical contexts nor did it give physicians a special status. Originally, the expression 'selfish motive' mainly referred to obtaining an inheritance or gaining in some other external way from aiding or facilitating the act of suicide. Suicides were motivated by honour and romance and these were considered legitimate and reasonable reasons for suicide.[39]

The law does not make the practice of assisted suicide legal, but only non-punishable provided that no selfish motive is present. Since non-governmental entities generally do not act upon selfish interests—although, as will be discussed below, some may be motivated by financial aspects—their involvement in assisting death could not typically be considered illegal and indeed no assisted suicide organization, or a director thereof, has been convicted to date under article 115 of the Penal Code.[40]

Second, a unique feature of the Swiss law is that it does not require assisted suicide to be performed by a doctor. Hence, in contrast to the regulation of assisted suicide in other countries, which can be classified as 'physician-assisted suicide', assisted suicide in Switzerland can take place in any form and by any person (although it is still a requirement that it must be a doctor who issues a prescription, under a decision of the Swiss Supreme Court).[41] Within reason, anyone can provide aid in dying, assuming that they do not act out of selfish motives and that they have access to a lethal drug or to other means by which a person can take her own life, such as gas masks. The rate of physician-assisted death in Switzerland

---

[39] Samia A. Hurst and Alex Mauron, 'Assisted Suicide and Euthanasia in Switzerland: Allowing a Role for Non-Physicians' (2003) 326(7383) *BMJ* 271 (hereafter: 'Hurst and Mauron, Assisted Suicide').

[40] However, the right-to-die organization, Dignitas, is suspected of receiving legacies from people seeking to commit suicide. If this practice is confirmed, the altruistic nature of the practice of Dignitas becomes doubtful. Roberto Andorno, 'Nonphysician-Assisted Suicide in Switzerland' (2013) 22 *Cambridge Quarterly of Healthcare Ethics* 1 (hereafter: 'Andorno, Nonphysician-Assisted Suicide') at 4. See also 'Dignitas Founder is Millionaire', *The Telegraph* (24 June 2010) https://www.telegraph.co.uk/news/worldnews/europe/switzerland/7851615/Dignitas-founder-is-millionaire.html (raising doubts over Dignitas' non-profitability), accessed on 23 January 2018.

[41] *Bundesgericht* 3 November 2006 (133 I 58) mentioned in Evelien Delbeke, 'The Way Assisted Suicide is Legalised: Balancing a Medical Framework Against a Demedicalised Model' (2011) 18 *European Journal of Health Law* 149 at 158.

remains relatively low although it increased from 1.0 per cent of all deaths in 2001 to 2.2 per cent in 2013.[42]

Another distinctive characteristic of the Swiss law is that one need not have a particular medical condition (e.g. terminal illness) to be qualified to request assistance in dying. In fact, as the cases of Sir Edward Downes,[43] Oriella Caszzenello,[44] Gill Pharaoh,[45] and the Stokes couple[46] demonstrate, a person can be non-terminal and yet choose to join a partner's request to commit suicide with the help of Swiss organizations or could ask for assisted suicide when she is tired or frustrated with modern life, experiencing loss of enthusiasm, or upset by one's physical appearance. The major requirement for assisted suicide is that the person involved has decisional capacity[47] and, as decided by the Federal Court in case of incurable and serious mental disorder, a psychiatrist's report must indicate that a person's wish to die is not the expression of the psychiatric disorder itself.[48]

Recently, it was reported that Exit, a major assisted suicide organization in Switzerland, had extended its services to elderly people who are not terminal but who suffer from psychological or physical problems associated with old age. The organization admitted that although people seeking their services would have to go through comprehensive checks,

---

[42] Georg Bosshard et al., 'Medical End-of-Life Practices in Switzerland: A Comparison of 2001 and 2013' (2016) 176(4) *JAMA Intern Med.* 555.

[43] 'Conductor Sir Edward Downes and Wife End Lives at Dignitas Clinic', *The Telegraph* (14 July 2009) http://www.telegraph.co.uk/culture/music/music-news/5823704/Conductor-Sir-Edward-Downes-and-wife-end-lives-at-Dignitas-clinic.html, accessed on 23 January 2018. Compare also the recent case of Anne, an 89-year-old retired art teacher who went to Switzerland to commit suicide because of the lack of interaction in modern life. Claire Carter, 'Retired Art Teacher Committed Suicide Because of Frustration with Modern Life', *The Telegraph* (6 April 2014) http://www.telegraph.co.uk/news/uknews/law-and-order/10747672/Retired-art-teacher-committed-suicide-because-of-frustration-with-modern-life.html, accessed on 24 January 2018.

[44] Hannah Roberts, 'Italian Woman, 85, Ends Her Life at Swiss Euthanasia Clinic Because She Was Upset about Losing Her Looks', *The Daily Mail* (20 February 2014) http://www.dailymail.co.uk/news/article-2564023/Italian-woman-85-ends-life-Swiss-Dignitas-clinic-upset-losing-looks.html, accessed on 25 January 2018.

[45] Ollie Gillman, 'Healthy Ex-Nurse, 75, Kills Herself at Swiss Clinic—Because Growing Old is "No Fun": Mother of Two Spent Years Caring for Frail Elderly, then Decided She Would Rather Die than Suffer Their Fate', (*MailOnline*, 2 August 2015) http://www.dailymail.co.uk/news/article-3182813/Healthy-former-nurse-75-died-Swiss-suicide-clinic-deciding-didn-t-want-risk-burden-family-NHS.html, accessed on 25 January 2018.

[46] BBC News, 'UK Couple Die at Suicide Clinic' (15 April 2003) http://news.bbc.co.uk/2/hi/uk_news/2948365.stm, accessed on 24 January 2018.

[47] Andorno, Nonphysician-Assisted Suicide, (n 40).

[48] Ibid. at 4.

the medical tests would be less stringent than those required for younger people.[49] Along with this anecdotal data, a recent study shows that almost 25 per cent of people that die by assisted suicide in Switzerland do not suffer from serious or terminal illness.[50]

It is difficult to know how much of an influence this characteristic of Swiss law has since, unlike other countries where assisted suicide is legal, in Switzerland there is no mandatory reporting of assisted suicide cases and there exists no national or cantonal registry of such cases. While every case of unnatural death must be reported and investigated, each canton may have a different approach to such an investigation.[51] Data on the practice of assisted suicide—which, as illustrated below, is carried out by many potential actors (organizations and individual physicians)—is scarce and dependent upon the willingness of these actors to publish it.

Another possible attraction may be the reassurance that every person who seeks assisted suicide in Switzerland must be examined by a medical doctor since the latter is the only one who can prescribe the lethal drugs (sodium pentobarbital) that are generally used. Having a doctor pre-scribe the lethal drug is not regarded as contrary to the patient's right to privacy[52] and is supported by the state obligation to protect life and take active measures to prevent abuse (in line with Article 2 of the European Convention on Human Rights).[53] If the doctor refuses to so prescribe, the assisted suicide organization can refer that person to a collaborating physician who may assess her capacity and eventually prescribe the drug.

Assessing a person's decisional capacity may be subject to court in-tervention and may lead—though very rarely—to criminal conviction. Thus, in 2009 the Federal Court convicted a psychiatrist for homicide in the suicide of two persons suffering from mental illness.[54] In a decision

---

[49] Maddy French, 'Swiss Group to Allow Assisted Dying for Elderly Who Are Not Terminally Ill', *The Guardian* (26 May 2014) http://www.theguardian.com/society/2014/may/26/swiss-exit-assisted-suicide-elderly-not-terminally-ill, accessed on 24 January 2018 (hereafter: 'French, Swiss Group').

[50] Andorno, Nonphysician-Assisted Suicide (n 40) at FN 4.

[51] Stephen J. Ziegler, 'Collaborated Death: An Exploration of the Swiss Model of Assisted Suicide for Its Potential to Enhance Oversight and Demedicalize the Dying Process' (2009) 37 *J. L. Med., & Ethics* 318.

[52] Federal Court, 12 April 2010, Decision 2C_9/2010, mentioned in Andorno, Nonphysician-Assisted Suicide (n 40) at 8.

[53] *Haas* (n 9).

[54] Federal Court, 11 June 2009, Decision 6B_48/2009, mentioned in Andorno, Nonphysician-Assisted Suicide (n 40) at 8.

the year before, the Federal Court upheld the decision not to renew the licence of a 70-year-old doctor who prescribed sodium pentobarbital to elderly patients after just one interview.[55] In another case, a Swiss doctor was acquitted by a court of appeals for giving drugs to an 89-year-old patient with a serious bowel illness who wanted to end his life but refused to be examined.[56]

Interestingly, the legal position in Switzerland on assisted suicide and the application of the regulation of assisted suicide to the medical context is not the result of an explicit liberal policy but was rather down to the initiative of non-governmental right-to-die organizations that took advantage of a gap in the legal system.[57]

To have a clearer understating of the current (and unique) situation in Switzerland, we should now look at the various options and right-to-die organizations that are available to people seeking aid in dying. While the first three associations discussed below are the most influential and well known, other organizations need to be considered to give a more accurate picture of the dynamics in place within the country in relation to the phenomenon of suicide tourism.

Exit ADMD (*association pour le droit de mourir dans la dignité*), established on 23 January 1982, was the first right-to-die association created in Switzerland. It counts around 15,000 members, mostly francophone. The procedure to be allowed to terminate one's life is not at all quick and simple. The request for assisted suicide is accepted only if it is serious and reiterated, and if the person is fully competent. In addition, the person needs to be in a particularly burdensome situation: she must be suffering from an incurable disease or some permanent disability that creates physical and psychological pain. Disability is defined by the association as an impossibility to carry out basic actions on a day-to-day basis (including putting on clothes, washing oneself, going to bed, eating, caring for one's personal hygiene, going to the bathroom, and moving), or being affected by blindness or a hearing impairment.

Exit DS (*Deutsche Schweiz*) is the 'German twin' of Exit ADMD. It was founded a few months later, on 3 April 1982, and it is the most

---

[55] Federal Court, 24 June 2008, Decision 2C_191/2008, mentioned in Andorno, Nonphysician-Assisted Suicide (n 40).

[56] French, Swiss Group (n 49).

[57] Andorno, Nonphysician-Assisted Suicide (n 40) at 2.

influential organization and dominant actor in the field of assisted suicide in Switzerland. This organization has about 108,000 members around Switzerland and has seventy employees. In addition to assisted suicide, Exit provides services around self-determination, living wills, and counselling. Every year, the organization deals with 750 cases of physician-assisted suicide.

According to Exit's statute, a person is eligible for assisted suicide only if they are terminally ill, suffer from terrible pain, or have undergone unsustainable disablements. As described above, assisted suicide is performed through the ingestion of sodium pentobarbital. If the person is able to do so, she will drink the lethal cocktail on her own. Otherwise, the process will involve nasogastric or intravenous feeding. In these latter instances, the person will always have control of the actions taking place, as she is the only one entitled to put an end to her life.

Exit is believed—and has presented itself to me this way—not to play a significant role in suicide tourism. First, it posits itself apart from Dignitas, which—as will be discussed below—is an organization that is highly associated with non-residents. The organization only accommodates Swiss residents or foreign residents who have lived in Switzerland for a while.[58] According to Bernhard Sutter, CEO of Exit DS, 1.25 per cent of their members live outside of Switzerland.[59] Secondly, it appears that, since the beginning of the twenty-first century at least, Exit accepts only terminally ill patients and does not provide help to people who suffer from depression or other mental diseases, even though it is not restricted in this way by Swiss law.

Dignitas is the main organization through which suicide tourism to Switzerland takes place. It was founded by the lawyer Ludwig Minelli on 17 May 1998. As of 31 December 2017, it had 8,432 members with only 688 of them from Switzerland. Dignitas is based in Forch (near Zurich) and until recently it also had an office in Hanover, Germany. Its explicit purpose is to ensure a life and death with dignity for its members and to allow other people to benefit from these values. Among its services, it provides counselling in end-of-life issues, carries out

---

[58] Alexander R. Safyan, 'A Call for International Regulation of the Thriving "Industry" of Death Tourism' (2011) 33 *Loy. L .A. Int'l & Comp. L. Rev.* 287 (hereafter: 'Safyan, Call for International Regulation') at 311.

[59] Personal interview, 9 June 2017.

patients' advanced directives, works for suicide prevention, and accompanies dying patients and assists with 'a self-determined end-of-life'.[60] In its brochure, Dignitas admits that only a small number of members who ask for the preparation of an accompanied suicide actually make use of this option.[61] In fact, the organization was established as a result of a scission within Exit due to an internal dispute focussing precisely on how to deal with requests for assisted suicide coming from outside Switzerland.

In contrast to other members of Exit, Ludwig Minelli decided that geographical borders were not a sufficient basis for selecting who may fulfil their right to die. Hence, he created an alternative that, in his view, provides the opportunity to live and die with dignity to anyone who is otherwise eligible for the procedure, regardless of their country of origin.

Dignitas provides the person seeking to advance her right to die with dignity with a living will that guarantees legal value and ensures support throughout the dying process. Until 2001 the personnel working in Dignitas were doing so on a voluntary basis, but the association has since decided (due to the drastic increase in the number of requests) to pay a salary to the people behind all the work of interviewing, interacting with the person seeking assisted suicide and her family, and providing the aid-in-dying process itself. This has involved certain costs, which has in turn increased the criticism of the association as a business speculating over the death and misery of someone else.

Once contacted, Dignitas provides background information on its activities, and examines whether there are other ways to address the applicant's wishes and needs, including palliative care.[62] Where the desire to end one's own life does not pass, the applicant should submit a letter of request to join the organization, along with her CV and updated medical information, including her diagnosis, treatment, and prognosis of her condition, as far as possible. People who simply turn up at the

---

[60] Dignitas, *Objectives and Purposes* http://www.dignitas.ch/index.php?option=com_content&view=article&id=9&Itemid=45&lang=en, accessed on 25 January 2017.

[61] Dignitas, *Information Brochure of Dignitas* (2018) at 9 http://www.dignitas.ch/images/stories/pdf/informations-broschuere-dignitas-e.pdf, accessed on 25 January 2018 (hereafter: 'Dignitas Brochure').

[62] But compare Materstvedt who argues against the view that purports to combine assisted death and palliative care. Lars Johan Materstvedt, 'Palliative Care Ethics: The Problems of Combining Palliation and Assisted Dying' (2013) 21(3) *Progress in Palliative Care* 158.

clinic or who do not provide the necessary medical documentation are turned away.[63]

Once Dignitas is able to locate a physician who will issue the lethal barbiturate prescription (usually within 2 months), the applicant must supply the organization with certain legal documentation (such as a birth certificate) before her first meeting with the physician is scheduled. In that meeting, the physician informs the applicant about the available alternatives and seeks to verify that the applicant's wish to die remains constant and is formed with competency, namely that she understands what is to be done to her and is able to demonstrate such an understanding by, at a minimum, responding 'yes' or 'no' to questions posed to her. Only then will the physician prescribe the lethal barbiturate.[64]

After consuming an anti-emetic drug (to prevent vomiting), the applicant has to confirm her wishes and sign a declaration of suicide. Following that, the barbiturates are ingested, either by drinking a solution, injecting it through a gastric tube, or activating a pre-prepared infusion. Sleep occurs within a few minutes and death usually occurs within half an hour. Following death, Dignitas contacts various authorities and the body is released, usually for cremation in Switzerland and subsequent burial in the applicant's home state.[65]

People seeking to end their lives through the assistance offered by Dignitas have to register with the society and pay a registration fee of 200 Swiss Francs and an annual fee of eighty Swiss Francs. The preparation for their assisted suicide requires a further fee, paid in advance, of 3,500 Swiss Francs. Additional costs of 1,000 Swiss Francs are incurred for two consultations with the physician and related administrative charges. Those wishing to be accompanied until the end of their life need to pay another 2,500 Swiss Francs, these fees covering payment to the person who acts as an escort/helper and use of Dignitas' apartment. In addition, those who delegate to Dignitas all the bureaucratic formalities linked to

---

[63] David Bryant, 'The Need for Legalization and Regulation of Aid-in-Dying and End-of-Life Procedures in the United States' (2015/16) 18 *Quinnipiac Health L.J.* 287 at 289.

[64] However, some reports suggest that Dignitas also experimented with oxygen deprivation, using helium and a common face mask and reservoir bag, as an alternative to sodium pentobarbital. Russel D. Ogden, William K. Hamilton, and Charles Whitcher, 'Assisted Suicide by Oxygen Deprivation with Helium at a Swiss Right-to-Die Organisation' (2009) 36 *JME* 174.

[65] Richard Huxtable, 'The Suicide Tourist Trap: Compromise Across Boundaries' (2009) 6 *Bioethical Inquiry* 327 at 329.

the services of the funeral director, including cremation, need to pay an extra 2,500 Swiss Francs. On request, Dignitas can also take care of the official procedures following a death in Switzerland for an additional contribution of 1,000 Swiss Francs. It follows that a person requesting the full service of an accompanied suicide through Dignitas must pay a total of 10,780 Swiss Francs.[66]

The organization maintains that an accompanied suicide can only be completed if it is convinced that all costs will be met. Hence, Dignitas normally requires advance payment. The organization allows for some discounts in the membership fees and the additional contributions if the person is in particularly needy financial conditions.[67]

As of 31 December 2017, according to data provided by Dignitas, 2,550 cases of accompanied suicides had been completed by Dignitas since its formation in 1998. The six countries from which most of the cases arose were: Germany (1,150 cases, 45.10%); UK (391 cases, 15.33%); France (299 cases, 11.73%); Switzerland (173 cases, 6.78%); Italy (110 cases, 4.31%); and Austria (55 cases, 2.16%). Non-residents from other continents also take advantage of Dignitas' services. Hence, data refers to ninety-one cases (3.57%) from the US, twenty-seven cases (1.06%) from Australia, and to a few other cases from various countries in Asia, Central and South America, and the Middle East.[68]

Another organization which may provide aid in dying to non-residents is Ex International. This organization was founded in Bern in 1996. According to some estimations it has roughly 700 members and, as suggested by its name, it has a much more internationally oriented mission, though most of its members are of German nationality.[69] It appears that members of this organization do not need to pay any fees, but the personnel involved in the suicide do get reimbursed for their time. Assisted suicide is provided to any member affected by unbearable pain, and all expenses are to be covered by person asking for assisted suicide. My attempts to interview staff from this organization were unsuccessful.

[66] Dignitas Brochure (n 61) at 14.

[67] Ibid.

[68] Dignitas, 'Accompanied Suicide of Members of Dignitas, by Year and by Country of Residency 1998–2017' (2018) http://www.dignitas.ch/images/stories/pdf/statistik-ftb-jahr-wohnsitz-1998-2017.pdf, accessed on 25 January 2018.

[69] Ex International, 'Offener Brief An Nachdenkliche Menschen' http://www.exinternational.ch/frame.html, accessed on 25 January 2018.

A fifth organization is Verein Suizidhilfe. It was created on 17 January 2002 by the psychiatrist (and former member of Exit DS) Peter Baumann. With this additional association, Baumann's intention was to guarantee easier access to assisted suicide for people with mental health issues. In 2007, Baumann was convicted of negligent homicide and sentenced to 4 years in prison. However, in 2010 he was given a pardon and in April 2011 he died from cancer. There are no official records concerning the number of members or the number of deaths assisted by the association. In its statute, the association affirms the use of dignified methods for the assisted suicide, making the intervention of a doctor superfluous.[70]

Another actor, which in recent years joined Dignitas in its contribution to suicide tourism in Switzerland, is Lifecircle-Eternal Spirit. This organization was founded in Basel in 2011 by a medical doctor named Erika Preisig and is the newest and smallest of the associations. It declares that it is open to non-residents and is committed to human dignity and self-determination.[71] The organization provides counselling, assistance in drafting living wills, and access to palliative care and what they call 'assisted voluntary death'.

Eligibility for assisted suicide is broadly defined. Anyone who suffers from an incurable disease, is severely disabled, and is in need of nursing care over a long period of time can apply. In addition, application can be made by people who do not wish to be nursed when there is no hope of improvement or by those with an incurable disease that leads to a reduction in quality of life even though death is not imminent, such as dementia, multiple sclerosis, motor neurone disease, and quadriplegia. According to the organization's brochure, minors, people who suffer from mental disease without serious physical suffering, or people who lack mental capacity are not eligible for assisted suicide.[72]

Requests for assisted suicide from non-residents must be followed by two detailed discussions with a Swiss doctor. The organization's brochure therefore mentions that a person from abroad must expect to stay in Switzerland for 3 to 4 days before an assisted suicide can be realized. Once a 'green light' is given by a Swiss doctor, assisted suicide can be scheduled within 1 to

---

[70] See http://www.suizidhilfe.ch/, accessed on 25 January 2018.

[71] Lifecircle, *Information Brochure* (2018) https://www.lifecircle.ch/pdf/lifecircle_Information_brochure.pdf, accessed on 25 January 2018.

[72] Ibid. at 12.

2 days. For non-residents, assisted suicide takes place in a rented studio that has been restructured for this purpose. The person signs her wish to die again on the day the assisted suicide takes place. She can then drink the lethal medication or take it by intravenous drip. It appears that Preisig is the one injecting the needle in the vein so the person herself autonomously activates the mechanism that opens the tab containing the sodium pento-barbital. She asks the person three questions: name, date of birth, and if he or she is fully aware of what is going to happen after the tab is opened. Only then can the procedure begin. Preisig's brother films everything to have proof for the police that everything was done in accordance with the law. After death occurs, the Preisigs call the Police Chief in Basel and the legal doctor and sign all the documents that confirm the event of death.

Here, too, one must pay membership and additional costs to obtain the services provided by this organization. The membership fee is at least fifty Swiss Francs per year and 1,000 Swiss Francs for a lifetime. The whole procedure costs around 10,000 Swiss Francs, including cremation. Interviews for this research reveal that Lifecircle is perceived by non-residents to be preferable to Dignitas as it maintains a more intimate relationship with the people seeking assisted suicide, plus it is run by a medical doctor and as such is perceived to be more professional. Since it is smaller than Dignitas and the medical review of requests for assisted suicide is usually made by Preisig herself, it is also perceived to be less bureaucratic and able to offer these services relatively quickly.

In Switzerland, most assisted suicide cases are made through Exit and Dignitas and take place within their premises. Assisted suicides in public hospitals only take place in Geneva and Lausanne and in these cases suicides are assisted by volunteers within these hospitals and not by physicians themselves.

Recent media reports indicate that the business of assisted-death organizations in Switzerland, especially Dignitas, is on the rise. Thus, citing from police figures presented in one of the local newspapers, it was held that the number of assisted deaths carried out by Dignitas rose by 35 per cent in 2011 to 144 cases, only five of which were not related to a foreign national. Exit also showed an increase of 17 per cent in that year.[73]

---

[73] Kathy Jones, '2011: Dignitas Assisted Deaths Rose by 35%' (20 February 2012) http://www.medindia.net/news/2011-dignitas-assisted-deaths-rose-by-35-97757-1.htm, accessed on 28 January 2018.

Publicized cases of suicide tourism refer to individuals, mostly famous or familiar to the public, who travelled to Switzerland to end their lives. These include, for example, Dr John Elliot from Australia,[74] English rugby player Daniel James,[75] English millionaire Peter Smedley,[76] Israeli radio broadcaster Adi Talmor,[77] and retired Canadian flight attendant Kathleen (Kay) Carter.[78] Through these 'celebrity' stories, ST receives recognition and legitimization, while also being accused of serving as an alternative for only those who can afford it.

Even though Switzerland has become the most popular destination for assisted suicide, there has been some opposition from within. As elaborated in Chapter 5, social attitudes were less accepting of suicide tourism than of assisted suicide for Swiss residents. In particular, some resistance was raised by people like Beatrice Wertli from the Swiss Christian Democrats[79] and by the Ministry of Justice, which issued statements suggesting that Switzerland 'has no interest, as a country, in being attractive for suicide tourism'.[80] However, public polls indicate large support for assisted suicide and even euthanasia,[81] including by right-to-die societies.[82]

---

[74] James Button, 'My Name is Dr John Elliot and I'm about to Die, with my Head Held High', *The Sydney Morning Herald* (26 January 2007) https://www.smh.com.au/world/my-name-is-dr-john-elliott-and-im-about-to-die-with-my-head-held-high-20070127-gdpc53.html, accessed on 28 January 2018.

[75] Jeremy Laurance, 'Agony of Helping a Son to Kill Himself', *The Independent* (27 May 2011) https://www.independent.co.uk/life-style/health-and-families/health-news/agony-of-helping-a-son-to-kill-himself-2289710.html, accessed on 28 January 2018.

[76] Michael Seamark, 'The 71-Year-Old Millionaire Who Died at Dignitas with Terry Pratchett at his Side in Controversial BBC Documentary', *Daily Mail* (9 June 2011) http://www.dailymail.co.uk/news/article-2000641/BBC-millionaires-Dignitas-death-controversial-documentary.html, accessed on 28 January 2018.

[77] Eran Baron, 'Radio Personality Adi Talmor Dead at 58' (*Ynet*, 8 August 2011) http://www.ynetnews.com/articles/0,7340,L-4106065,00.html, accessed on 28 January 2018.

[78] The Search, 'B.C. Woman Chooses a "Dignified" Death in Switzerland' (31 January 2010) http://blogs.vancouversun.com/2010/01/31/b-c-woman-chooses-a-dignified-death-in-switzerland/, accessed on 28 January 2018.

[79] BBC, 'Dignitas: Swiss Suicide Helpers' (20 January 2003) http://news.bbc.co.uk/2/hi/health/4643196.stm, accessed on 28 January 2018.

[80] Michael Leidig and Philip Sherwell, 'Swiss to Crack Down on Suicide Tourism', *The Telegraph* (14 March 2004) https://www.telegraph.co.uk/expat/4191761/Swiss-to-crack-down-on-suicide-tourism.html, accessed on 28 January 2018.

[81] Joachim Cohen, Paul Van Landeghem, Nico Carpentier, and Luc Deliens, 'Public Acceptance of Euthanasia in Europe: A Survey Study in 47 Countries' (2014) 59(1) *International Journal of Public Health* 143.

[82] General support varies from 50 per cent to 82 per cent of respondents. See Miller and Gonzalez, When Death Is the Destination (n 37) at 299. In the study they refer to 22 per cent of respondents supporting assisted suicide by right-to-die societies.

In a survey of the Swiss public conducted in 1999, 82 per cent of 1,000 respondents agreed that 'a person suffering from an incurable disease and who is in intolerable physical and psychological suffering has the right to ask for death and to obtain help for his purpose'. Interestingly, 68 per cent of those who so agreed mentioned that physicians should supply such help.[83] Attempts to change the law and revise the permission given for assisted suicide apparently did not involve proposals to otherwise regulate suicide tourism in Switzerland.[84]

While the vast majority of medical doctors in Switzerland is reluctant to be directly involved with assisted suicide,[85] professional guidelines published by the Swiss Academy of Medical Sciences convey a mixed message with regard to the ethics of assisted suicide and the involvement of physicians in this phenomenon. On the one hand, the guidelines stipulate that the physician's task is not 'to directly offer assistance in suicide, he rather is obliged to alleviate any suffering underlying the patient's wish to commit suicide'.[86] On the other hand, it is stated that consideration of the patient's wishes is fundamental for the physician–patient relationship, and thus, along with a physician's right to refuse to give help in committing suicide, the decision to provide assistance in suicide must be respected as such.[87]

Under these guidelines, when providing aid in dying, the physician must verify that: the patient's disease justifies the assumption that she is approaching the end of life; alternative possibilities for providing assistance have been discussed and implemented (if desired); the patient is cable of making the decision, and her wish has been well considered and is persistent;[88] and that the final action leading to death must be taken by the patient herself.

[83] Hurst and Mauron, Assisted Suicide (n 39) at 272.

[84] But see Mary Papenfuss, 'Swiss Politicians Battle "Suicide Tourism"' (*Newser*, 21 September 2009) http://www.newser.com/story/69889/swiss-politicians-battle-suicide-tourism.html, accessed on 28 January 2018 (reporting that, according to one Swiss initiative, only Swiss residents would be allowed to commit suicide).

[85] Andorno, Nonphysician-Assisted Suicide (n 40) at FN 6.

[86] Swiss Academy of Medical Sciences, *End-of-Life Care* (2013) at p. 9 https://www.samw.ch/en/Publications/Medical-ethical-Guidelines.html, accessed on 28 January 2018.

[87] Ibid.

[88] The guidelines stipulate that this condition has been checked by a third person who is not necessarily a physician.

However, in practice, it is not clear at all whether these guidelines are met in full. This chapter has already referred to cases under which non-terminally ill people sought and received aid in dying in Switzerland. In addition, some reports suggest that people have managed to obtain the lethal drugs on the day they arrived in Switzerland and after only a short interview.[89]

More generally, despite extensive public consultation on end-of-life issues[90] and a few attempts to revise the Swiss law on assisted suicide and contextualizing it in the medical sphere, the law remained the same as no consensus on whatever direction the law should take could be realized. An signed agreement between the canton of Zurich and one of the assisted suicide organizations (Exit), regulating the method and medical condition required for assisted suicide as well as the maximum payment to be received by the organization for carrying out this service, was invalidated by the Federal Court in 2010.[91]

In 2001, the Swiss Parliament rejected a bill that would have barred physicians from providing aid in dying.[92] Two bills were introduced by the Federal Council (the executive body) in 2009 but did not result in amendments to article 115 of the Penal Code. Under one of the bills, which was preferred by the majority of the Federal Council, assisted suicide would be restricted to terminal illness and would not be available to people with chronic or mental diseases, assisted suicide organizations would be prevented from becoming profit-driven businesses, and suicidal individuals with a terminal illness would be offered major alternatives (e.g. palliative care). Under the second bill, proposed by Council member Mr Pascal Couchepin, organized assisted suicide would be banned completely and suicide would remain a private issue.

Other initiatives by the ultra-conservative Federal Democratic Union and the Evangelical People's Party in 2011 to introduce a general national ban on assisted suicide and/or to restrict access to assisted suicide to those who had been living in the canton of Zurich for at least 1 year

---

[89] Andorno, Nonphysician-Assisted Suicide (n 40) at 4.

[90] Swiss Federal Council, 'Swiss Federal Council Acknowledges Results of Consultation Process' (Federal Office of Justice, 17 September 2010) https://www.bj.admin.ch/bj/en/home/aktuell/news/2010/ref_2010-09-17.html, accessed on 28 January 2018.

[91] Andorno, Nonphysician-Assisted Suicide (n 40) at 5–6.

[92] Hurst and Mauron, Assisted Suicide (n 39) at 272.

were rejected by 85 per cent and 78.4 per cent of voters respectively in this canton. Following considerable controversy and debate, the legislative proposals were abandoned and the Swiss government decided to leave the current legal position as it was and to adopt measures to prevent or reduce the incidence of suicides.[93]

Aside from the specific dynamics and methods implemented by any of the right-to-die associations present in Switzerland and the structure of Swiss federalism and Swiss law, one aspect common to all of them stands out when discussing suicide tourism: the accessibility granted to all citizens of the world. Before discussing the legal, philosophical, and sociopolitical aspects of suicide tourism, it is important to underline briefly the peculiar status of those other countries and states where assisted suicide is permitted so as to shed more light on the possible scope and potential for them to take part in the practice of suicide tourism.

The Netherlands

Since 2002, the Termination of Life on Request and Assisted Suicide (Review Procedures) Act[94] has allowed doctors in the Netherlands to carry out voluntary euthanasia in a number of circumstances. The law evolved over 3 decades from a series of judicial decisions and professional guidelines,[95] and in many ways can be regarded as liberal.

While assisted suicide still carries criminal liability under the Dutch penal code, the 2002 Act permits the active intervention of a doctor in the death of a patient following a consultation with at least one other independent physician, who has seen the patient, and a discussion with the patient about the medical condition and options available.

---

[93] Andorno, Nonphysician-Assisted Suicide (n 40) at 6–7.

[94] Available at: http://www.patientsrightscouncil.org/site/wp-content/uploads/2012/03/Netherlands_Ministry_of_Justice_FAQ_Euthanasia_2010.pdf, accessed on 28 January 2018.

[95] Prior to the law, few physicians had been accused of criminally ending patients' lives. There were five cases that had been decided by the highest legal institution, the Hoge Raad. However, all but one of these cases ended with light and often suspended sentences for technicalities or resulted in a verdict of not guilty. In the one exception, a conviction of a physician by a lower court was upheld since the patient did not express a request to die. Gerrit K. Kimsma, 'Death by Request in the Netherlands: Facts, the Legal Context and Effects on Physicians, Patients and Families' (2010) 13(4) Med Health Care Philos 355 (hereafter: 'Kimsma, Death by Request'). See also Safyan, Call for International Regulation (n 58) at 305.

Physician-assisted suicide is also legal in the Netherlands. Interestingly, the law does not distinguish between euthanasia and assisted suicide and uses 'euthanasia' as a term that encompasses both phenomena. Physicians and patients may choose one or the other depending on the circumstances. If a choice can be made, the Royal Dutch Society for the Advancement of Medicine recommends that physicians prefer assisted suicide for psychological reasons although this is not a binding recommendation.[96]

A request for euthanasia or assisted suicide must be well informed and voluntary. As a general rule, the patient's health condition must be such that there is no hope of improvement and the patient must be at least 16 years old. In addition, there must be no other reasonable alternatives in light of the patient's medical condition.

In rare instances, euthanasia is also possible where the patient is between 12 and 16 years—as long as they have a 'reasonable understanding of their interests'. In this scenario, the doctor is not allowed to refuse to euthanatize the patient if their legal guardians (parents or otherwise) agree with the end-of-life decision. However, the patient is expected to consult at least one other independent physician before formalizing the request.

Dutch doctors can also prescribe lethal drugs following a patient's request if she suffers from an unbearable physical or psychological condition for which there is no prospect of improvement. Following the Supreme Court decision in *Chabot*, while physicians should be extremely cautious, physician-assisted suicide can be justified when the patient is under mental suffering as well.[97] The law also respects such requests if made by minors aged between 12 and 15 with parental consent, or aged 16 to 17 with parental involvement in decision-making.

The Dutch law requires a report and investigation of each euthanasia/assisted suicide case. Five regional administrative bodies, entitled Euthanasia Review Committees, supervise on these cases; if they find that a case has not been carried out with due care, the case is referred to the criminal prosecution service and the medical inspectorate.[98] However,

---

[96] *Carter v. Canada (Attorney General)* [2012] B.C.J. No. 1196 (hereafter: '*Carter v. Canada lower court*') § 461.

[97] *Chabot*, Supreme Court [1994] N.J. No. 656 mentioned in *Carter v. Canada lower court* (n 96) at § 469.

[98] Kimsma, Death by Request (n 95).

research reveals that not all cases of the administration of lethal drugs are being reported. One of the main reasons for this under-reporting is that physicians do not regard the course of action as euthanasia or physician-assisted suicide and therefore do not believe a report is necessary.[99]

The Health Ministry recently put forward a proposal to allow elderly people over the age of 75, who are not suffering from a medical condition, to receive assisted suicide if they feel their lives are 'complete'. The decision whether to allow such assistance in any given case would be made by two specially trained life-ending consultants (each a qualified doctor, nurse, psychologist, or psychotherapist) and/or a committee. Support for such a proposal is based on the premise that restricting assisted suicide to patients with terminal or unbearable psychological conditions is insufficient and that older people have a right to end their life with dignity if they so choose. The proposal is aimed at older people who are struggling with a loss of independence, reduced mobility, and/or with loneliness. It is considered to be the first bill to assist healthy people to die to be proposed anywhere in the world.[100]

A study reviewing death certificates in the Netherlands reveals an increase in cases of euthanasia over a 20-year period (from 1.7% of all deaths in 1990 to 2.8% in 2010) and a decrease in deaths resulting from physician-assisted suicide (from 0.2% of all deaths in 1990 to 0.1% in 2010). Data also shows a significant decrease in cases of ending life without an explicit patient request (from 0.8% of all deaths in 1990 to 0.2% in 2010). The study also refers to the fact that 77 per cent of euthanasia or assisted suicide cases were reported to the Euthanasia Review Committees in 2010. The reporting rate is similar to that observed in 2005 (80%) and much higher than in 1990 (18%).[101] As will be discussed in Chapter 5, provided that the legal conditions are met, the Netherlands could be a potential destination for euthanasia/suicide tourism.[102]

[99] *Carter v. Canada lower court* (n 96) at § 482.

[100] Dan Bilefsky and Christopher F. Schuetze, 'Dutch Law Would Let Healthy Older People Choose Death', *New York Times* (14 October 2016) A5; Martin Bagot, 'Suicide Law Could Give Healthy Over-75s the Right to End Lives', *Daily Mirror* (20 December 2016) http://www.mirror.co.uk/news/world-news/suicide-law-could-give-healthy-9491792, accessed on 28 January 2018.

[101] Bregje D. Onwuteaka-Phillipsen et al., 'Trends in End-of-Life Practices Before and After the Enactment of the Euthanasia Law in the Netherlands from 1990 to 2010: A repeated Cross-Sectional Survey' (2012) 380(9845) *Lancet* 8.

[102] As will be discussed in Chapter 5, the Dutch law does not require that the person seeking assisted suicide or euthanasia be a resident.

Belgium

In 2002, Belgium passed a law on euthanasia while at the same time introducing new legislation on patients' rights and palliative care. This latter legislation covers the right to be informed of diagnosis and prognosis, the right to give medical consent, and the right to receive palliative care. While assisted suicide is not specifically covered under the legal definition of euthanasia, the Belgian oversight body on this issue, the Federal Control and Evaluation Commission (FCEC), ruled that the law covers this phenomenon as well.[103] Hence, if an assisted suicide case meets all the criteria for euthanasia under the law and it is reported to the FCEC, it will be treated as a euthanasia case.

The law, which is based on the Dutch law, establishes that a physician who performs euthanasia may not be criminalized if she ensures that the patient is adult, conscious, and competent in making a voluntary request to die. Additional requirements are that the request, which should also be in writing, is repeated and does not derive from external pressure, and that the patient is in a medical condition of constant and unbearable physical or mental suffering which cannot be alleviated and which results from a serious and incurable disorder caused by illness or accident. It should be noted that the law does not necessarily require that the patient is expected to die within months or to have a terminal condition.[104]

Similarly to Dutch law, the law in Belgium provides procedural safeguards such as imposing a duty to: inform the patient about her condition and to discuss the request for euthanasia with her; conduct several conversations with the patient over a reasonable period of time; consult another physician who will examine the patient independently about her medical condition and prognosis; discuss the matter with relatives (following the patient's consent); and have the patient discuss her wishes with loved ones.

In cases where the physician believes that the patient is unlikely to die in the near future, the law calls for an additional independent consultation with a third physician and requires the lapse of at least one month from the patient's written request to the act of euthanasia. Importantly,

---

[103] *Carter v. Canada lower court* (n 96) at § 508.

[104] Tinne Smets, Johan Bilsen, Joachim Cohen, Mette L. Rurup, and Luc Deliens, 'Legal Euthanasia in Belgium: Characteristics of All Reported Euthanasia Cases' (2009) 47(12) *Med Care* 1.

the law does not include a formal requirement for Belgian residency in order to be entitled to make an enforceable request for euthanasia. Yet, the prescribing physician has to know the patient well and, as mentioned above, to have several discussions with her about her explicit wish to die.

Physicians who complete an act of euthanasia are required to report it to the FCEC, and this supervisory body (consisting of sixteen members including doctors, lawyers, and individuals from various groups) must determine if the cases reported to it have been made in accordance with the law.[105]

In December 2013, the Parliament voted for an extension to the law so that it would also apply to minors.[106] This made Belgium the first country to allow euthanasia for incurably ill children. The amended law states that children afflicted with 'constant and unbearable physical suffering' and equipped 'with a capacity of discernment' will be allowed to be euthanized. The law—as well as the issue of euthanasia for children in general—attracted much criticism and debate.[107]

Studies show that the rate of euthanasia cases in Flanders (Belgium) decreased from 1.1 per cent of all deaths in 1998 to 0.3 per cent in 2001, shortly before the legalization of euthanasia in 2002, and then increased to 1.9 per cent of all deaths in 2007.[108] From 2007 to 2013 the rate of euthanasia increased significantly to 4.6 per cent of all deaths. This increase is attributable to an overall increases in the number of requests (from 3.5% to 6% of deaths) and the proportion of requests granted (from 56.3% to 76.8% of requests). The rate of ending life without an explicit request from the patient remained stable between these years at 1.7 per cent of all deaths.[109] Data from recent years refers to an increased rate

---

[105] When a majority of 2/3 of the FCEC decides that the act reported was not made under the law, the case then moves to the public prosecutor.

[106] Andrew Higgins, 'Belgian Senate Votes to Allow Euthanasia for Terminally Ill Children', *New York Times* (12 December 2013) http://www.nytimes.com/2013/12/13/world/europe/belgian-senate-votes-to-allow-euthanasia-for-terminally-ill-children.html?_r=0, accessed on 28 January 2018. The law was approved on 13 February 2014.

[107] Brian S. Carter, 'Why Palliative Care for Children is Preferable to Euthanasia' (2016) 33(1) *American Journal of Hospice & Palliative Medicine* 5; Giulia Cuman and Chris Gastmans, 'Minors and Euthanasia: A Systematic Review of Argument-Based Ethics Literature' (2017) 176(7) *European Journal of Paediatrics* 837.

[108] Johan Bilsen et al. 'Medical End-of-Life Practices under the Euthanasia Law in Belgium' (2009) 361(11) *NEJM* 1119.

[109] Kenneth Chambaere et al., 'Recent Trends in Euthanasia and Other End-of-Life Practices in Belgium' (2015) 372(12) *NEJM* 1179 (hereafter: 'Chambaere, Recent Trends').

of euthanasia among those aged 80 or older, those living in a nursing home, those with a disease other than cancer, and those not expected to die in the near future.[110] Overall, assisted suicide is a rare phenomenon in Belgium, comprising 0.5 per cent of all deaths, while euthanasia is a much more common phenomenon, representing 4.6 per cent of all deaths in 2013.[111]

Luxembourg

Luxemburg was the last member of the Benelux to adopt legislation legalizing voluntary euthanasia and assisted suicide. Although the law was passed by Parliament on 19 February 2008 (with a minimal majority of thirty votes in favour and twenty-six against), some bureaucratic and political controversies meant that it only came into force in March 2009. Under the law, which draws on the experience in Belgium, doctors can prescribe lethal drugs to a terminally ill patient under her repeated request to die if they consult an independent colleague to ensure that the patient has a terminal illness and is in a grave and incurable condition. Prescribing physicians should also consult with the patient's medical team and a 'person of trust' appointed by the patient.

Since no clause regarding residency or nationality is included in the law, non-residents can also ask for physician-assisted death. However, in an official document issued by the Ministry of Health it is stated, in this regard, that the law requires a close doctor–patient relationship. The doctor must know the patient well so that she should be able to confirm that the request to die is made freely. She must also interview the patient on several occasions, and certify and check that the suffering is indeed unbearable and with no prospects of improvement. Hence, it is emphasized that the treating physician must have treated the patient continuously and for a sufficiently long time.[112] Here, too, doctors are obliged to

---

[110] Sigrid Dierickx, Luc Deliens, Joachim Cohen, and Kenneth Chambaere, 'Euthanasia in Belgium: Trends in Reported Cases Between 2003 and 2013' (2016) 188(16) *CMAJ* E 407.

[111] Chambaere, Recent Trends (n 109).

[112] Luxemburg Ministry of Health, *Euthanasia and Assisted Suicide: Law of 16 March 2009* (Ministry of Health, 2010) at p. 26 http://www.sante.public.lu/fr/publications/e/euthanasie-assistance-suicide-questions-reponses-fr-de-pt-en/euthanasie-assistance-suicide-questions-en.pdf, accessed on 21 June 2017.

report each case to a national committee. The committee must verify if actions were taken in accordance with the law.[113]

Germany

Until 2015, there was no criminal prohibition on assisted suicide in Germany. In addition, a large majority (around 80%) of the public supported assisted suicide in Germany.[114] In 2014, an attempt to legalize assisted suicide in Germany was carried out by a few politicians representing various political and social parties.[115] Under this proposal, any person who suffered from acute pain should be able to decide, in a trusted conversation with her doctor, how much pain she should bear. The proposal set conditions for physician-assisted suicide: the patient must be an adult and have the ability to think rationally; she must suffer from an incurable disease which will inevitably lead to death; she should be suffering tremendously and should have undergone palliative care; a medical diagnosis of the patient is confirmed by a second physician; the person has to commit suicide herself. This proposal attempted to regulate physician-assisted suicide under the civil law rather than including it as a matter of criminal law. However, its discussion did not continue in Parliament.

A year later, four bills were introduced to Parliament. Three of them were considered unconstitutional as the definitions they contained would be hard to enforce.[116] The strictest version was proposed by lawmakers Michael Brand (the Christian Democratic Union) and Kerstin

[113] Rory Watson, 'Luxemburg is to Allow Euthanasia from 1 April' (2009) 338 *BMJ* b1248; Owen Dyer, Caroline White, and Aser R. Garcia, 'Assisted Dying: Law and Practice around the World' (2015) 351 *BMJ* h4481.

[114] Ben Knight, 'Proposed Assisted Suicide Controls in Germany "Are Unconstitutional"', *Deutsche Welle* (27 August 2015) http://www.dw.com/en/proposed-assisted-suicide-controls-in-germany-are-unconstitutional/a-18674011, accessed on 28 January 2018.

[115] The politicians who were involved in the proposal were vice-president of the Parliament, Peter Hintze, social democrats Karl Lauterbach, Burkhard Lischka, and Carola Reimann (SPD), Christian democrat Katherina Reiche (CDU), and member of the Christian social union Dagmar Woehrl. Deutsche Welle, 'German Parliament Discusses Euthanasia for Terminally Ill Patients' (*Deutsche Welle*, 16 October 2014) http://www.dw.com/en/german-parliament-discusses-euthanasia-for-terminally-ill-patients/a-18000591, accessed on 28 January 2018.

[116] Ibid. This was also evidenced from the interviews that I conducted with German participants.

Griese (the Social Democratic Party). According to their proposal, a punishment of 3 years' imprisonment would be likely to be given to anyone who offered or mediated the suicide of others on a regular basis, even where not undertaken for monetary purposes, including charities.

In November 2015, Germany passed a new revision to the criminal code (§ 217 StGB) prohibiting organizations and individuals from providing regular and repetitive assistance to others to commit suicide, including on a not-for-profit basis. As elaborated in Chapter 5, this new law was mainly prompted by the activities pursued by the society Sterbehilfe Deutschland and also by the growing rates of suicide tourism from Germany to Switzerland.

A recent study of the opinions of 457 physicians and nurses who participated in a conference on palliative care reveals that only half of respondents supported the new law, with 54 per cent of them believing the law did not sufficiently differentiate between illegal and legal forms of assisted suicide. The law did not make sense for more than 40 per cent of respondents.[117] At the time of writing this book, thirteen complaints have been submitted to the Federal Constitutional Court (*Bundesverfassungsgericht*) against the new law, claiming that it is unconstitutional.[118] Most of the claimants are palliative physicians arguing that the law violates the constitutional right to self-determination, specifically at end of life.

France

In France, a 2005 law allows the limitation or discontinuation of treatment and sedation until death occurs.[119] Following extensive public

---

[117] J. Zenz, R. Rissing-van Saan, and M. Zenz, 'Physician Assisted Suicide—Survey on §217 StGB in Germany' (2017) 142(5) *Dtsch Med Wochenschr* e28–e33 [in German].

[118] Complaints numbers are: 2 BvR 2347/15, 2 BvR 651/16, 2 BvR 1261/16, 2 BvR 1494/16, 2 BvR 1593/16, 2 BvR 1624/16, 2 BvR 1807/16, 2 BvR 2354/16, 2 BvR 2494/16, 2 BvR 2506/16, 2 BvR 2507/16, 2 BvR 2527/16, 2 BvR 2667/16. See: http://www.bundesverfassungsgericht.de/EN/Verfahren/Jahresvorausschau/vs_2017/vorausschau_2017.html.

[119] LOI n° 2005-370 du 22 avril 2005 relative aux droits des malades et à la fin de vie 23 April 2005 https://www.legifrance.gouv.fr/eli/loi/2005/4/22/SANX0407815L/jo/texte, accessed on 27 June 2017.

debate and a parliamentary commission (chaired by Didier Sicard) discussing issues relating to end-of-life care, an amendment was made to the Public Health Act (effective as of February 2016) which acknowledges an explicit right to deep and continuous sedation for terminally ill patients.[120] Palliative sedation applies in two situations: when the patient is a victim of refractory symptoms and when she decides to discontinue vital treatment.

The new law requires that sedation will normally be accompanied by the withholding of life-sustaining treatment including artificial nutrition and hydration.[121] Sedation in this context may be defined as 'the use of a pharmacological agent(s) to induce unconsciousness for treatment of truly distressing and refractory symptoms in the terminally ill'. While causing death is not intended, it is implicit that it may not be possible to achieve adequate symptom control except at risk of shortening life.[122]

Under the law it is not a requirement that the patient would otherwise experience severe or unbearable suffering. Although the practice of palliative sedation is not identical to euthanasia or physician-assisted suicide, it may be regarded as being similar to them.[123] It is also argued in the literature that the legalization of continuous deep sedation is made to avoid having to decriminalize physician-assisted suicide, thereby detracting from the debates on euthanasia and physician-assisted suicide more generally.[124] A lack of public and professional support for assisted suicide was also evidenced in the interviews that I conducted, as elaborated in Chapter 5.

---

[120] LOI n° 2016-87 du 2 février 2016 créant de nouveaux droits en faveur des malades et des personnes en fin de vie 2 February 2016 https://www.legifrance.gouv.fr/eli/loi/2016/2/2/AFSX1507642L/jo/texte, accessed on 27 June 2017.

[121] Alexandre de Nonneville et al., 'End-of-Life Practices in France under the Claeys-Leonetti Law: Report of Three Cases in the Oncology Unit' (2016) 9(3) *Case Rep Oncol* 650.

[122] John D. Cowan and Declan Walsh, 'Terminal Sedation in Palliative Medicine: Definition and Review of the Literature' (2001) 9 *Supportive Care in Cancer* 403 at 403–4.

[123] Henk Ten Have and Jos V.M. Welie, 'Palliative Sedation Versus Euthanasia: An Ethical Assessment' (2014) 47(1) *Journal of Pain and Symptom Management* 123.

[124] Kasper Raus, Kenneth Chambaere, and Sigrid Streckx, 'Controversies Surrounding Continuous Deep Sedation at the End of Life: The Parliamentary and Societal Debates in France' (2016) 17 *BMC Medical Ethics* 36; Kasper Raus, Sigrid Streckx, and Freddy Mortier, 'Is Continuous Sedation at the End of Life an Ethically Preferable Alternative to Physician-Assisted Suicide?' (2011) 11(6) *AJOB* 32.

The UK

Assisted suicide is illegal in the UK under section 2 of the Suicide Act 1961. The law was passed following the decriminalization of suicide in the UK. Since its enactment, several public committees and parliamentary discussions have addressed the issue of the legalization of assisted suicide. In 1994, a House of Lords select committee on medical ethics refused to recommend changing the law because of the possible message to be sent to vulnerable and disabled people in society. The committee was also unanimous in its conclusion that the right to refuse medical treatment is far removed from the right to request assistance in dying. The British government agreed and held that a change in the law would be open to abuse and may put the lives of the weak and vulnerable at risk.[125]

Following the European Court of Human Rights decision in the case of *Diane Pretty* (analysed in the next chapter), Lord Joffe introduced the Patient (Assisted Dying) Bill in 2003. In 2004 he then introduced the Assisted Dying for the Terminally Ill Bill.[126] Both bills sought to legalize assistance for those who suffered from unbearable suffering and who could not commit suicide without the help of others, which was debated in Parliament. A House of Lords select committee, set up to consider the issue, collected evidence from experts and the public and released its report in 2005.[127] The committee feared that a change in the law would be a 'slippery slope', leading to assisted suicide and euthanasia practices in inappropriate circumstances. It also suggested that the bill would put some vulnerable groups of people, such as the disabled and the elderly, at risk. The bill was rejected by Parliament in 2006.

In November 2008, the House of Commons had an adjournment debate on assisted dying. A year later, during the passage of the Coroners and Justice Bill, Lord Falconer of Thoroton proposed an amendment to

---

[125] Select Committee on Medical Ethics, *Report (HL Paper 21-I)* (HMSO, 1994). See http://hansard.millbanksystems.com/lords/1994/may/09/medical-ethics-select-committee-report, accessed on 29 January 2018.

[126] See https://api.parliament.uk/historic-hansard/lords/2004/mar/10/assisted-dying-for-the-terminally-ill.

[127] House of Lords, *Select Committee on the Assisted Dying for the Terminally Ill Bill (HL Paper 86-I)* (2005) https://publications.parliament.uk/pa/ld200405/ldselect/ldasdy/86/86i.pdf, accessed on 29 January 2018.

the Suicide Act under which those who assisted terminally ill people to travel to other countries where assisted suicide was legal would not be at risk of prosecution. This amendment was defeated in the House of Lords and the effect of section 2 of the Suicide Act has been preserved.[128]

Following the *Purdy* case (also discussed in the next chapter),[129] the Director of Public Prosecutions (DPP) revised its policy on prosecutions of people who provided assistance in suicides and Parliament discussed this policy in 2012. In 2013, the House of Lords held a debate on end-of-life care as well as on section 2 of the Suicide Act. A further debate on the DPP policy and the Act was held in the House of Lords in 2014.[130]

In 2014, before judgment in the *Nicklinson* case was given, Lord Falconer of Thoroton introduced a bill in the House of Lords. The bill was prepared following the work of the Falconer Commission.[131] It sought to enable competent adults who are terminally ill (defined as an inevitably progressive condition leading to death within 6 months) to receive aid in dying.[132] The bill was debated for 2 days but Parliament was prorogued before it made any progress. Rob Marris MP introduced a similar private member's bill in the House of Commons. It was debated in the House of Commons for only a few hours and rejected by 330 votes to 118.[133]

The Assisted Dying Bill (in similar terms to the earlier draft) has since been introduced in the House of Lords by Lord Falconer, in June 2015, and by Lord Hayward, in June 2016. However, neither of these attempts resulted in parliamentary debate.

According to recent research conducted by the British Medical Association, a majority of doctors in the UK believe that legalization of physician-assisted suicide can have a professional and emotional impact on doctors as well as having a detrimental effect on the physician–patient relationship. Most doctors taking part in this research did not want to

---

[128] *R (Conway) v. The Secretary of State for Justice* [2017] EWHC 2447 (Admin) (hereafter: *Conway*) at para. 50 (iv–vi).

[129] *R (Purdy) v. DPP* [2009] UKHL 45 (hereafter: *Purdy*).

[130] *Conway* (n 128) at para. 50 (vii–ix).

[131] The Commission on Assisted Dying, *Final Report* (Demos, 2011) https://www.demos.co.uk/files/476_CoAD_FinalReport_158x240_I_web_single-NEW_.pdf?1328113363, accessed on 29 January 2018.

[132] Assisted Dying Bill (HL) 2014–2015 https://publications.parliament.uk/pa/bills/lbill/2014-2015/0006/15006.pdf, accessed on 29 January 2018.

[133] Assisted Dying (No. 2) Bill 2015–2016 https://services.parliament.uk/bills/2015-16/assisteddyingno2/stages.html, accessed on 29 January 2018.

be involved in such practices.[134] Other recent surveys undertaken by the Royal College of General Practitioners,[135] the Royal College of Physicians,[136] and the Association of British Neurologists[137]—as well as a report by the British Geriatrics Society[138]—all demonstrate largescale opposition to a change in the law on assisted suicide in the UK and a reluctance to perform acts which may lead to a patient's death.

Public support for assisted suicide has been indicated in polls in 2010 and 2012, with about 60 per cent of Britons thinking that people who help another person to commit suicide should not be prosecuted.[139]

The legalization of assisted suicide in the UK has been discussed in case law in recent years. The next chapter elaborates on the *Nicklinson* case. Suffice it to mention here that in this case, a majority of the Supreme Court of the UK held that the absolute prohibition on assisted dying interfered with the claimant's right to respect for private life under Article 8 of the European Convention on Human Rights while finding the evidence on safeguards insufficient. However, the court did not find it institutionally appropriate to grant a declaration on the current law. It nonetheless

---

[134] Ruth Campbell and Veronica English, *End-of-Life Care and Physician-Assisted Dying*, vol. 3 (British Medical Association, 2016) https://www.bma.org.uk/collective-voice/policy-and-research/ethics/end-of-life-care, accessed on 29 January 2018.

[135] Royal College of General Practitioners, *Assisted Dying Consultation Analysis* (2014) http://www.rcgp.org.uk/policy/rcgp-policy-areas/assisted-dying.aspx, accessed on 29 January 2018.

[136] Under this survey, 32.3 per cent of respondents support a change in the law and another 10.2 per cent of them are in favour of such a change while objecting to assisted suicide by doctors. The remaining majority opposes any change in the law. Interestingly, 62.5 per cent of respondents believe changes and improvements in palliative care make the change in legislation unnecessary. Royal College of Physicians, *Assisted Dying Survey 2014* (2014) https://www.rcplondon.ac.uk/news/rcp-reaffirms-position-against-assisted-dying, accessed on 29 January 2018.

[137] Association of British Neurologists, *Assisted Dying: Conclusions of the Working Party of the Association of British Neurologists* (2011) http://www.livinganddyingwell.org.uk/sites/default/files/ABN%20-%20Assisted%20Dying%20-%20Conclusions%20-%20April%202011.pdf, accessed on 30 January 2018. The Association states on its website that this statement is out of date and is replaced by the Royal College of Physicians 2014 survey (n 136). See https://www.theabn.org/resources/other-publications/a/assisted-dying.html, accessed on 30 January 2018.

[138] British Geriatrics Society, *Physician Assisted Suicide: The British Geriatrics Society Position* (2015) https://www.bgs.org.uk/sites/default/files/content/attachment/2018-04-06/2015_bgs_on_assisted_suicide.pdf, accessed on 30 January 2018.

[139] Moreover, under this survey 67 per cent of respondents support the legalization of euthanasia in the UK. Angus Reid Institute, *Two Thirds of Britons Are Willing to Legalise Euthanasia* (Angus Reid Institute, 2010) http://www.gilanifoundation.com/homepage/GlobalOpinion145.htm#15/, accessed on 18 June 2017. The large amount of support for euthanasia had increased to 71 per cent in another poll conducted 2 years later. Angus Reid Institute, *Legal Euthanasia Supported by Majority in Great Britain* (Angus Reid Institute, 2012) https://angusreid.org/legal-euthanasia-supported-by-majority-in-great-britain/, accessed on 18 June 2017. See also, Raphael Cohen-Almagor, 'The Assisted Dying Bill for England and Wales' in Michael J. Cholbi (ed), *Euthanasia and Assisted Suicide* (Praeger, 2017) 29.

ruled that Parliament should have the opportunity to debate and consider the amendment of this legislation.[140]

A more recent case for judicial review in the matter of Noel Conway was heard by the English High Court.[141] This case involved a man who suffered from motor neurone disease consisting of a gradual deterioration and weakening of the muscles. When Conway's prognosis was that he had less than 6 months to live he wished to take actions to end his life through the help of a medical professional. Conway did not find acceptable the alternative of withdrawing the non-invasive mechanical ventilation which helped him breath accompanied with medication to ensure he was unaware of it and did not suffer. Neither did he regard the possibility of travelling to Switzerland to be an acceptable option. At court, Conway argued that the current law interfered with his private life under Article 8 of the European Convention on Human Rights. He sought a declaration of incompatibility under the Human Rights Act, arguing that the law could be modified to allow people in his position, with proper safeguards suggested by him (relatively similar to those included in Lord Falconer's bill),[142] to receive medical aid in dying.

While previous case law affirmed that the law did indeed represent an interference with Conway's right to respect for private life,[143] the Ministry of Justice argued that the law was not incompatible with Article 8 since it was justified under Article 8(2) to the Convention as being necessary in a democratic society as a proportionate measure for the protection of the health, morals, and rights of others. It was argued that this law gave proper respect to the weak and vulnerable and to the sanctity of life. From an ethical perspective the law also promoted trust between patients and physicians, thereby safeguarding the provision of appropriate treatment.[144]

The court held that the current law was compatible with Article 8. In this case it found that, since Mr Conway was expected to die soon and because of the palliative care available to him, the public interest in

---

[140] *Nicklinson* (n 2).

[141] *Conway* (n 128); *R (Conway) v. The Secretary of State for Justice* [2017] EWHC 640 (Admin); *R (Conway) v. The Secretary of State for Justice (Rev 1)* [2017] EWCA Civ 275.

[142] *Conway* (n 128).

[143] *Pretty* (n 15) at para. 67; *Haas* (n 9); *Purdy* (n 129); and *Nicklinson* (n 2). This position was also endorsed in *Koch v Germany* (2013) 56 EHRR 6.

[144] *Conway* (n 128) at paras 12, 13.

maintaining section 2 of the Suicide Act 1961 outweighed the price he had to pay. The court commented that Parliament was better placed than the court to make an assessment on the impact of changing the law and concluded that section 2 was necessary to protect the weak and vulnerable.[145]

North America

United States of America

Assisted suicide is legal in seven jurisdictions in the US covering almost 20 per cent of Americans[146] and more states are now witnessing some pressure to change their laws in this direction.[147] In *Washington v. Glucksberg*,[148] the US Supreme Court rejected the argument that a competent terminally ill patient has a constitutional right to assisted suicide derived from the right to withdraw life-support and to refuse treatment under the Fourteenth Amendment's Due Process Clause. The court, nonetheless, conferred upon states the discretion to legalize this medical practice should they so desire. It also followed from this ruling that states can make assisted suicide illegal without violating the Equal Protection Clause.[149] The validity of a state's jurisdiction in this context was approved in a later Supreme Court decision which merely focussed on an administrative issue relating to the interpretation of a federal regulation and its effect on the Oregon Death with Dignity Act.[150]

Most of the jurisdictions have legalized physician-assisted suicide via legislation, while only one state (Montana) reached its decision via a court ruling. The subsections below will explore the different models of legalization of assisted suicide in the US.

---

[145] *Conway* (n 128) at paras 110, 111, 128.

[146] Paula Span, 'Physician Aid in Dying Gains Acceptance in the US', *New York Times* (16 January 2017) https://www.nytimes.com/2017/01/16/health/physician-aid-in-dying.html?smid=pl-share, accessed on 31 January 2018 (hereafter: 'Span, Physician Aid').

[147] These jurisdictions are: California, Colorado, District of Columbia, Montana, Oregon, Vermont, and Washington. Moreover, three of these seven jurisdictions enacted their laws between 2015 and 2017: California, Colorado, and District of Columbia. Thaddeus M. Pope, 'Legal History of Medical Aid in Dying: Physician Assisted Death in the U.S. Courts and Legislatures' (2018) 48 *New Mexico L. Rev.* 267 (hereafter: 'Pope, Legal History').

[148] *Glucksberg* (n 10) at 702, 728, 735.

[149] *Vacco* (n 10); Lewis, Graceful Exit (n 1).

[150] *Gonzalez v. Oregon* 546 U.S. 243 (2006).

Oregon

Back in 1997, Oregon was the first state in the US to introduce the possibility of receiving aid in dying through the Death with Dignity Act.[151] Interestingly, Washington was the first state to offer aid in dying to its voters but without success. The following year, a ballot initiative on this issue was offered in California but failed to pass by a small margin. Given these failures, the law in Oregon was tailored to pass, which it did by a margin of 51 per cent to 49 per cent.[152]

Under this law, terminally ill[153] capable[154] adult patients who are residents of Oregon are allowed to voluntarily self-administer lethal medications (prescribed by a physician for that purpose only) to end their lives. Factors demonstrating Oregon residency include, but are not limited to: possession of an Oregon driving licence; registration to vote in Oregon; evidence that the person owns or leases property in Oregon; or filing an Oregon tax return for the most recent tax year.[155]

However, participants in the programme only need to provide proof of residency to their prescribing physician, and there is no minimum length required for participation, nor must they necessarily have a long-standing relationship with the prescribing physician. Moreover, the Oregon Health Authority does not collect data on the length of residency.[156] It is also not required that the person take the lethal drug in Oregon. Indeed, under Oregon law (as well as the Washington statute which is based on the Oregon law model) it is easy and inexpensive for persons to become residents in order to meet the qualifying requirements.[157]

The law provides various procedural safeguards to ensure that eligibility criteria for physician-assisted suicide are met, including: the

---

[151] Oregon Death with Dignity Act, Oregon Rev. Stat. (1994) § 127.800–127.897. Available at: http://www.oregon.gov/oha/PH/PROVIDERPARTNERRESOURCES/EVALUATIONRESEARCH/DEATHWITHDIGNITYACT/Documents/statute.pdf, accessed on 31 January 2018.

[152] Kathryn L. Tucker, 'When Dying Takes Too Long: Activism for Social Change to Protect and Expand Choice at the End of Life' (2011/12) 33 *Whittier L. Rev.* 109, 115.

[153] A terminal condition refers to an incurable and irreversible disease which has been confirmed as such that will lead to death within 6 months. Oregon Death with Dignity Act, Oregon Rev. Stat. (2004) at § 127.800 § 1.01(12).

[154] Defined as having the ability to make and communicate health care decisions. Ibid. at § 127.800 § 1.01(3).

[155] Ibid. at § 127.860 § 3.10.

[156] Email correspondence with Craig New, Research Analyst, Oregon Health Authority on 19 June 2017.

[157] Lewis, Graceful Exit (n 1) at 480.

patient must, over 15 days, make two oral requests and one written request signed by two witnesses (one of the witnesses should be a person who is not related to the patient); a confirmation by the attending physician that the patient is indeed in a terminal condition; a second opinion by a consulting physician confirming both the diagnosis and that the patient is capable and acting voluntarily; and a minimum period of 48 hours between the patient's written request and the writing of the prescription.[158]

The Oregon Health Authority is required to collect detailed information about the physicians and patients involved in the practice, and it publishes an annual statistical report and highlights the numbers and trends of the Act within the state. According to data presented in 2017, the number of prescriptions under the Act has increased from twenty-four prescriptions in 1998 to 204 in 2016, while the number of these prescriptions almost doubled between 2013 and 2016 (from 121 to 204). The number of deaths has dramatically risen as well throughout the years: from sixteen incidents in 1998 to 133 in 2013. Here, too, the number of deaths almost doubled within 3 years (from 73 in 2013 to 133 in 2016). Since the law was passed, 1,749 people have had prescriptions written under the law and 1,127 patients have died from ingesting the drugs. During 2016, the rate of deaths under the law was 37.2 per 10,000 total deaths. About 17 per cent of those who received prescriptions in 2016 did not take the medication and died of other causes.[159]

Washington

The Washington Death with Dignity Act passed in November 2008 and was first implemented in 2009.[160] Very much in line with its predecessor in Oregon, the Act is limited to the terminally ill (with a life expectancy of less than 6 months) who are residents of the state, and it requires the involvement of physicians in the prescription of lethal drugs and in

---

[158] Oregon Death with Dignity Act, Oregon Rev. Stat. § 127.800; Institute of Public Opinion and Market Research –127.897 (1994) at § 127.860 § 3.01; 3.08.

[159] Oregon Health Authority, Public Health Division, *Oregon Death with Dignity Act: Data Summary 2016* (Oregon Health Authority, 10 February 2017) http://www.oregon.gov/oha/PH/ PROVIDERPARTNERRESOURCES/EVALUATIONRESEARCH/DEATHWITHDIGNITYACT/ Documents/year19.pdf, accessed on 18 June 2017.

[160] Washington Death with Dignity Act. Wash. Rev. Code s. 70.245 (2009). Available at: http:// apps.leg.wa.gov/RCW/default.aspx?cite=70.245, accessed on 31 January 2018.

the supervision of the procedure. Here, too, evidence demonstrating Washington residency includes possession of a state driver's licence, registration to vote in Washington, or owning or leasing property in the state.[161] Also, the names of patients and of healthcare providers are kept and made public through the publication of an annual report aimed at updating the general public on the real impact of the Act.

Recent data on the application of the law in Washington indicates a similar pattern to that observed in Oregon. The number of people receiving prescriptions for lethal drugs and of deaths occurring has gradually risen since the law came into effect, with a significant increase in these numbers over the last 3 years. Hence, while in 2009 there were sixty-five cases of prescriptions leading to sixty-four deaths, in 2015 there were 213 participants in the programme and 202 deaths. It should be noted that these latter figures are almost double those in 2012. In that year, there were 121 cases of prescriptions and 121 reported deaths.[162] Reviewing the data from Washington, it also suggests a close proximity between the number of actual deaths and the number of people receiving prescriptions, unlike in Oregon where a larger gap between these figures is observed.

Vermont

Chronologically speaking, this is the next state to have lifted legal penalties for doctors providing prescriptions for patients willing to put an end to their lives. A consulting doctor and the patient's primary physician must assess the patient and confirm that she is suffering from a terminal illness and that she is fully competent when requesting death-inducing drugs. The Vermont bill[163] was implemented on a 3-year trial period. In 2015, the Vermont legislature repealed this sunset provision and Vermont became another state under the Oregon model of the Death with Dignity Act where physician-assisted suicide is legal.

---

[161] Ibid. at § 70.245.130.

[162] Washington State Department of Health, *Washington State Department of Health 2015 Death with Dignity Act Report Executive Summary* (Washington State Department of Health, 2016) http://www.doh.wa.gov/portals/1/Documents/Pubs/422-109-DeathWithDignityAct2015.pdf, accessed on 19 June 2017.

[163] No. 39. An act relating to patient choice and control at end of life. Available at: http://www.procon.org/sourcefiles/ACT039_Vermont_Death_with_dignity.pdf. See VT.STAT.ANN. title 18, §§ 5281–5293 (2013).

Montana

Although no legal protocol is in place in Montana, the 2009 four-to-three ruling of the Montana Supreme Court (affirming a district court decision) found that there is no indication in Montana law that a physician providing aid in dying to a terminally ill, mentally competent adult patients is acting against public policy. The court ruled that a physician whose role is to provide a terminally ill patient with the means to end her life does not force her to take the medication. Under this rationale, if the person commits suicide and dies, the death is not a direct result of the physician's actions.[164]

As a result, any physician assisting a competent person wishing to die does not risk criminal liability if they have been granted the patient's consent. There are no reporting requirements in Montana and little is known about the practice of assisted suicide in this state.[165]

New Mexico

Another attempt to legalize assisted suicide in the courts was made in a lower court in New Mexico in 2014. In *Morris v. Brandenburg*, the court held that a competent terminally ill individual has a right to receive aid in dying under the state's constitution. Interestingly, the court invalidated the state's prohibition against assisted suicide not only on the grounds that it violated the rights to enjoy life and liberty but also the right to seek and obtain happiness.[166] However, the court of appeals and the New Mexico Supreme Court reversed the decision. It held that the law represents a rational response to the legitimate public interest in protecting individuals and making sure that end-of-life decisions are informed and safe. If a revised balance between this interest and the interest in preventing a painful and debilitating life is to be made, it is the legislature and not the courts to make it.[167] The New Mexico legislature has not responded.

---

[164] *Baxter v. Montana*, 224 P.3d. 1211, 1222 (Mont. 2009).

[165] Linda Ganzini and Anthony L. Back, 'The Challenge of New Legislation on Physician-Assisted Death' (2016) *JAMA Intern Med.* 427; Lewis, Graceful Exit (n 1).

[166] *Morris v. Brandenberg*, 2014 WL 10672977 (2d Jud. D. Ct. Bernalillo County, N.M. 31 January 2014).

[167] *Morris v. Brandenburg*, 376 P.3d. 836 (N.M. 30 June 2016).

California, District of Columbia, and Colorado

While four bills on physician-assisted suicide had been introduced in California since 1995, the journey of 29-year-old Brittany Maynard from California to Oregon to die in November 2014 gave the issue a renewed visibility and increased the public support, and as a result the political support, for such a law.[168] In October 2015, the End of Life Option Act passed, making California the fourth state in the US to enact a law allowing physician-assisted suicide.[169] Based on the Oregon law model, this law will be effective until 1 January 2026.

Another statute, which is also based on the Oregon law model, was enacted in 2017 in the District of Columbia. The law has been effective since February 2017.[170]

In November 2016, Colorado voters approved proposition 106—Medical Aid in Dying—which allows physician-assisted suicide for terminally ill patients. The Colorado End of Life Options Act became effective on 16 December 2016.[171] This law is also based on the Oregon law model.

In addition to these successful attempts at legislation, other states have been very close in recent years to passing ballot initiatives on assisted suicide while many others are considering introducing them in the next few months. The most prominent include Massachusetts, Maine, Michigan, and Maryland.[172]

Legalization of assisted suicide increased (and reflected) public support, shifting aid in dying in America from a rich white person's issue to a phenomenon that can be found in more diverse localities.[173] Indeed, the Oregon experience shows that the number of prescriptions has increased annually since the legalization of physician-assisted suicide.[174] On the other hand, aid in dying is not covered under Medicare or the Department of Veterans Affairs. The states of California and Oregon

---

[168] 'California's Right to Die Bill', *New York Times* (22 September 2015) http://www.nytimes.com/2015/09/22/opinion/californias-right-to-die-bill.html?_r=0.

[169] Cal. Health & Safety Code §§ 443.2–443.22 (effective 9 June 2016).

[170] D.C. Act 21-577, D.C. Law L21-0182, 64 D.C. Reg. 2691 (17 March 2017).

[171] Colo. Rev. Stat. §§ 25-48-101 to 123 (effective 16 December 2016) .

[172] Pope, Legal History (n 147) at 14.

[173] Span, Physician Aid (n 146).

[174] Charles Blanke, Michael LeBlanc, Dawn Hershman, Lee Ellis, and Frank Meyskens, 'Characterizing 18 years of the Death with Dignity Act in Oregon' (2007) *JAMA Oncol.* doi:10.1001/jamaoncol.2017.0243

agreed to cover it for Medicaid recipients, but other states did not. As the cost of the most commonly used lethal drug, Seconal, reaches $3,000–$4,000 this could be a serious hurdle.[175] There is also a reported problem of a shortage of participating physicians who could prescribe.[176] Overall, after almost 20 years in Oregon and 8 years in Washington, less than 1 per cent of annual deaths involve a lethal prescription. It follows that although assisted suicide is legal in a growing number of states, most Americans do not choose to die.[177]

Moreover, the gradual spread of legislation allowing physician-assisted suicide in the US should be reviewed in light of some recent data suggesting that assisted suicide in Oregon and Washington may involve abuse and complications. Allegations in this direction include physician shopping to get around safeguards, an absence of psychiatric consultation, nurse-assisted suicide (with no orders from physicians), assisted suicide of an unconscious patient or where there has not been a specific request from the patient, and economic pressure and coercion (e.g. denying Oregon Medicaid patients cancer treatment while offering coverage for assisted suicide).[178]

Canada

In June 2014, the Province of Quebec approved Bill 52,[179] which legalized euthanasia, although it used the term 'medical aid in dying'. It is argued that the term was used to allow support for the bill by not explicitly informing the general public that euthanasia was being legalized.[180] The new law, which has been in effect since December 2015, stipulates a few conditions to be met before allowing a request, namely the person

---

[175] As a result, it is reported that physicians use an alternative which is less well understood, namely the combination of opioids and sedatives. Ibid.

[176] Ibid.

[177] Ibid.

[178] Kenneth R. Stevens and William L. Toffler, 'Euthanasia and Physician-Assisted Suicide: A Letter to the Editor' (2016) 316(5) *JAMA* 1599.

[179] Bill 52: An Act Respecting End-of-Life Care. Available at: http://www.assnat.qc.ca/en/travaux-parlementaires/projets-loi/projet-loi-52-40-1.html, accessed on 21 June 2017.

[180] Brian L. Mishara and David N. Weisstub, 'Legalization of Euthanasia in Quebec, Canada as "Medical Aid in Dying": A Case Study in Social Marketing, Changing Mores and Legal Manuvering' (2015) 1(4) *Ethics, Medicine and Public Health* 450.

must: submit a free and informed request in writing; be 18 years old or over and be able to give consent to care; be suffering from a serious and incurable disease; be in a medical condition characterized by an advanced and irreversible decline in her faculties; and be experiencing constant and unbearable physical or psychological suffering which cannot be tolerably alleviated.

As a result of lobbying from suicide prevention organizations and the fact that Canadian law contained a criminal prohibition against assisted suicide at the time it was passed, the law in Quebec does not legalize assisted suicide but explicitly permits the ending a person's life at her request by physicians through the idea of medical assistance.[181] Physicians acting under this law must report to a monitoring body, although the law does not specify which practices constitute medical aid in dying and research shows that even healthcare professionals are confused on this question.[182]

In February 2015, an anonymous decision of the Supreme Court of Canada in *Carter v. Canada* ruled that the Criminal Code prohibitions against voluntary euthanasia (section 14) and assisted suicide (section 241(b)) were unconstitutional as they violated the right to life, liberty, and security of the person under section 7 of the Canadian Charter of Rights and Freedoms. The case heard a claim by a patient suffering from ALS, Gloria Taylor, who refused to die slowly as her disease progressed and sought aid in dying. Taylor did not have the financial means to go to Switzerland and was left with a cruel choice given the prohibition under the Criminal Code.[183]

The claim was also brought by Lee Carter and Hollis Johnson who assisted Ms Carter's mother, Kay Carter, in travelling to Switzerland for assisted suicide. The two, who were at risk of prosecution, described how their plan and arrangement of the trip to Switzerland was difficult, partly because it had to be kept secret. They claimed that Kay ought to have died at home rather than undergoing a stressful and expensive procedure abroad.[184] Also joined to the legal proceedings were a physician from

---

[181] Ibid.

[182] Isabelle Marcoux, Antoine Boivin, Claude Arsenault, Melanie Toupin, and Joseph Youssef, 'Health Care Professionals' Comprehension of the Legal Status of End-of-Life Practices in Quebec' (2015) 61(4) *CFP* e196.

[183] *Carter v. Canada* (n 3) at § 13.

[184] Ibid. at § 18.

British Columbia, who was willing to practice physician-assisted suicide if it became legal, and the British Columbia Civil Liberties Association, which advocated for respect to be given to end-of-life choices, including assisted suicide.

The court held that the prohibitions against euthanasia and assisted suicide were void when the person affected clearly consented to the termination of life and she had a grievous and irremediable condition (including an illness, disease, or disability) causing her enduring and intolerable suffering.[185] The Court suspended its decision for 16 months to allow the Canadian government time to make new laws or regulations.

By this judgment, the court reversed its previous ruling in *Rodriguez v. British Columbia*,[186] decided 21 years earlier. The *Rodriguez* case upheld, by a slim majority, the prohibition of assisted suicide in Canada, holding that such a prohibition did not violate section 7 to the Charter, thereby prompting extensive public and political debate on assisted suicide in Canada.[187]

Indeed, the story of Rodriguez resulted in much public debate which was followed by a Special Senate Committee on Euthanasia and Assisted Suicide. This committee recommended against legalization of these practices in Canada.[188] Further deliberations of this committee in 2000 resulted in no other recommendations, in terms of legalization of assisted suicide, but it called for a continued search for better and more adequate solutions for the dying and the hopelessly ill members of the community.[189]

In June 2016, the prohibition against assisted suicide in the Criminal Code was amended through a new law on assistance in dying. The new

[185] Ibid. at § 4.

[186] *Rodriguez* (n 18).

[187] This extensive debate resulted in the publication of two reports supporting assistance in dying under some circumstances: Royal Society of Canada, *The Royal Society of Canada Expert Panel: End-of-Life Decision Making (Chair: Udo Schuklenk)* (RSC, November 2011) https://rsc-src.ca/en/expert-panels/rsc-reports/end-life-decision-making, accessed on 18 June 2017; National Assembly of Quebec, *Select Committee: Dying with Dignity: Report* (NAC, March 2012) http://www.rpcu.qc.ca/pdf/documents/rapportcsmden.pdf accessed on 18 June 2017.

[188] Parliament of Canada, Special Senate Committee on Euthanasia and Assisted Suicide, *Of Life and Death: Final Report* (Parliament of Canada, 1995) https://sencanada.ca/content/sen/committee/351/euth/rep/lad-e.htm, accessed on 21 June 2017.

[189] Parliament of Canada, Standing Senate Committee on Social Affairs, Science and Technology, *Quality End-of-Life Care: The Right of Every Canadian: Final Report* (Parliament of Canada, 2000) https://sencanada.ca/content/sen/committee/362/upda/rep/repfinjun00-e.htm, accessed on 21 June 2017.

amendment added an exemption for medical assistance in dying that is provided by a medical practitioner or a nurse. Medical assistance in dying includes the direct administration of a substance that causes the death of the person who requested it as well as prescribing to a patient a substance that they can self-administer to cause their own death.[190] Under section 241.2(1)(a) of the law, a person may receive medical assistance in dying if they are eligible or, but for any applicable minimum period of residence or waiting period, would be eligible for health services funded by a government in Canada.[191]

This residency requirement goes further than the proposals set by the Senate advisory committee and a provincial-territorial expert group, where it was recommended that eligibility for medical-assisted suicide should be based on existing eligibility for public healthcare insurance. The rationale for the residency requirement according to the Senate Joint Committee Report was twofold: 'MAID (medical assistance in dying) should occur in the context of a patient–physician relationship and the Committee does not want Canada to become a destination for people seeking MAID'.[192] Furthermore, it is evidenced from the process leading to this legislation that such a provision was intended not only to limit suicide tourism to Canada but also within Canada:[193]

Although imposing a Canadian residency requirement would prevent residents of foreign countries from visiting Canada to receive physician-assisted dying, imposing limits based on citizenship or permanent residency status could also create a barrier to access for some in Canada. As a result, we recommend that all—and only—those eligible for publicly-funded health services also qualify for physician-assisted dying.

[190] Medical Assistance in Dying Law (Bill C-14), Statutes of Canada 2016, Chapter 3 at § 241.1 http://laws-lois.justice.gc.ca/PDF/2016_3.pdf accessed on 6 July 2017 (hereafter: 'Medical Assistance in Dying Law').

[191] Ibid. at § 241.2(1).

[192] Parliament of Canada, *Medical Assistance in Dying: A Patient-Centered Approach—Report of the Special Joint Committee on Physician-Assisted Dying* (2016) p. 24 http://www.parl.ca/Content/Committee/421/PDAM/Reports/RP8120006/pdamrp01/pdamrp01-e.pdf, accessed on 31 January 2018.

[193] Government of Canada, *Provincial-Territorial Expert Advisory Group on Physician-Assisted Dying—Final Report* (2015) p. 37 http://www.health.gov.on.ca/en/news/bulletin/2015/docs/eagreport_20151214_en.pdf, accessed on 31 January 2018.

In addition, it is required that the person seeking assistance in dying: is at least 18 years old and capable of making healthcare decisions; has a grievous and irremediable medical condition, defined as a serious and incurable disease or disability (whereby natural death is reasonably foreseeable); and is in an advanced state of irreversible decline in capability, leading to enduring intolerable physical or psychological suffering that cannot be relieved.[194] She must also have made a voluntary request for medical assistance in dying that does not result from external pressure, and given informed consent to receiving medical assistance in dying after having been informed of the means that are available to relieve suffering, including palliative care.[195]

The law stipulates several safeguards to secure the voluntariness of the request to receive medical assistance in dying, including the requirement for the request to be signed before two independent witnesses; a second opinion, written by a medical practitioner or nurse, attesting to the person's meeting all necessary criteria; the lapse of at least 10 days between the day on which the request to receive assistance was signed and the day on which the medical assistance is provided;[196] providing an opportunity immediately before the medical assistance for the person to withdraw their request, and ensuring that express consent is given to receiving such medical assistance; and taking all necessary measures to provide a reliable means of providing information so that the person would understand it, in case she has difficulty communicating.[197]

The monitoring system as well as data collection and reporting activities, to be set under regulations, are expected in 2018. Implementation of the law rests upon the provinces and territories. Public reporting by all provinces and most territories reveal that between 10 December 2015 (the date on which the law in Quebec came into effect) and 31 December 2016 there were 803 cases of medically assisted deaths in Canada comprising less than 0.6 per cent of all deaths. Only 0.4 per cent of medically

---

[194] The law does not require delivering a prognosis on the specific length of time that the person has remaining. It may be that, to err on the side of caution, medical assistance in dying may be provided only to those whose deaths are imminent.

[195] Medical Assistance in Dying Law (n 190) at § 241.2(1), § 241.2(2).

[196] If death or loss of capacity to give informed consent is imminent, the law allows for a reduced period of time.

[197] At § 241.2(3).

assisted deaths have been self-administered; most cases are classified as voluntary euthanasia.[198]

The court's decision and the new law corresponds with the public view on the matter. According to recent polls, 90 per cent of Canadians think some form of assisted suicide should be permitted, although they are split on whether regulation should be strict or minimal. About 80 per cent of respondents say assisted suicide should not be allowed to people who have severe psychological suffering but with no terminal disease. More than 70 per cent of them refer to severe pain and imminent terminal prognosis as legitimate conditions for assisted suicide.[199]

South America

Colombia

Following two cases in the Constitutional Court of Colombia in 1997 and 2014, in which the prohibition against euthanasia and assisted suicide was challenged, Colombia became a country where euthanasia and assisted suicide are legal.[200] Effective since 2015,[201] The law on euthanasia and assisted suicide mandates that the patient requesting assisted suicide or euthanasia must be adult, legally capable, and in a terminal state (as certified by two physicians), that is she is suffering from a disease which is expected to lead to her death within 6 months. She must also be experiencing intensive pain or a continued condition of great dependency and disability that the person herself considers unworthy. Another requirement

---

[198] Government of Canada, *Interim Report on Medical Assistance in Dying in Canada June 17 to December 31, 2016* (Government of Canada, 2017) https://www.canada.ca/en/health-canada/services/publications/health-system-services/medical-assistance-dying-interim-report-dec-2016.html#intro, accessed on 6 July 2017.

[199] Angus Reid Institute, 'Physician-Assisted Suicide: Canadians Reject Certain Commons Committee Recommendations' (Angus Reid Institute, 1 April 2016) http://angusreid.org/assisted-suicide-law/, accessed on 18 June 2017.

[200] Emanuel et al., Attitudes and Practices (n 1); Julia Nicol and Marlisa Tiedemann, *Euthanasia and Assisted Suicide: The Law in Selected Countries* (Library of Parliament, 2015) https://lop.parl.ca/staticfiles/PublicWebsite/Home/ResearchPublications/BackgroundPapers/PDF/2015-116-e.pdf, accessed on 1 February 2018.

[201] Senate Bill regulating the practices of euthanasia and assisted suicide in Colombia and other provisions (2015). See https://www.ambitojuridico.com/BancoMedios/Documentos PDF/pl117-14senado.pdf.

to be eligible for assisted suicide or euthanasia is that the person must be Colombian or have been a resident of Colombia for at least 1 year.[202] No reports have been found on the exercise of this law.

Conclusion

It is worth mentioning that there are other countries that could be considered when portraying a global picture of the development of suicide tourism. In the past, there have been other attempts to implement laws decriminalizing assisted suicide and euthanasia. For example, between 1996 and 1997, Northern Territory in Australia had legislation in place that permitted assisted suicide (Rights of the Terminally Ill Act)[203] but it was quickly invalidated by the central Australian government. Presently, a few countries or states that are pushing forward changes to the laws in their respective communities include Scotland,[204] New Zealand,[205] Victoria (Australia),[206] and Israel.[207] Some reports claim that assisted suicide is also legal in Japan if certain requirements are satisfied.[208] Although significant, their discussion is beyond the scope of this book.

Analysis of legislation on assisted suicide around the world, especially in Europe and North America, reveals some common features that may be important in the discussion of suicide tourism. Assisted suicide is

---

[202] Article 2(1).

[203] Rights of the Terminally Ill Act. Available at: http://www.austlii.edu.au//au/legis/nt/consol_act/rottia294/, accessed on 1 February 2018.

[204] In 2012, Member of the Scottish Parliament Margo MacDonald lodged a proposal for the 'Assisted Suicide (Scotland) Bill', although the bill ultimately fell following the Stage 1 debate in 2015. Available at: http://www.scottish.parliament.uk/parliamentarybusiness/Bills/46127.aspx, accessed on 1 February 2018.

[205] NewsHub, 'David Seymour Introduces End of Life Choice Bill' (14 October 2015) https://www.parliament.nz/en/pb/bills-and-laws/bills-proposed-laws/document/BILL_74307/end-of-life-choice-bill, accessed on 1 February 2018; Pam Oliver et al., 'New Zealand Doctors' and Nurses' Views on Legalising Assisted Dying in New Zealand' (2017) 130(1456) *N Z Med. J.* 10.

[206] Jean Edwards, 'Assisted Dying: Victorian Government to Introduce Bill in Second Half of 2017' (ABC News, 8 December 2016) http://www.abc.net.au/news/2016-12-08/assisted-dying-bill-to-be-introduced-in-victoria-in-2017/8102972, accessed on 1 February 2018.

[207] Shimshon H. Nadel, 'Physician-Assisted Suicide and the Struggle for the Soul of the State of Israel' *The Jerusalem Post* (18 June 2014) http://www.jpost.com/Opinion/Op-Ed-Contributors/Physician-assisted-suicide-and-the-struggle-for-the-soul-of-the-State-of-Israel-359823, accessed on 1 February 2018.

[208] Said M. Ladki, Maya El Hajjar, Yara Nacouzi, Lama Nasereddine, and Nizar Mahmoud, 'Euthanasia Services: The Next Health Tourism Wave' (2016) 1(2) *Int. J. of Health Manag. and Tourism* 1.

mostly regulated in secular and democratic societies, at times following legal cases which prompted public consultation and parliamentary action. It is a practice to which a majority of physicians in most of these societies are opposed. Laws permitting assisted suicide are usually positioned independently of a patient's right to palliative care and the protection of one's right to withdraw medical treatment. Outside the Benelux countries and Canada, most laws distinguish between euthanasia and assisted suicide, prohibiting the former and allowing the latter.

In almost all countries (excepting Switzerland), assisted suicide is regulated in a medical context, focussing on prescribing physicians; the person seeking assisted suicide must be terminal and/or suffering from unbearable pain and incurable disease; and there is a centralized monitoring and reporting system which tracks evidence on the phenomenon, making its participants accountable to the system. All of their respective laws include safeguards to prevent abuse and coercion, and to ensure that end-of-life decision-making is informed and appropriate. Yet, in some of them (Switzerland, the Netherlands, Belgium) proposals to expand the medical conditions meeting the eligibility criteria for assisted suicide/euthanasia have been introduced in recent years.

In many of the legal schemes of assisted suicide (states in the US, Colombia) there is also a residency requirement for the person seeking assisted suicide or some other substantial requirements emphasizing a local context—such as eligibility for public health insurance (Canada)—or the existence of a long-standing relationship between the prescribing physician and patient (the Netherlands) expressed, for example, as a mandatory requirement for two separate meetings or several discussions confirming her wish to die (Belgium and Luxemburg). In some cases, such as the US laws, these requirements are relatively easy to overcome.

The residency requirements, in particular, make it difficult for non-residents to access assisted suicide in these territories. Limiting access to assisted suicide to residents only, or to people whom the prescribing physicians know well, does not stem from a conceptualization of the right to die or to access assisted suicide but from consequential considerations pointing to a possible harm caused by suicide tourism. Some of the countries (most notably, Canada) refer to such considerations in their law-making procedure, affirming an interest in not becoming a destination for assisted suicide.

The analysis of these laws thus far helps understand why Switzerland—where assisted suicide is not restricted to residents or terminal patients only, and does not include a centralized monitoring and reporting system—became the destination for many people around the Globe to access assisted suicide. The next chapter discusses the legality of such a practice and the legal response to it.

2

The Legality of Suicide Tourism

Given the relative ease with which people can seek information and travel outside their country or state to receive aid in dying, the practice of suicide tourism (ST) has introduced a number of challenges to the countries involved. A few strategies have been adopted by countries to respond to citizens who travel to other countries to escape local laws. One involves a complete ban on citizens performing an action whether in one's country or outside of it. An example of this strategy is the recent amendment of the Penal Code of Turkey to prohibit gamete donation and surrogacy of Turks outside Turkey. Section 231 of the Code reads that it is illegal to change or obscure the child's ancestry. If it is discovered that an individual travelled abroad to receive fertility treatment using donor eggs, donor sperm, or surrogacy then that individual, as well as the donor and any intermediary, will be reported to the state prosecutor and may be subject to imprisonment for up to 3 years.[1]

A second example of prohibition to engage in unlawful action outside one's country can be found in the case of female genital mutilation. Section 4 of the Female Genital Mutilation Act 2003[2] extends the offences under sections 1–3 to any act done outside the UK by a UK national or resident, including section 3 of the Act which provides that a person is guilty of an offence if he assists, counsels, or procures another person who is not a UK national or permanent resident to perform an act of female genital mutilation outside the UK upon a UK national or permanent resident.

The practice of suicide tourism creates its own challenges both for countries whose citizens leave for assisted suicide and for those allowing non-residents to access such services. Countries which allow

---

[1] Zeynep B. Gürtin, 'Banning Reproductive Travel: Turkey's ART Legislation and Third-Party Assisted Reproduction' (2011) 23 *Reproductive Biomedicine Online* 555.
[2] Female Genital Mutilation Act 2003, c. 31.

Suicide Tourism. First Edition. Daniel Sperling. © Daniel Sperling 2019. Published 2019 by Oxford University Press.

non-residents to access assisted suicide in their territories will have to deal with a rising number of people coming to their region to die. This may have as much to do with their residents and the practice of assisted suicide as with their reputation and international appearance.[3]

If these countries did not anticipate this ahead of legalizing assisted suicide, they can change their laws—for example restricting it to residents only, establishing a minimum waiting period between the patient's request to die and receipt of the medical prescription, or imposing a stricter supervision of international assisted suicides—or can completely ignore such practice.

The most difficult challenges come into play with regard to countries of origin where assisted suicide is illegal. It can be argued that these countries will find it difficult to monitor the use and distribution of lethal drugs by its residents outside their territory. More substantially, ST undermines the public policy of these countries, which have chosen to criminalize assisted suicide and apply the moral standing represented by this prohibition to its residents.[4] These challenges call for some actions to be taken by countries of origin.

From legal and ethical perspectives there are several alternatives for jurisdictions whose citizens are embarking on assisted suicide tourism. These include restricting particular benefits and services to residents and/or preventing residents from leaving to take up options available elsewhere; providing a unified and harmonized moral stance with regard to ST; or permitting ST on the grounds that ST can be justified by an appeal to the principle of interstate moral pluralism. Yet, the choice between such alternatives derives from moral justifications that in themselves are linked to the symbolic and emotional meanings carried by assisted suicide, dying, and death in each and every society. The next chapter analyses and discusses these justifications and provides a prima facie argument in support of the practice of ST. Before discussing these justifications, it may be useful to describe the current legal position towards suicide tourism in selected countries from which people travel to commit suicide. Such

---

[3] Alexander R. Safyan, 'A Call for International Regulation of the Thriving "Industry" of Death Tourism' (2011) 33 *Loy. L .A. Int'l & Comp. L. Rev.* 287, 289 (hereafter: 'Safyan, Call for International Regulation').

[4] Browne C. Lewis, 'A Graceful Exit: Redefining Terminal to Expand the Availability of Physician-Facilitated Suicide' (2012) 91 *Oregon L. Rev.* 457 at 479.

an investigation is important, not because the existing laws, regulations, and policies necessarily reflect the required position on the subject but because the analysis within this chapter may shed more light and serve as a tool to reflect on and scrutinize the opinions expressed by them for a more comprehensive and justified approach. This will be the focus of this chapter.

Restrictions within permissive countries

As discussed in the previous chapter, Switzerland plays a major role in the practice of suicide tourism, being the primary destination for people seeking assisted suicide. In Switzerland there is no residency requirement for enjoying access to aid in dying and there are no restrictions in terms of the nature of the relationship between the prescribing physician and the person who seeks aid in dying. The person need not necessarily have a terminal condition and her request for a prescription can be met by just one physician.

In 2011, a draft bill was introduced that sought to restrict access to assisted suicide to only those who had been living in the canton of Zurich for at least 1 year.[5] The suggestion arose in the canton of Zurich, where most ST (and assisted suicide) cases arise,[6] especially because of its proximity to Germany. However, the bill was rejected by the population of the canton and no similar bill has been introduced since then. Switzerland remains the only country in the world where assisted suicide is legal and where there is no residency or other substantial requirements impeding non-residents from receiving assistance with suicide.

The residency requirement for assisted suicide based on, for example, the Oregon law model (discussed in the previous chapter) can be justified by the idea of a state's sovereignty. As the US Supreme Court held with regard to divorce tourism, 'A state such as Iowa may quite reasonably decide

---

[5] I. Glenn Cohen, 'Travelling for Assisted Suicide' in Michael J. Cholbi (ed), *Euthanasia and Assisted Suicide: Global Views on Choosing to End Life* (Praeger, 2017) p. 373 (hereafter: 'Cohen, Travelling for Assisted Suicide'); Saskia Gauthier, Julian Mausbach, Thomas Reisch, and Christine Bartsch, 'Suicide Tourism: A Pilot Study on the Swiss Phenomenon' (2015) 41(8) *JME* 611.

[6] Swiss Federal Statistical Office, *Cause of Death Statistics 2014: Assisted Suicide and Suicide in Switzerland* (FSO, 2016).

that it does not wish to become a divorce mill for unhappy spouses ...'[7] It also follows that states like the Netherlands or Belgium can impose a required duration on a physician–patient relationship to prevent unwanted travel by outsiders merely taking advantage of the permissive laws on assisted suicide or euthanasia.[8]

However, there is much criticism of such restrictions. It is correctly argued that the fundamental rights to liberty and autonomy, which are at the basis of legalization of assistance in dying, and whose expression can usually be found in the constitutions of Western democracies, do not apply to citizens or permanent residents only. Neither can limitations be explained by reference to the idea of the protection of the vulnerable as surely not all of the people who travel from one country to another for assisted suicide are vulnerable. In fact, one can argue the opposite: the many preparations needed ahead of the travel itself serve as a de facto barrier and an apparatus by which people can change their mind, affirm their willingness to receive aid in dying, and explore other alternatives. These many opportunities reduce the odds that vulnerable people will participate in ST. Another justification for imposing restrictions, namely that countries do not want 'a stampede of "suicide tourists" in their country', does not hold either. As one can see from the Swiss experience, numbers of people who travel for assisted suicide are relatively small and this fear is exaggerated and unrealistic.[9]

Justifications under international law

In general, laws do not have extraterritorial application.[10] As a general rule, while assisted suicide may be illegal in one's home country, this prohibition does not apply to conduct carried out outside the country. In order to extend the criminal prohibition existing within one's country,

---

[7] *Sosna v. Iowa* 419 U.S. 393 (1975) at 407.

[8] Brian H. Bix, 'Physician-Assisted Suicide and Federalism' (2003) 17 *Notre Dame Journal of Law, Ethics & Public Policy* 53, 60.

[9] Konstantin Tretyakov and I. Glenn Cohen, 'Medical Assistance in Dying and "Suicide Tourism" to Canada: Bill C-14 from a Comparative Perspective' (2016) 1 *JEMH* 1, 4 (hereafter: 'Tretyakov & Cohen, Medical Assistance in Dying').

[10] Cohen, Travelling for Assisted Suicide (n 5) at p. 380.

the law has to specifically say so, as can be seen, for example, with regard to criminalization of child sex tourism under the US Federal law.[11]

A state's exercise of extraterritorial jurisdiction in criminal matters—as opposed to civil matters—is uncontroversial. A country may exercise its enforcement jurisdiction so that it will enforce a local prohibition concerning an action carried out outside the county. An example of this includes the federal Defense of Marriage Act that authorizes states not to recognize same-sex marriages carried out in other states.[12] It may also apply to current discussions regarding states' powers to criminalize the use or buying of marijuana by their residents in other states where such acts are legal.[13] Alternatively, a country could exercise its jurisdiction to prescribe to make certain actions illegal if they are carried out outside the country but legal if carried out within it. Under international law, a country's exercise of its jurisdiction to prescribe is given more deference than the exercise of its enforcement.

A state's exercise of its extraterritorial jurisdiction could be defended by reference to one of the following principles: the territoriality principle; the nationality principle; the protective principle; the passive personality principle; and the universality principle.[14] The territoriality principle assumes that every state has jurisdiction over crimes that are committed within its territory. However, where an offence commenced within the territory of another state is completed in the territory of the state concerned ('objective territory') or where the offence is commenced within the territory of the state but completed in the territory of another country ('subjective territory'), the territorial principle holds that the state may still exercise its jurisdiction with regard to such offences.[15] Neither of these situations seems to apply in the case of ST. Although one can argue that some of the assistance leading to the actual suicide may begin within one's home country, it is only with the prescribing of the lethal drug that the main aid in dying takes place. This is

---

[11] The Protect Act of 2003, 18 U.S.C. § 2252B(b).

[12] 28 U.S.C. § 1738C (2006).

[13] G.J. Chin, 'Policy, Preemption and Pot: Extraterritorial Citizen Jurisdiction' (2017) 58 *B.C.L. Rev.* 929.

[14] Alina Kaczorowska-Ireland, *Public International Law* (5th edn, Routledge, 2015) (hereafter: 'Kaczorowska-Ireland, Public International Law').

[15] Ibid. at p. 359.

done outside one's country of origin. As such, the potential crime also ends outside one's country of origin.

The nationality principle justifies extraterritorial jurisdiction under the rationale that a person charged with a crime is the responsibility of the state of which that person is a national. Hence, the state may prosecute its nationals for crimes committed outside the state.[16] Here, too, this rationale seems not to apply. As will be explored in the next chapter, arguments against suicide tourism possibly leading to its criminalization do not posit such a crime as one that is substantially related to ideas of nationality but focus on liberty interests or on unwanted outcomes that violate public morality. Providing aid in dying is not to be regarded as an offence against the state or what it symbolizes.

Under the protective principle, a state can exercise its extraterritorial jurisdiction in order to protect itself and its vital interests, such as for political matters, spying, forging currency, immigration, and economic offences.[17] Important as they are, these are not the types of interests that can serve as umbrella interests leading to the criminalization of assisted suicide and to the enforcement of such a crime when made outside one's state.

According to the passive personality principle, a state has jurisdiction to punish foreigners for actions committed against its nationals even if outside its territory, for example attacking diplomats or killing citizens abroad.[18] By its very nature, this principle is not applicable to ST cases, which represent acts that heavily involve the participation, consent, and execution of the person seeking aid in dying.

Finally, the universality principle permits extraterritorial jurisdiction with regard to international crimes committed anywhere in the world and irrespective of the nationalities of the accused and the victim. Under this principle, the prosecuting state acts on behalf of all states in punishing an act which is considered *hostis humani generis*, that is enemies of all mankind.[19] For example, in extending exterritorial jurisdiction for Congress' ban on child sex acts to an American defendant in Mexico, the 9th Circuit Court of Appeals held that the decision of whether to apply

---

[16] Ibid. at p. 360. See e.g. *Skiriotes v. Florida* 313 U.S. 69 (1941).
[17] Kaczorowska-Ireland, Public International Law (n 14) p. 361.
[18] Ibid. at p. 364.
[19] Ibid. at p. 365.

exterritorial jurisdiction is based on the nature of the offences and the legislative efforts to eliminate the type of crime involved.[20]

However, it should be doubted whether providing aid in dying by, for example, prescribing a lethal drug in a country where such an action may not be illegal amounts to a moral crime against humanity. The fact that aid in dying is becoming more accepted and legally permitted in Western and democratic countries proves that this is not the case.

Glenn Cohen argues that if patient protection is the motivation in countries where assisted suicide is prohibited then these countries have good reason to extend their criminalization when it is carried out by their citizen in a destination country.[21] However, Cohen himself rejects the claim that paternalism is a strong justification for criminal prohibition of assisted suicide, rather than the more general harm principle.[22] He also presents other rationale for criminalization which—as this section demonstrates—are not sufficient to justify extraterritorial jurisdiction. Moreover, in another publication, Cohen discusses the new Canadian bill on assistance in dying and argues that from the perspective of individual autonomy 'it is not clear why one should make the right for medical assistance in dying available only to the citizens and permanent residents of Canada.'[23] Cohen is, of course, right to ask this question. It, nonetheless, emphasizes the tension with his previous argument that provides a prima facie reason for criminalization of ST based on welfare justifications.

One of the moral rationales for extraterritorial jurisdiction is based on the idea that, by virtue of being a citizen, one owes a duty of obedience to the laws of the country of origin even when outside its borders. Seth Kreimer discusses this duty in the context of abortion tourism. He follows a Razian conception of the duty to obey the law according to which such a duty is premised on the practical authority of the state, by which he means the state's ability to resolve moral conflicts more accurately than any other citizen.[24]

---

[20] *US v. Thomas* 893 F.2d. 1066, 1068 (9th Cir. 1990).

[21] I. Glenn Cohen, 'Circumvention Tourism' (2012) 97 *Cornell L. Rev.* 1309 at 1391 (hereafter: 'Cohen, Circumvention Tourism'); I. Glenn Cohen, 'Medical Tourism and Ending Life: Travel for Assisted Suicide and Abortion' in I. Glenn Cohen, *Patients with Passports* (Oxford University Press, 2015) ch. 8, at FN 75: Cohen comments that he imagines that the home country legislature will be explicitly extending its domestic prohibition extraterritorially by statute.

[22] Cohen, Circumvention Tourism (n 21) at 1389.

[23] Tretyakov & Cohen, Medical Assistance in Dying (n 9).

[24] Joseph Raz, *The Morality of Freedom* (Clarendon Press, 1986).

Yet, as Kreimer rightly argues, when there is a moral disagreement between countries as to the proper response to a specific phenomenon or practice (e.g. assisted suicide), it does not follow from such a conception that one necessarily has to follow the rules and laws of her home state rather than the laws of the country to which she may be travelling. Hence, under this view a person can travel to shop for the laws of the state which better suits her own moral values on that specific issue or practice.[25]

A few years ago, a very exceptional proposal to regulate ST on the international level was called for.[26] This proposal suggested that, regardless of one's personal views on the legality of assisted suicide, a practice whereby non-terminally ill individuals are allowed to travel to another country to receive aid in dying 'offends both notions of international comity and respect for the obligations of domestic law'.[27] It argued that, because of the moral implications of assisted suicide and its irreversibility, suicide tourism is different to other forms of tourism in which citizens engage while abroad. Assisted suicide transcends domestic restrictions and involves core principles of sovereignty and international comity.

Hence, international regulation of assisted suicide was called for. This proposal recommended the adoption of an instrument of 'soft law' as the most effective tool for 'curtailing' ST, namely a non-binding, informal instrument of international law imposing moral or political commitments on nations, rather than legal obligations. This soft law grants flexibility to countries in shaping their responsibility towards non-residents receiving aid in dying in their territories and provides a framework to comply with such responsibilities.

It is further argued that soft law has many advantages over hard law, one of which address the assumption that Switzerland has no incentive in ratifying a treaty restricting the practice of assisted suicide on the basis of residency (perhaps because of the financial benefit it enjoys from being virtually the sole destination for suicide tourism). Instead of countries signing a treaty to decrease the incidence of suicide tourism, the proposal suggested a non-binding recommendation by the United Nations

---

[25] S.F. Kreimer, ' "But Whoever Treasures Freedom . . .": The Right to Travel and Extraterritorial Abortions' (1993) 91(5) *Michigan L. Rev.* 907 at 930–1. *Bigelow v. Virginia* 421 U.S. 809, 822–5.

[26] Safyan, Call for International Regulation (n 3).

[27] Ibid. at 289.

General Assembly calling on nations to recognize and accept other nations' assisted suicide laws.

The recommendation made under this proposal would not ban assisted suicide or attempt to influence its local regulation within states. It would rather call on states to abide by the laws of their neighbour states and prevent the spread of suicide tourism. Hence, for example, a non-terminally ill British citizen would not be able to travel to Switzerland for assistance with suicide in disregard of UK's ban against such a practice. The proposal assumes that many, if not all, of the states that would be asked to adopt the recommendation (including those where assisted suicide is legal) would do so. Refusing states would still be subject to international pressure while still being able to preserve their right as sovereign nations to regulate and govern the practice of assisted suicide as they wished within their own territory.

While this proposal attempts to offer relatively mild and non-binding means to address the practice of ST, it is not clear what the moral basis is for such an intervention, even in this weak form. Thus, there still needs to be a solid justification for any UN recommendation to decrease ST, assuming that ST does not cause any harm to nations or to residents facilitating it.

One also has to question the premise of this proposal, according to which ST is different to other forms of what Glenn Cohen has termed 'circumvention tourism', namely 'avoiding the penalties set by the citizen's home country's criminal law by going abroad to engage in the same activity where it is not criminally prohibited'.[28] It is claimed that ST is different because of its morality and irreversibility. However, given that suicide is not generally considered immoral and no longer amounts to a criminal offence, and assuming that not all cases of assisted suicide result in the actual deaths of those requiring aid, it is not clear why ST is necessarily irreversible and why the morality of ST and assisted suicide is more troubling and should receive more weight and consideration than other practices such as abortion tourism or cross-border surrogacy. While the first of these examples also involves travel to perform an act terminating a potential for life, the second may be associated with the exploitation of poor and disadvantaged women, putting them at risk of physical and

---

[28] Cohen, Circumvention Tourism (n 21).

emotional harm, merely for the promotion of the autonomy-based interests of would-be parents. It is of no surprise that this proposal has not
been followed up since its publication.

Prosecution of accompanying family members and third parties

People who travel to another country to receive aid in dying are usually
supported and helped by their family members. As in other forms of assisted suicide, these family members play a pivotal role as advocates for
the patients and in helping to obtain assistance with the suicide, in addition to their role as caregivers.[29] One of the legal aspects of ST, however,
concerns the prosecution of such family members once they return to
their country of origin.

Any decision to prosecute a person who assists another in travelling
for the purpose of assisted suicide will undoubtedly intensify their pain
and grief following the tragic event. In most cases, family members will
have to cope with investigations, publicity, and fear of penalty on their
return, while not yet coming to terms with their loss. This encourages
people who would like to choose assisted suicide to travel in the earlier
stage of their disease so that they are able to travel alone and do not require the physical or emotional help of another person who might otherwise be prosecuted.

One of the countries in which existing laws and policies already provide for the prosecution of family members who are involved in the practice of suicide tourism is the UK. Although suicide is no longer a crime,
anyone who does an act capable of encouraging or assisting the suicide
or attempted suicide of another person and intends it to so encourage
or assist them is liable to imprisonment for up to 14 years.[30] To be held

---

[29] C. Gamondi, M Pott, N. Preston, and S. Payne, 'Family Caregivers' Reflections on
Experiences of Assisted Suicide in Switzerland: A Qualitative Interview Study' (2018) *Journal of
Pain and Symptom Management*. doi: 10.1016/j.jpainsymman.2017.12.482.

[30] Suicide Act 1961, s. 2(1C). However, in practice the penalties imposed tend to be non-
custodial or at the lower end of the sentencing scale. Richard Huxtable, 'The Suicide Tourist
Trap: Compromise Across Boundaries' (2009) 6 *Journal of Bioethical Inquiry* 327, 330 (hereafter: 'Huxtable, The Suicide Tourist Trap'). The wording was amended by the Coroners and
Justice Act 2009 (see http://www.legislation.gov.uk/ukpga/Eliz2/9-10/60).

criminally responsible, the person who assists in the suicide must intend to assist another person in committing suicide or foresee this as a consequence of one's behaviour.[31] It is accepted that 'even if he had not known the intended time and place, but had known the nature of the crimes that were planned, there could be no question of his guilt.'[32] In terms of her *actus reus*, the accused should have entered into an agreement with that person, encouraged him to commit suicide, or provided some assistance before or at the time of suicide.

The assisted suicide offence covers an almost infinite range of scenarios, under which a person could be considered assisting another in committing suicide.[33] However, one can question whether, because the act of assisted suicide takes place (mostly or solely) within another territory, the lawfulness of any such assistance depends on the intended site of the suicide and the lawfulness of the suicide in that jurisdiction.[34]

Despite numerous investigations and much criticism,[35] there have—apart from one recent case in Italy[36] —been no prosecutions in assisted suicide tourism cases in any of the countries from which people travel for aid in dying.[37] This is mostly explained by the argument that prosecution

[31] *R v. Woollin* [1998] 4 All ER 103.

[32] *Director of Public Prosecutions for Northern Ireland v. Maxwell* [1978] 1 WLR 1350, 1361.

[33] *R (on the application of Purdy) v. DPP & Another* [2008] EWHC 2565.

[34] Charles A. Foster, 'Rapid Response: Time to Test the Law' (17 June 2004) *British Medical Journal* http://www.bmj.com/rapid-response/2011/10/30/time-test-law.

[35] See e.g. House of Lords, 'Health: End of Life' motion to take note, *Official Report* vol. 750, col. 916 (UK Parliament, 12 December 2013) https://hansard.parliament.uk/Lords/2013-12-12/debates/13121261000539/HealthEndOfLife?highlight=%22assisted%20suicide%22%20 Switzerland#contribution-13121261000086, accessed on 18 January 2018 ('What is the difference between taking someone to Switzerland to help them die and driving a bank robber to a bank? Both are equally guilty of a crime. However, when it comes to assisting someone to die, the Director of Public Prosecutions says "Sometimes I will decide it is a crime and sometimes not. It is entirely for me to decide". She would never say that in a case of assisting a bank robbery. This practice brings the whole system of justice into disrepute. It makes the law, to quote Mr Bumble, "a ass". Indeed, that most eminent judge, the late Lord Bingham, said that the law was a mess and needed revision', Lord Taverne).

[36] This case involves the prosecution of Marco Cappato (discussed later in this section) whose trial was ongoing at the time of writing.

[37] Huxtable, The Suicide Tourist Trap (n 30) p. 331; Rohith Srinivas, 'Exploring the Potential for American Death Tourism' (2009) 13(1) *Mich St. J. Med & Law* 91 at 111 (hereafter: 'Srinivas, Exploring the Potential'); House of Commons, 'Assisted Suicide' debate, *Official Report* vol. 542, col. 1365 (UK Parliament, 27 March 2012) https://hansard.parliament.uk/Commons/2012-03-27/debates/12032752000001/AssistedSuicide?highlight=%22assisted%20suicide%22%20 Switzerland#contribution-12032752000402, accessed on 18 January 2018 ('records show that more than 180 Britons have travelled to die in Switzerland in the last 10 years. No one has been prosecuted for accompanying them or assisting them with their arrangements, even when there has been sufficient evidence to prosecute', Richard Ottoway MP). It appears that even with regard to non-ST cases, there has been only one prosecution under section 2 of someone who

in such circumstances is not in the public interest.[38] A number of legal cases have discussed the possibility of prosecuting accompanying family members in this context. All cases involved the seeking of a declaration of immunity from prosecution or a requirement to establish a transparent and accountable prosecution policy that referred explicitly to such cases.

In the UK, the High Court confirmed that a 65-year-old person was competent to make an informed decision to travel to Switzerland with the aid of her husband, thereby overruling the local authority decision to prevent her from such a travel on the grounds of her being a 'vulnerable person'.[39] The court ruled that it had 'no basis in law for exercising the jurisdiction so as to prohibit Mrs Z from taking her own life'. It was ruled that the right and responsibility for such a decision belonged to Mrs Z alone.[40]

A previous attempt to guarantee immunity from prosecution for the husband of a patient wanting to go to Switzerland for assistance with suicide was unsuccessful in the case of *Pretty*.[41] At the time of the hearing, Dianne Pretty was a 43-year-old paralysed woman who suffered from motor neurone disease—an incurable and progressive disease resulting in the weakening and wasting of the voluntary muscles of the body. Pretty had no decipherable speech and was fed with a tube. Her life expectancy was measured only in weeks or months. However, being of full mental capacity she decided to end her life by suicide with the help of her husband.

The family wrote to the Director of Public Prosecutions (DPP) asking for an undertaking that her husband would not be prosecuted if he assisted her. The DPP replied that immunity could not be granted, no matter how exceptional her circumstances. Pretty applied for judicial

provided petrol and a lighter to a vulnerable person with suicidal intent and who—as a result—suffered severe burns. *R (Nicklinson) v. Ministry of Justice* [2014] UKSC 38; [2015] AC 657 at § 48 (hereafter: *Nicklinson*).

---

[38] Srinivas, Exploring the Potential (n 37).

[39] *Re Z (Local Authority: Duty)* [2005] 1 WLR 959. However, the judge commented that it seemed inevitable that by making arrangements and escorting his wife, Mr Z would have contravened section 2(1) of the Suicide Act. It nonetheless implied that such a prosecution might not always be in the public interest (at § 14).

[40] Ibid. at § 12.

[41] *Pretty v. UK* (2002) 35 EHRR 1; *R (On the application of Pretty) v. DPP* [2002] 1 AC 800; *R (On the application of Pretty) v. DPP* [2001] EWHC Admin 788; *R (On the application of Pretty) v. DPP (Permission to move for judicial review)* [2001] EWHC Admin 705.

review of the DPP's decision, arguing that it was unlawful. The application was unsuccessful and the court ruled that the DPP did not have the power to give an undertaking not to prosecute. Pretty appealed to the House of Lords and ultimately to the European Court of Human Rights. She claimed that the DPP decision violated her right under Article 8 of the European Convention of Human Rights to respect for privacy and family life.[42]

In dismissing her case, it was held that, given the concerns about abuse and the need to create safeguards as well as the flexibility that existed in the prosecution process, the blanket prohibition against assisted suicide was not arbitrary, and it had not been arbitrary or unreasonable for the DPP to refuse to give an undertaking not to prosecute.[43]

A call for clarification of the prosecution policy in this area was subsequently made in 2008, in the case of *Purdy*.[44] The case examined whether the DPP acted unlawfully in not publishing guidance as to the circumstances in which individuals would or would not be prosecuted for assisting in the suicide of another person.[45] Purdy, who suffered a debilitating illness and declared her wish to travel with her husband to Switzerland for assisted suicide, applied to the High Court seeking an order that the DPP issue guidelines concerning the facts and circumstances that he would take into account in deciding whether to prosecute under the Suicide Act 1961. In this case, it was clear that Purdy wanted to know in advance if her husband could be prosecuted if he aided her suicide.

The court ruled that, while the DPP had power to issue such guidance, he did not have a duty to do so, and as long as the DPP and his delegates took into account only relevant factors and followed the Code for the Crown Prosecutors reasonably and rationally in making a decision about whether to prosecute an offence under the Act, it could not be said that

---

[42] Pretty also claimed, although to a lesser extent, that her rights under Articles 9 (freedom of thought, conscience, and religion) and 14 (equality in enjoyment of the rights under the Convention) were also violated. The Court rejected these claims as well.

[43] *Pretty v. UK* (2002) 35 EHRR 1.

[44] *R (on the application of Purdy) v. DPP* [2008] EWHC 2565.

[45] Ibid. at § 1: the court emphasized that it did not discuss the question of whether assisted suicide should continue to be criminal in the UK or whether someone could obtain immunity from prosecution in advance for helping another person travel to another country where assisted suicide was lawful.

the exercise of the DPP's discretion constituted an arbitrary or unfettered power of the executive.[46]

Although that decision may have been legally defensible, a call for the publication of guidance seems reasonable given that suicide tourism attracts great public and state interest.[47] Indeed, following an unsuccessful appeal to the Court of Appeal, a further appeal to the House of Lords was allowed and the previous decisions were overturned. It was held that, although few cases had been referred to the DPP for such an offence, this should not be a reason for excusing him 'from the obligation to clarify what his position is as to factors that he regards as relevant for and against prosecution.'[48]

Following this ruling and after considering public views on this issue, the DPP published his policy on prosecutions in respect of cases of encouraging or assisting suicide.[49] The guidelines apply to encouragement or assistance taking place in England although the suicide or attempted suicide itself can take place outside the UK.[50] It specifies some of the evidential requirements as well as the public interest factors for and against prosecution. Interestingly, among others, the guidelines mention the full voluntariness of the suspect, the compassionate motive of the suspect, and the fact that the actions of the suspect have been minor as factors serving against prosecution.[51] These may apply to many of the cases represented by the practice of suicide tourism.

It may be that the new prosecuting guidelines, which can now be interpreted as offering a more lenient approach towards family members accompanying people travelling for aid in dying, resulted in an increase in the number of British people becoming members at Dignitas and travelling overseas to die in the years that followed their publication.[52] Such an increase should also be attributed to the fact that legislative bills on aid

---

[46] Ibid. at § 75.

[47] John Coggon, 'Assisting "Death Tourism": Possible Prosecution or Pragmatic Immunity?' (unpublished paper) https://www.escholar.manchester.ac.uk/api/datastream?publicationPid=uk-ac-man-scw:217849&datastreamId=FULL-TEXT.PDF.

[48] R (Purdy) v. DPP [2010] 1 AC at § 55.

[49] The Crown Prosecution Service, Policy for Prosecutors in Respect of Cases of Encouraging or Assisting Suicide (February 2010, updated October 2014) https://www.cps.gov.uk/legal-guidance/policy-prosecutors-respect-cases-encouraging-or-assisting-suicide, accessed on 2 March 2019.

[50] Ibid. at § 8.

[51] Ibid. at § 45.

[52] According to data published on the Dignitas website, the number of British members at Dignitas increased from 842 in 2013 to 1,139 in 2016. The number of accompanied suicides of Britons also increased in this period from 29 to 47, respectively.

in dying and relevant case law had made the likelihood of the UK legalizing such a practice more remote.

A few years after the DPP guidelines were published, another case was brought to the highest court in the UK, the Supreme Court. This was the case of *R. (Nicklinson and Lamb) v. Ministry of Justice* and *R. (AM) v. Director of Public Prosecutions.*[53] The case involved three claimants, two of whom suffered from locked-in syndrome and were almost completely immobile so that they were unable to carry out their suicide themselves.[54] They argued that their right under Article 8 of the Convention required the law to allow a third party to take actions to end their lives. The third claimant, 'Martin', was also in a state of locked-in syndrome but retained the capacity to make hand movements and was thus able to end his own life with assistance. He showed interest in travelling to Switzerland for this purpose. Because of the criminal offence, his wife did not want to be involved and he did not want to involve any other member of his family in this journey. He therefore required help from one of his healthcare providers or from an organization like Friends at the End.

In his petition, Martin called for clarification and modification of the DPP guidelines so that the people who cared for him could be assured that they were at no risk of prosecution when they assisted him. More specifically, he argued that while it may be clear from the guidelines that if a third party who is a relation or a friend provides assistance, purely out of compassion and exerting no pressure on the person, she may not be at risk of prosecution, this may not be the case with regard to other third parties, most frequently a doctor or other professional-care provider who would also usually be receiving payment for such requests. None of the claimants was terminally ill or facing a short life expectancy.

The court referred to the fact that people who assisted relatives and friends that wished to commit suicide by taking them to Switzerland were routinely not prosecuted whereas those who lacked the physical ability and/or the means to travel and/or could not receive such

http://www.dignitas.ch/index.php?option=com_content&view=article&id=32&Itemid=72 &lang=en, accessed on 18 January 2018.

[53] *Nicklinson* (n 37).
[54] The only way for them to end their lives was by refusing food and water and starving to death—an act involving considerable pain and distress.

assistance were left to suffer at home until death came.[55] It held that, while many may regret that the DPP policy were not clearer in relation to assistance given by people who are neither family members nor close friends, it would not be right for the court to dictate to the DPP what her policy should be.

More specifically, the court documented an unexpected statement made by the DPP through her counsel during the hearing. According to this statement, an individual member of a profession, or a professional carer, who did not have previous influence or authority over the person who was seeking assisted suicide and who was brought in for this purpose after the person had made a settled decision to end her life, and who provided services which a family member would not be prosecuted for, would be most unlikely to be prosecuted.[56] It, nonetheless, called on the DPP to review the written policy because of this gap between what it meant and what it was intended to mean.[57]

The *Nicklinson* ruling should be read as offering some direction to British doctors who may participate and provide aid to people seeking to travel for assisted suicide. In 2009, the legal status of suicide tourism was discussed by the British Medical Association (BMA). In a report entitled *End-of-Life Decisions*, the BMA referred to queries from doctors asking if they could write medical reports for terminally ill patients to use abroad or whether they could accompany a patient travelling for assisted dying. The BMA report stated that while no doctor had been prosecuted for such actions, in such circumstances doctors should be aware of the possible legal implications of these or other actions which may be regarded as encouraging or facilitating suicide.[58]

Another professional guideline issued on this subject concerns an opinion by the General Medical Council (GMC) published in 2015. Under section 5 of the guideline, 'where patients raise the issue of assisting suicide, or ask for information that might encourage or assist them in ending their lives, respect for a patient's autonomy cannot justify

---

[55] *Nicklinson* (n 37) at § 109.

[56] Ibid. at §§ 142, 143, 251.

[57] Ibid. at § 143.

[58] BMA Ethics, *End-of-Life Decisions: Views of the BMA* (BMA, 2009) http://bmaopac.hosted. exlibrisgroup.com/exlibris/aleph/a23_1/apache_media/VITJEQ4TGE1SQBYYUCDDQ2T93SAHVT. pdf, accessed on 22 January 2018.

illegal action'. The guideline calls on doctors who are uncertain about the legal position to seek up-to-date legal advice. It is, however, clear from the introduction to this guideline that assisted suicide remains a criminal offence in the UK.[59]

Recent litigation, brought by a 50-year-old man suffering from locked-in syndrome, challenged the GMC policy stating that doctors who give advice and supply the medical reports required by Dignitas, in connection with requests for assisted suicide, may be subject to investigations into their fitness to practice and disciplinary actions. The claim argued that the GMC should have followed the laxer and more compassionate DPP policy evolving from the same issue.

However, the High Court dismissed the claim and ruled that since, in accordance with R (Nicklinson) v. Ministry of Justice, the blanket ban on assisted suicide did not infringe Article 8 of the European Convention on Human Rights, nor would any step taken to discourage a doctor from assisting a suicide do so. Moreover, the court ruled that the GMC guidelines could be justified by the need to protect vulnerable patients. It was also ruled that there was no reason why the analysis of the public interest in the context of public prosecutions should dictate the way the GMC determined what was required to protect the reputation of the medical profession.[60]

It follows that these legal cases involving people who considered travelling to Switzerland for assisted suicide prompted a clarification and change in guidelines concerning the prosecution of accompanying family members and professionals. These cases helped better frame existing law so that family members and friends who are asked to help a person in her request to end her life will not be put at so much risk. The Nicklinson case also demonstrates that while the compassionate application of these guidelines was not intended to apply to other third parties offering aid in dying within the UK, in cases where these third parties are asked to act in the absence of family members or friends, they may also be effectively immune from possible prosecution. However, professional guidelines

---

[59] General Medical Council, *When a Patient Seeks Advice or Information about Assistance to Die* (General Medical Council, Updated June 2015) https://www.gmc-uk.org/18_JUNE_2015_When_a_patient_seeks_advice_or_information_about_assistance_to_die.pdf_61449907.pdf, accessed on 22 January 2018.

[60] *R (on the application of AM) v. General Medical Council* [2015] P.T.S.R. D38.

published by the BMA and GMC call for a careful management of requests for information or help which may lead to assisted suicide. As discussed in Chapter 5, these guidelines create much difficulty for patients seeking medical information in connection with their travel for assisted suicide. Nonetheless, the DPP's revised guidelines and subsequent case law (especially *Nicklinson*) provide more solid safeguards for those who wish to choose death by the means of travelling to another country where assisted suicide is legal.

An exceptional case recently took place in Italy, in which a third party who provided help to people travelling to Switzerland for assisted suicide was prosecuted. In fact, this is the only reported case to date in which a person has been prosecuted and brought to trial for offering assistance that may have led to assisted suicide outside one's own country. Marco Cappato was the former president of an association for the freedom of scientific research, a pro-euthanasia campaigner, and a former member of the European Parliament. He was prosecuted under article 580 of the Italian Penal Code, which prohibits assisted suicide in Italy. Cappato had provided aid and advice to more than 450 people who wanted to receive aid in dying, including by means of travel to Switzerland. One of the most publicized cases in which Cappato helped, and for which he was actually prosecuted, was that of Italian disc jockey, DJ Fabo (Fabiano Antoniani). Fabo took his life in Switzerland after a car accident in 2014 left him blind and tetraplegic.

Cappato's trial commenced in November 2017 and, if he had been found guilty, he could have been subject to up to 12 years' imprisonment. In my interview with him, he claimed that the Italian authorities were obliged to prosecute him because he denounced himself publicly. Other interviews in Italy suggest this case is intended to raise Cappato's publicity as he would like to return to politics. An update from 17 January 2018 suggests that Milan prosecutors asked that Cappato be acquitted since he had no role in the execution of the assisted suicide of Fabo, and it was claimed that Fabo had a firm wish to die and that Cappato even delayed his plan by trying to involve him in his political campaign.[61]

---

[61] Radazione ANSA, 'No Crime, Acquit Cappato for DJ Fabo', *NASA en Business* (17 January 2018) http://www.ansa.it/english/news/business/2018/01/17/no-crime-acquit-cappato-for-dj-fabo_4f28353a-0e61-429d-8072-e6aa3ec189fd.html, accessed on 22 January 2018.

The case went to the Constitutional Court of Italy and was put off to be discussed further during the year 2019.[62]

Another issue associated with the legality of suicide tourism concerns the treatment of the remains or body of the deceased. Under the UK legal system, for example, if the family of the deceased returns from Switzerland with their ashes, there is no inquest and they can scatter them in privacy. However, if they bring the body back for burial, the coroner is obliged to open an inquest, as death is deemed to be uncertain. There may also be an autopsy followed by a criminal investigation although, as previously discussed, the chances are low that a prosecution will take place. Such a procedure not only causes significant distress for families but also provides a different treatment under the law, depending on one's preference for cremation or burial, and consumes time and public expenses.[63]

Guardianship law issues

Another area of law where ST can be addressed and governed is that relating to guardians. Indeed, a guardian may be faced with making decisions concerning life-sustaining treatment,[64] including assisted suicide (where the patient can take his or her life) or euthanasia. When these latter alternatives are unavailable or illegal in one's own country, ST may arise.

Interestingly, many state guardianship statutes do not make specific reference to end-of-life decisions.[65] As in other fields of practice, a guardian's decision-making involves reflecting on a person's values and acting to promote her best interests. In general, it is accepted that guardians can make decisions about whether to continue or discontinue life-sustaining treatment, while deferring decision-making authority to the

---

[62] Redazione ANSA, 'Current Norms Insufficient on DJ Fabo', *ANSA General News* (24 October 2018) www.ansa.it/english/news/general_news/2018/10/24/current-norms-insufficient-on-dj-fabo_3142153f-ef5d-4f2b-836a-0de5d8000eac.html, accessed on 2 March 2019.

[63] A proposal to change the law has been debated in the House of Commons. See UK House of Commons, 'Prisons and Courts Bill' second reading debate, *Official Report* vol. 623, col. 729 (UK Parliament, 20 March 2017) https://hansard.parliament.uk/Commons/2017-03-20/debates/1C7C8083-7F13-4FA6-9648-A4B4D5716FF5/PrisonsAndCourtsBill#debate-379250, accessed on 28 June 2017.

[64] See e.g. *In Re Biersack*, No. 10-04-03, 2004 WL 2785963 (Ohio. Ct. App. 2004); *In Re L.M.R.*, No. 4392-S-MG, 2008 WL 398999 (Del. Ch. 2008).

[65] Andrew B. Cohen, Megan S. Wright, Leo Cooney, and Terri Fried, 'Guardianship and End-of-Life Decision Making' (2015) 175(10) *JAMA Intern Med.* 1687.

courts when they believe it would be more appropriate for a neutral judge to exercise it.[66]

In 1991, the Court of Appeals in Missouri heard a case involving guardianship decision-making which may have affected travel at the end of life. This case involved a father acting as guardian of his incapacitated and disabled 20-year-old daughter, who had been in a permanent vegetative state for 3 years following an automobile accident. She was kept alive through gastric feeding and hydration tubes. The father sought to remove her from the hospital to take her to Minnesota where she could be re-evaluated through tests that Missouri refused to perform.

The court accepted the state's objection to such a request on the basis that the father's intention was to remove his daughter's gastrostomy tube, Minnesota's requirements on this being less stringent than those in Missouri. Indeed, the guardian did not rule out the possibility of removal of his daughter's feeding tube. He stated at court that he wanted to move her to Minnesota where it was clear he could stop the life-sustaining medical treatment. The majority ruled that the trial judge could not have been convinced that the guardian acted in the best interests of his daughter when he decided to move her to Minnesota; more evidence would have been needed to clarify this.

However, in his dissenting opinion, Judge Gerald did not believe the majority's opinion was necessary. Holding for the defendant and crediting his actions to make the right decision for his daughter, he wrote,

> Finally, I am offended by the concept that the state or the judiciary can restrict the guardian's movement to another state in this country because of a perception that the guardian is doing so to avoid the Laws of Missouri. Unrestricted travel and movement throughout the country is a privilege of the citizens of each state and of the United States. Shapiro v. Thompson, 394 U.S. 618, 89 S.Ct. 1322, 22 L.Ed.2d 600 (1969) ... A state cannot prevent its residents from traveling to another state to take advantage of the laws of that state.[67]

---

[66] *In Re Guardianship of Schiavo*, 916 So. 2d 814 (Fla. Dist. Ct. App. 2005).

[67] *In re: The Matter of Christine Busalacchi*, 1991 Mo. App. Lexis 305. For a similar view in relation to such a scenario see Lea Brilmayer, 'Interstate Preemption: The Right to Travel, the Right to Life, and the Right to Die' (1993) 91(5) *Mich. L. Rev.* 873, 905.

While no other similar case has been found, with the evolution of end-of-life jurisprudence it is reasonable to argue that a guardian's right and duty to make decisions in the best interests of an incapacitated patient, including whether to continue or stop life-sustaining treatment, should be extended to ST decisions. As long as there is evidence that a decision by a guardian, supporting the travel of a formerly capacitated patient to another country to take advantage of its permissible laws on assisted suicide, is in her best interest, such a decision should be legally respected. Here, the expected challenge should rest upon securing proper safeguards to establish the patient's previous opinions on choosing to end her life in such a way.

Constitutional justifications

One can argue that, besides the criminal risk to those who assist a person in travelling abroad, the residency requirements for assisted suicide in some legal systems may violate and impede the constitutional right of people to travel, in particular violating and impeding their right to engage in interstate travel originating as a form of interstate commerce, at least within the US. Although the nature and constitutional sources of such rights are far from being clear,[68] it may well be that their application to the case of ST can create a strong justification not to legally interfere with it.

As in other contexts of personal movement, such as movement for purposes of work, establishment, and service provision or receipt, the movement to a different state to take advantage of its unique legal system and privileges should be supported. It is argued that in order for individuals to be as free as possible with regard to their choices and given the diversity between states and the unequal distribution of opportunities across geographical areas, the capacity to move and settle in another place is instrumentally important.[69] The right to interstate travel and movement

[68] Kathryn E. Wilhelm, 'Freedom of Movement at a Standstill: Toward the Establishment of a Fundamental Right to Intrastate Travel' (2010) 90 *B.U.L. Rev.* 2461; S.F. Kreimer, 'The Law of Choice and Choice of Law: Abortion, the Right to Travel and Extraterritorial Regulation in American Federalism' (1992) 67 *N.Y.L. Rev.* 451.

[69] Joseph H. Carens, 'Migration and Morality: A liberal Egalitarian Perspective' in Barry Brian and Robert E. Goodin (eds), *Free Movement: Ethical Issues in Transnational Migration of People and of Money* (Pennsylvania State University Press, 1992); Rainer Bauböck, 'Global Justice, Freedom of Movement and Democratic Citizenship' (2009) 50(1) *European Journal of Sociology* 1.

is so well acknowledged that it is ruled that an act which deters or penalizes it should be regarded unconstitutional unless shown to be necessary to promote a compelling governmental interest.[70] This is especially true with regard to 'necessities of life',[71] as is usually evident in ST cases. Limiting or otherwise curtailing a person's freedom to travel for assisted suicide when access to it may not be allowed in her own state is therefore unconstitutional and violates that right to free movement.

Conclusion

This chapter discussed the alternatives that countries of origin and host countries may exercise with regard to ST. It explored whether actions to limit or prohibit either travel for assisted suicide or access to it within a country can be legally valid, looking at the issue from various legal perspectives.

It was shown that, on the one hand, legally restricting access to assisted suicide to residents or to patients who have had a long-standing relationship with prescribing doctors suffers from much criticism and is difficult to justify.

On the other hand, from the perspective of countries of origin, it is difficult and inappropriate to apply the doctrine of extraterritorial jurisdiction to the criminality of assisted suicide. Suggestions for international 'soft law' regulation on this practice are not sufficiently strong or convincing.

In addition, case law and guidelines concerning the prosecution of accompanying family members and third parties, especially doctors who provide information facilitating travel for assisted suicide, indicate that these parties may not be at high risk of prosecution. Although professional opinions may refer to some uncertainty in this regard, such a conclusion may be clearer on the legal side.

Finally, it was argued that, by securing proper safeguards, a guardian's decision regarding assisted suicide that is in the patient's best interest should be respected. Moreover, any prohibition on or limitation of one's

---

[70] *Shapiro v. Thompson* 394 U.S. 618, 634 (1969).
[71] *Memorial Hospital v. Maricopa County* 415 U.S. 250, 254 (1974).

ability to access assisted suicide where it is legal may violate a constitutional right to free movement, linked to personal autonomy, and should not be validated.

Based on this legal analysis, it is fair to suggest that the practice of suicide tourism does not suffer from illegality and its practising members are acting in an area that should not be limited or prohibited as such.

PART II

PHILOSOPHICAL ASPECTS OF SUICIDE TOURISM

3

The Morality of Suicide Tourism

The question of whether there are justifications for suicide tourism has practical implications in law, ethics, and public policy. Legally, if one argues that suicide tourism may be permissible and justified, there would be no prosecution of subjects of failed suicide attempts, nor of any third party assisting a person to travel for assisted suicide, including the agency or organization, medical doctor, or lawyer who supported it. From a moral and ethical perspective, the argument that suicide tourism can be justified implies, or may lead to, an analysis exempting health or legal professionals from moral or ethical condemnation when supplying, for example, information that may support an application for assisted suicide, or advice and help in carrying out such plans. On a public policy level, normative support for suicide tourism provides the state with regulatory authorization on the subject and affects the extent, content, and limit of its regulatory power, should it exist.

The previous chapter examines the legal response to suicide tourism. This chapter goes further to discuss and provide the moral basis for a response. Whether countries from which people travel to receive aid in dying should shape, regulate, and enforce policies pertaining to such a practice depends on the moral and philosophical justifications for and against suicide tourism. These should be distinguished from the justifications for and against assisted suicide. There is, of course, a connection between the two. One who regards suicide tourism as a morally sound practice will, almost certainly, also believe that assisted suicide should be permitted. But the opposite is not necessarily true: even when there are good reasons to believe that assisted suicide is morally permissible, this does not (automatically) lead to the argument that the travel from one country to another for assisted suicide is morally acceptable. The following sections will provide a detailed analysis of such a query.

Suicide Tourism. First Edition. Daniel Sperling. © Daniel Sperling 2019. Published 2019 by Oxford University Press.

Justifications for suicide tourism

In this section, I will refer to three key arguments in support of suicide tourism: the argument from the right to die; the argument from freedom of movement; and the argument from humanitarian aid.[1]

The argument from the right to die

While still subject to some conceptual debate and criticism,[2] the right to die requires that people should have power to determine the way, time, and place they depart the world. Usually such a right refers to the concepts of liberty, autonomy, dignity, respect, concern, quality of life, and suffering. Thus, the right to die is supported by the patient's liberty, her autonomy to make fatal decisions, her desire to maintain her dignity, and the healthcare profession's obligation to guarantee that the patient's dignity is preserved. Furthermore, the right is justified by a shared commitment to respect, and to show concern for, vulnerable patients, and to evaluate and reflect on quality-of-life considerations, alleviation of pain, and avoidance of suffering.[3]

The right to die is strongly associated with the concept of human dignity, and thus it is often referred to as the right to die with dignity. The value of dignity, in this respect, cannot be solely understood as an absolute and incomparable inner worth that of itself meets the condition for

---

[1] A fourth justification involves arguments pertaining to a moral obligation to respond to human suffering or to alleviate pain. However, this chapter seeks to provide general justifications for suicide tourism so that they apply to cases of people who travel to another country to die as a specific recourse to e.g. loss of autonomy and loss of interest in life as well as to suffering and pain. The three types of justification chosen for the discussion relate more specifically to travelling with the intention to die rather than to other, more general reactions to human suffering or alleviation of pain.

[2] See e.g. Leon Kass who argues that there is no sense in arguing for the right to die as we cannot serve a patient's good by deliberately eliminating her. Leon R. Kass, 'Is There a Right to Die?' (1993) 23(1) *Hastings Center Report* 34. See also Scott Shershow who raises a question as to whether the political and legal concepts of 'right' can apply to something which marks the limit of all rights and freedoms: Scott C. Shershow, 'The Sacred Part: Deconstruction and the Right to Die' (2012) 12(3) *CR: The New Centennial Review* 153.

[3] For an elaboration of such a right see: Raphael Cohen-Almagor, 'Right to Die' in Henk ten Have (ed), *The Encyclopedia of Global Bioethics* (Springer-Kluwer, 2015); Raphael Cohen-Almagor, *The Right to Die with Dignity: An Argument in Ethics, Medicine and Law* (Rutgers University Press, 2001).

the Kantian requirement that an individual be an end in herself. This is because of the contradiction that exists between supporting the right to die with a concept of human dignity which is not relational and arguing (as Kant did when he objected to suicide) that human dignity cannot be lost or diminished.[4] It may nonetheless be developed from a Millian idea of personal autonomy as self-determination, entailing a person's capacity to make her own decisions, control her desires, and determine her individuality at end-of-life.[5]

Moreover, it will be argued that the right to die is so essential to human flourishing and well-being that it should be viewed as a human right, namely a right that is part of 'the subclass of moral rights that are said, in virtue of their fundamentally important and essential connection with human well-being, to belong equally and unconditionally to all human beings, simply in virtue of their being human'.[6] Under a secular, natural law approach to human rights, a person's right pertaining to her death derives from her being a freely thinking individual and from her individual liberty. It is based on being a part of the human nature reflected in one's moral status but also in its connection with human need and vulnerability.[7] Under this argument, a person who regards her life as unworthy and who expresses no wish to continue living is at her most frail. Human frailty derives from conditions of scarcity, disease, and danger; facing inevitable death is a common feature to all human beings.[8]

The right to die includes all of the major characteristics of human rights: it has a right holder, relevant parties who are assigned responsibilities pertaining to it, and a clear scope; it has a pluralistic account referring to the combined values of autonomy, liberty, and human vulnerability; it is universal and does not depend on the existence of a particular society or nation applying it to a creature who has the potential for normative

---

[4] Milene Tonetto, 'Is There a Human Right to Be Assisted in Dying?' (2016) 23(41) *Principios: Revista de Filosofia* 75 at 82–3 (hereafter: 'Tonetto, Is There a Human Right').

[5] Ibid. at 85–6.

[6] Joel Feinberg, 'Voluntary Euthanasia and the Inalienable Right to Life' (1 April 1977) The Tanner Lecture on Human Values (hereafter: 'Feinberg, Voluntary Euthanasia').

[7] Corinna Mieth, 'The Double Foundation of Human Rights in Human Nature' in Marion Albers et al. (eds), *Human Rights and Human Nature* (Springer, 2014) p. 11.

[8] Bryan S. Turner, 'Outline of a Theory of Human Rights' (1993) 27(3) *Sociology* 489.

agency; and it has meaningful and significant norms supporting the high priority placed on it (as a human right).[9]

The human right to die is also expressed by the idea of the human right to end one's life. As Thomas Szasz argues, 'suicide is a fundamental human right. This does not mean that it is morally desirable. It only means that society does not have the moral right to interfere, by force, with a person's decision to commit this act'.[10] This is not to say that society should not propose and introduce programmes to prevent suicide and to promote life. This is to argue that one has a negative human right (as opposed to a claim right) to have her wish to die respected when it is well informed and properly supported. It is also argued that if suicide and the right to die can be classified as human rights,[11] it follows that such rights cannot be interfered with when a person needs to travel for assisted suicide, given that she is unable to exercise these rights fully in her country of origin.[12]

While, like other human rights,[13] the right to die may not be absolute—so that the state can interfere with the fulfilment of such a right, especially as it contradicts another human right, most notably the right to life—the human right to die should receive full protection universally and regardless of the legal regime that applies to the person. Following Alan Gewirth's thesis, according to which human rights entail a communitarian conception of human relationships characterized by mutuality and social solidarity,[14] and given that individuals possess these rights

---

[9] James Nickel, *Making Sense of Human Rights* (Blackwell, 2007); Tonetto, Is There a Human Right (n 4).

[10] Thomas S. Szasz, *The Second Sin* (1973), mentioned in Walter W. Steele and Bill B. Hill, 'A Plea for a Legal Right to Die' (1976) 29 *Oklahoma L. Rev.* 328 at 340 (at FN 80). See also Margaret P. Battin, *The Least Worse Death* (Oxford University Press, 1994) (arguing that suicide is a human right because of its connection with human dignity).

[11] For a legal positivist analysis supporting an opposite conclusion, see Maria C. Lucan, 'The Right to Death: Fiction or Reality' (2016) 17(31) *Journal of Legal Studies* 37.

[12] It does not follow from this argument, however, that there is necessarily a claim right to employ an agent to assist with one's wish to die: Martin Gunderson, 'A Right to Suicide Does Not Entail a Right to Assisted Death' (1997) 23 *JME* 51, nor that there are circumstances under which a person has a duty to die, especially for utilitarian considerations: James M. Humber and Robert F. Almeder, *Is There a Duty to Die?* (Humana Press, 2000); John Hardwig, 'Is There a Duty to Die?' (1997) 27(2) *Hastings Center Report* 34.

[13] Feinberg, Voluntary Euthanasia (n 6).

[14] Alan R. Gewirth, 'The Community of Rights' in Edgar Morscher, Otto Neumaier, and Peter M. Simons (eds), *Applied Ethics in a Troubled World* (Philosophical Studies Series, vol. 73; Springer, 1998) p. 225.

qua human beings so that they stand for the equality of all human beings, their application is and should be universal.[15]

If one accepts this argument from universalism, it follows that a human being should be able to exercise this right to die in another country if her own country limits or otherwise prohibits such an act by, for example, the prohibition of assisted suicide. Hence, suicide tourism can be justified on the grounds that it allows and guarantees the human right to die. Moreover, without defending this practice, the human right to die does not receive any practical meaning, and instead remains on a theoretical level.

The argument from freedom of movement

Another justification for suicide tourism concerns the value placed on the moral right to move about freely, and its application in the context of access to health or, more specifically, health-related services. The right to freedom of movement underpins one's sense of liberty through the expansion of one's opportunities and insights. From a liberal perspective, the principal argument for the moral right to free movement lies in its strong link with individual autonomy. It can be argued that allowing people to move to other geographical settings within and outside one's country[16] according to their wishes and needs is not only instrumentally important in enabling them to determine—as much as possible—the circumstances under which they live and die,[17] but it is also intrinsically important to their value of autonomy. This is because being confined in one's movement can be experienced as a constraint on freedom itself.[18] Other justifications for the moral right to free movement may apply particularly

---

[15] Tibor R. Machan, 'A Reconsideration of Natural Rights Theory' (1982) 19(1) *American Philosophical Quarterly* 61; Linda Hajjar Leib, *Human Rights and the Environment: Philosophical, Theoretical and Legal Perspectives* (Brill, 2011).

[16] Most philosophers would agree that there is no basis for distinguishing between one's right to move within one's country and one's right to move across countries. Sarah Fine, 'The Ethics of Immigration: Self-Determination and the Right to Exclude' (2013) 8(3) *Philosophy Compass* 254.

[17] Joseph H. Carens, 'Migration and Morality: A Liberal Egalitarian Perspective' in Barry Brian and Robert R. Goodin (eds), *Free Movement: Ethical Issues in Transnational Migration of People and of Money* (Pennsylvania University Press, 1992).

[18] Rainer Baubök, 'Global Justice, Freedom of Movement and Democratic Citizenship' (2009) 50(1) *European Journal of Sociology/Archives* 1–31.

to suicide tourism, insofar as the place of birth is morally arbitrary and people should not be held to it; a commitment to moral equality of humanity cannot justify limitation of a person's right to freely move from her place of birth,[19] thereby also to escape from its laws.

On a political and macro level, movement to another country to fulfil one's wishes by escaping a state's laws and moral conventions prevents moral homogeneity and promotes diversity and experimentation.[20] Following Albert Hirschman's theory of exit and voice[21] it may also prompt policy change, supported by an increased voice within the country from which travel is made. Applying this rationale to suicide tourism can refer to the significance which such a practice may have in its contribution to liberalizing laws on assisted suicide in countries of origin.

Perhaps it can be argued—as in other contexts of tourism that involve accessing health services or resources, such as medical tourism, reproductive tourism, transplant tourism, etc.—that one's right to access assisted suicide services in countries where provision of such services is not illegal provides strong justification for one's freedom to travel to another country, without fear of moral condemnation or legal prosecution/sanction.

An attempt to legally recognize physician-assisted suicide within more permissive jurisdictions as 'services' under the Treaty on the Functioning of the European Union (so that any restrictions on the provision of such services would be removed) has already been considered in the literature.[22] Along with this line of reasoning, Irene Glinos and colleagues introduced a typology of the concept of cross-border patient mobility that goes beyond conventional territorial logic. It is supported, inter alia, by the right to freedom of movement to allow citizens moving to another state to have access to health care. Within this typology is the 'law evasion' patient mobility, which includes travel to Switzerland for medically assisted suicide.[23]

---

[19] Phillip Cole, *Philosophies of Exclusion: Liberal Political Theory and Immigration* (Edinburgh University Press, 2000).

[20] S.F. Kreimer, '"But Whoever Treasures Freedom ...": The Right to Travel and Extraterritorial Abortions' (1993) 91(5) *Michigan L. Rev.* 907 at 915–16.

[21] Albert O. Hirschman, *Exit, Voice, and Loyalty* (Harvard University Press, 1970).

[22] Ben P. Slight, 'Could Physician-Assisted Suicide Be Classified as a Service under Article 49 of the European Community Treaty?' (2009) 10(2) *Medical Law International* 139.

[23] Irene A. Glinos, Rita Baeten, Matthias Helble, and Hans Maarse, 'A Typology of Cross-Border Patient Mobility' (2010) 16 *Health & Place* 1145.

Finally, following on from this latter argument, if one accepts the World Health Organization's definition of health, referring to the well-being of a person as a major component of 'health', then accessing services to pursue a person's well-being, including assisted suicide services, may be justified by a person's right to freely and deliberately move from one place to another to access services that promote her complete health.[24] At a minimum, under these circumstances a person's condition can, if left to continue, be considered a state worse than death so that accessing assisted suicide is not contrary to her well-being and at times may also improve it.[25] Thus, there is a prima facie moral justification for respecting such a right.

The argument from humanitarian aid

States, and perhaps also their citizens, hold a moral obligation to offer international humanitarian aid to their fellow humans when the latter face a state of natural disaster that potentially or actually affects a significant number of people. Traditionally, international aid, which usually involves the donation of domestic resources, is provided to victims of such disasters as floods, famine, epidemics, earthquakes, etc. Corollary to such an obligation is a person's moral right to receive such aid, including through being allowed to travel to the donor country to receive it.

Countries that offer international aid usually do this for some political gain and with some strategic interest.[26] Foreign aid is also seen as a means to facilitate commerce and trade resulting in economic growth and prosperity.[27] It may also lead to an increase in the international prestige of the giving country.[28]

---

[24] This argument assumes that a person can also be benefited—as much as she can be harmed—after she is dead. See Daniel Sperling, *Posthumous Interests: Legal and Ethical Perspectives* (Cambridge University Press, 2008).

[25] Dan W. Brock, 'A Critique of Three Objections to Physician-Assisted Suicide' (1999) 109(3) *Ethics* 519.

[26] Tobias Heinrich, 'When Is Foreign Aid Selfish, When Is It Selfless?' (2013) 75(2) *The Journal of Politics* 422.

[27] Howard B. White (ed), *Aid and Macroeconomic Performance: Theory, Empirical Evidence and Four Country Cases* (MacMillan Press, 1998).

[28] Hans Morgenthau, 'A Political Theory of Foreign Aid' (1962) 56(2) *American Political Science Review* 301.

More generally, international aid can be justified by three schools of thought. A deontological justification for foreign aid holds that foreign aid usually reflects an imperfect moral obligation owed by the more- to the less-industrialized and developed countries to provide basic needs which are characterized as a human right.[29] These needs can pertain to basic medical care or access to safe food and water. A consequentialist justification holds that foreign aid is a moral response to problems that can be fixed by technical or practical expertise. Under this argument, the giving country is best placed to offer services and resources to reduce or repair the detrimental effects of these natural disasters. Most commonly, this argument is applied to the medical context, in which physicians from a foreign country offer aid and support to victims of a natural disaster who may have been harmed as a result.[30]

However, providing humanitarian aid is also influenced by humanitarian considerations and can be justified as a reaction to human suffering.[31] Countries that consider providing international aid, it is argued, do and should go beyond their own national self-interests. Under this argument, the expression of human nature in international politics requires prudence, wariness, and moral concern. This may be realized in three ways: applying domestic political conceptions of justice to international life; holding a social and moral dialogue with the international society; and attaching normative meanings to international regimes and practices, for example foreign aid.[32]

Indeed, countries with strong domestic social welfare programmes are the most generous foreign aid donors and those politicians, parties, and interest groups who dislike the welfare state and related values and principles also dislike foreign aid. Similarly, public polls show that citizens who felt strongly about, for example, alleviating poverty in their home country were more likely to favour foreign aid. Foreign aid was referred to as a type of international welfare state and the realization of norms pertaining to such a concept.[33]

---

[29] Tomohisa Hattori, 'The Moral Politics of Foreign Aid' (2003) 29 *Review of International Studies* 229, 233, 230 (hereafter: 'Hattori, Moral Politics').

[30] Ibid.

[31] Ibid. at 231; David H. Lumsdaine, *Moral Vision in International Politics* (Princeton University Press, 1993).

[32] Ibid. at 4–5.

[33] Ibid. at 23–4.

The moral obligation to offer humanitarian foreign aid is supported by the value of solidarity that applies to all citizens, regardless of territorial limitations. It can be argued that such an obligation could be applied to the situation where people in some parts of the world, who suffer from pain or poor quality of life, cannot fulfil their right and wish to die, due to legal or social limitations. It is contended that such a situation, classified as a 'social disaster', equates to a natural disaster justifying humanitarian intervention.

The potential causality between the state's omission or refusal to legalize assisted suicide and the social disaster nonetheless does not disqualify the moral obligation to provide humanitarian aid under these circumstances. As is shown with regard to natural disaster cases, the receiving state could have established policies to prevent natural disasters or to manage them more efficiently (in terms of casualties and harm). The lack of such policies does not make the donor countries exempt from offering moral aid to their fellow humans.

That a moral obligation is owed by the Swiss people (including right-to-die organizations)—who are not only subject to permissive laws on assisted suicide but are also capable of offering such services to non-residents—can be established by reference to the idea of an unreciprocated gift and, more generally, as an expression of the power relations between Switzerland and other countries and their residents.[34] Like any other gift, providing access to assisted suicide to foreign residents establishes both interested and disinterested relationships between Switzerland and the other countries.[35] It allows the former to preserve and perpetuate its image as the oldest neutral country in the world and, by giving (to others) the means of providing assistance in death (an act which is so widely inaccessible and impermissible), to maintain what Pierre Bourdieu calls symbolic domination,[36] or a practice that signals and euphemizes social hierarchies.[37] Furthermore, the Swiss gift/humanitarian aid to non-residents makes them escape conscious scrutiny

---

[34] Rosalind Eyben, 'The Power of the Gift and the New Aid Modalities', (2006) 37(6) *IDS Bulletin* 88; Hattori, Moral Politics (n 29).

[35] Marcel Mauss, *The Gift: Forms and Functions of Exchange in Archaic Societies* (Trans.: Ian Cunnison) (Cohen & West, 1954).

[36] Pierre Bourdieu, *The Logic of Practice* (Polity Press, 1990).

[37] Tomohisa Hattori, 'Reconceptualizing Foreign Aid' (2001) 8(4) *Review of International Political Economy* 633–60.

of their law and their unique attitude towards assisted suicide that is exercised relatively widely by application to non-terminal individuals and performed also by non-physicians.

From non-political or institutional reasons, it may also be argued that not providing assistance to people who would otherwise die without dignity or through an agonizing and unjustly long process, may even constitute a 'crime against humanity', namely a serious attack on human dignity, a grave humiliation, or a degradation of human beings amounting to an inhumane act causing great suffering or serious bodily or mental injury.[38] Hence, humans in places where the law permits them to do so have a moral (and perhaps also legal) duty to provide assistance in dying to their international fellows.

Arguments against suicide tourism

Along with the above justifications in favour of suicide tourism, one should consider four major justifications (or groups of justifications) against such a phenomenon. These include the argument from consequentialism; the argument from the right to commit suicide; the argument from respect for one's body; and the argument from the nature of dying.

The argument from consequentialism

One of the strongest arguments against suicide tourism refers to the implications for serious and detrimental outcomes raised by such a practice. This group of considerations relates to consequentialist considerations pertaining to the person seeking assisted suicide, to parties accompanying the person in her travel to Switzerland or to another country where non-residents can access assisted suicide, and to third parties and society more generally.

---

[38] United Nations, 'Crimes Against Humanity' https://www.un.org/en/genocideprevention/crimes-against-humanity.shtml, accessed on 1 July 2019.

Allowing people to travel to other places for the purpose of committing suicide may be harmful in cases where ending their lives may be the result of abuse (financial or otherwise),[39] and/or does not follow a candid wish to die. If unsuccessful, attempts to commit suicide which are illegal in one's home country may make the people involved behave more immorally, and incentivize them to engage in more dangerous, immoral, or even criminal activities. If people who explore travelling to another country for assisted suicide reconsider their decision to commit suicide or are recklessly being assisted and, as a result, their health status worsens, this may aggravate their suffering, extend their terminal condition and the dying process, and create serious financial and emotional burdens for them.

As to accompanying partners, it can be argued that these people can be exposed to criminal prosecutions or otherwise social condemnation when they are back in their homeland. While attending suicides of their loved ones, they may suffer trauma and feel hurt and guilt for not supporting an opposing position. They may also be exposed to financial pressure and abuse by the right-to-die organization or other mediators who facilitate the proposed travel or are providing professional help for it. Overall, their close involvement in this experience may make them behave more immorally or engage in dangerous or criminal activities in the future.

As to consequentialist considerations pertaining to third parties and society at large, these include so-called 'slippery slope' arguments concerning the detrimental effect that suicide tourism may have on vulnerable people e.g. children, the elderly, patients who lack mental capacity, poor people, and otherwise marginalized people within a society. Specifically, such a practice, it can be argued, will increase disrespect towards these groups of people and increase the ease with which ending their lives can be brought about.[40]

---

[39] For one of the worst cases of abuse involved in assisted suicide see Jack Kevorkian, *Prescription: Medicine* (Prometheus Books, 1991).

[40] In this respect, there will be some commonality between this argument and slippery slope arguments concerning the effects of the practice of assisted suicide more generally. Recent empirical findings from the Netherlands and Belgium may support these arguments. See Barron H. Lerner and Arthur L. Caplan, 'Euthanasia in Belgium and the Netherlands: On a Slippery Slope?' (2015) 175(10) *JAMA Internal Medicine* 1640.

Validating the practice of suicide tourism may also lead to unethical and illegal practices by physicians and caregivers, and reconstitution of their professional obligations towards their patients. This will erode patient trust and damage the reputation of the medical profession. On the state level, suicide tourism may hurt the image of the permissive country (i.e. Switzerland) and may also affect its relations with countries of origin. Although it may bring some economic growth, it may lead to abusive and illegal activities being performed by its members and expose innocent parties to criminal and immoral behaviour.

It follows from this argument that the practice of suicide tourism leads to and may result in more detrimental and damaging outcomes than advantageous ones, and from this perspective it cannot be justified.

The argument from the right to commit suicide

Under this second rationale, human beings should not enjoy or hold a moral right to travel to another country to commit suicide, or to be assisted to do so, to pursue their wish in this regard, and therefore suicide tourism cannot be morally supported or justified. While this argument stems from the more general objections to suicide, it nonetheless holds that the practice of suicide tourism intensifies the conditions under which these objections apply. There are several aspects to this argument.

One aspect concerns the inviolability or sanctity of life and regards the intrinsic value that life has so that it must not be taken by human action. It is argued that the practice of suicide tourism emphasizes the 'artificial' or unnatural aspect of dying, increasing the involvement of others in this process including family members, friends, agencies, assisted suicide organizations, professionals, bureaucrats from both countries, etc. As dying becomes more human-made and dominated by 'unnatural' factors, the value attached to life diminishes and, if at all, receives weight only for its instrumental contribution to other external values. The substantial diminution of the value attached to life makes a strong case against the practice of suicide tourism.

Another aspect to the opposition to suicide tourism concerns the irrationality of suicide that becomes more evident by the practice of suicide tourism. This argument could be based on two modes of thinking. The first concerns the argument put forward by Immanuel Kant. Kant argues that since our rational wills are the source of our moral duty, it is a contradiction to assume that the same will can destroy itself. Moreover, because autonomous rational wills have distinctive worth, and given that rational wills are the source of morality, suicide acts against the very source of moral authority. In Kant's words:

> To annihilate the subject of morality in one's person is to root out the existence of morality itself from the world as far as one can, even though morality is an end in itself. Consequently, disposing of oneself as a mere means to some discretionary end is debasing humanity in one's person...[41]

A second type of argument leading to the conclusion that a decision to commit suicide is irrational can be evidenced in the writings of John Stuart Mill. In Mill's view, since the essence of human freedom lies in a person's ability to make choices, she cannot make a choice that would deprive her of her ability to make further choices, thereby defeating her own freedom. Mill writes,

> The reason for not interfering, unless for the sake of others, with a person's voluntary acts, is consideration for his liberty. His voluntary choice is evidence that what he so chooses is desirable, or at the least endurable, to him, and his good is on the whole best provided for by allowing him to take his own means of pursuing it. But by selling himself for a slave, he abdicates his liberty; he forgoes any future use of it, beyond that single act. He therefore defeats, in his own case, the very purpose which is the justification of allowing him to dispose of himself. He is no longer free; but is thenceforth in a position which has no longer the presumption in its favour, that would be afforded by his voluntarily remaining in it. The principle of freedom cannot require that he should

---

[41] Immanuel Kant, *The Metaphysics of Morals* (Trans.: Mary Gregor) (Cambridge University Press, 1996) at 177 (§6: 423). Moreover, universal laws of nature serve to impel the continuation of life. Kant believed suicide makes more ill than it promises agreeableness. This is why the maxim of ending one's life cannot become a universal law of nature. Hoa T. Dinh, 'Autonomy Trumps All? A Kantian Critique of Physician-Assisted Death' (2017) 94(4) *Australian Catholic Record* 466.

be free not to be free. It is not freedom, to be allowed to alienate his freedom.[42]

It is argued that the practice of suicide tourism emphasizes the advance planning of the act of suicide, including the place, manner, conditions, surroundings, and possible consequences of taking one's life—all of which are dominated by the rules of the market (especially supply and demand of assisted suicide services), operating under the assumption that more and better information results in a better and, from this aspect, a more rationalized 'outcome'. Whether rational autonomous decisions can or cannot pertain to committing suicide, following the concept of humanity or deriving from the content of such decision,[43] suicide tourism cannot be supported morally as such a practice rests on and heavily emphasizes the making of rational decisions that by themselves cannot stand in a coherent and morally justified relationship with the act of suicide.

The argument from respect for one's body

Under this argument, while suicide tourism empowers one's dominion over the body as it reflects intimate choices pertaining to one's body, it is through the movement (travel) of such a body that it transforms and annihilates itself. One can argue that a person has a moral duty to respect one's body and to make it function, thereby realizing one's humanity to the full. In this respect, suicide tourism is different to other forms of medical tourism where the body is altered, fixed, and revitalized but is not annihilated.

In support of such a view, one can refer to Kant's significant approach towards the human body. In Kant's view, 'a man is not his own property and cannot do with his body as he wills. The body is part of the self; in its togetherness with the self it constitutes the person.'[44] It follows that a person cannot use her body to dispose of herself because she is not a

---

[42] John S. Mill, *On Liberty* included in the collection *Utilitarianism, Liberty and Representative Government* (Dent, 1910) at 157–8.

[43] See also Susan Stefan, *Rational Suicide, Irrational Laws: Examining Current Approaches to Suicide in Policy and Law* (Oxford University Press, 2016).

[44] Kant, *Lectures on Ethics* (Cambridge University Press, 1963) p. 166.

thing; she is not her own property, for if she were her property she could give or sell it to someone to make use of it and thus to transform it (her person) to a thing. Because the human body is significant and constitutes one's self, Kant argued that human beings have a natural duty of self-preservation, an aspect of which is not to mutilate oneself. The rationale for this moral right is that acts of mutilation or even giving away one's body (or even one's body parts) results in 'depriving oneself of one's capacity for the natural (and so indirectly the moral) use of one's powers' which would be detrimental to personhood.[45]

If one follows this conceptualization, one would argue against a practice that refers to the (travelling) body as a means to annihilate the body through the assistance of another person not just as a mere contradiction to morality but as an act of disrespect towards the person (through its body).

The argument from the nature of dying

While the physical move from the familiarity of home to a hospital setting transformed the 'person' to a 'patient', with suicide tourism, the dying process takes place in a totally unfamiliar, remote, and alien environment, at times even isolated and artificial.[46] It can be argued that the practice of suicide tourism substantially alters the process of dying so that it empties the symbolic and emotional meanings attached to it and depletes the dying person's personality and identity linked to her original culture. Moreover, accompanying parties are sometimes investigated when they return to their home land, and thus their experience of the death of a loved one becomes one from the perspective of potential criminals.

In addition, because suicide tourism involves parties other than physicians—such as those who facilitate the travel and are responsible for administrative, legal, and technical issues—suicide tourism involves financial compensation and gives rise to a market which in turn

---

[45] Nicole Gerrand, 'The Misuse of Kant in the Debate about a Market for Human Body Parts' (1999) 16(1) *Journal of Applied Philosophy* 59, 62.

[46] For the importance of dying at home see Stephen J. Ziegler, 'Collaborated Death: An Exploration of the Swiss Model of Assisted Suicide for Its Potential to Enhance Oversight and Demedicalize the Dying Process' (2009) 37(2) *J. Law, Med., & Ethics* 318.

fosters profit-based motivations amongst the people involved. The travel itself is being regarded as an insurance plan, as advertised by Exit International: 'You do this trip because you want an insurance policy; you make it in good health so that if you become terminally ill this can guarantee you a quicker exit'.[47] Note that under this campaign, dying and death are not mentioned. It is the trip resulting in the product of the insurance plan which is at stake here.

As this becomes a major characteristic of suicide tourism, dying under this practice is transformed from a humane and incentive-free process to a commercialized, self-interested, and uncaring practice which is unjustly accessible only to those who can afford it. As a former nurse who worked at Dignitas testified, Dignitas is 'less about ethical euthanasia and more of a money-making machine'.[48] It is thus argued that because these changes are a threat to human life (which also consists of the way we die), suicide tourism should be warned against and cannot be justified.

Conclusion

While the justifications for suicide tourism are powerfully convincing, those against it suffer from theoretical problems and, in some cases, cannot necessarily be supported by empirical evidence. Indeed, suicide tourism provides individuals with much freedom and choice in exercising a right to die, which should receive greater weight than is the case within current moral and legal understandings. The tourism adventure secures an element of escapism (from e.g. the physical and psychological effects of chronic or terminal disease) and a sense of achievement following some fantasy (over the place, manner, and personnel involved in the dying process). These advantages accord with people's expectations

---

[47] Robin Emmott, 'Euthanasia Tourists Snap Up Pet Shop Drug in Mexico' (Reuters, 3 June 2008) https://uk.reuters.com/article/uk-mexico-euthanasia/euthanasia-tourists-snap-up-pet-shop-drug-in-mexico-idUKN0329945820080603, accessed on 18 February 2018 (citing Dr Michael Irwin).

[48] Allan Hall, 'Cashing in On Despair? Suicide Clinic Dignitas Is a Profit Obsessed Killing Machine, Claims Ex-Worker' (Mailonline, 25 January 2009) http://www.dailymail.co.uk/news/article-1127413/Cashing-despair-Suicide-clinic-Dignitas-profit-obsessed-killing-machine-claims-ex-worker.html, accessed on 22 February 2018.

when pursuing suicide and assisted suicide.[49] They also correspond to peoples' right to free movement which is more secured and valued in a globalized world and can also be supported by a revised—and more courageous—interpretation of the moral duty to provide humanitarian aid to citizens of less permissive states.

Meanwhile, the consequential considerations against suicide tourism have not been proven. While there is only a little anecdotal and indirect evidence to suggest that cases of suicide tourism involve abuse, there are hardly any cases reporting regret, inclination to be involved in other morally or criminally impermissible acts, or other health-inflicted injuries in cases of unsuccessful attempts to commit suicide pertaining to main actors and more generally to accompanying members. As to the latter, data suggests that there has not been even a single case of successful criminal prosecution in any of the countries from which travel has originated. As discussed in the previous chapter, the only case in which a prosecution was brought (against an Italian activist) does not seem to have resulted in an actual charge. Moreover, there are some positive affirmations (especially in the UK, following the revised guidelines of the Director of Public Prosecutions) to suggest some degree of legal immunity under such circumstances.

The argument from the moral right to commit suicide should have force if one accords higher moral weight to the right to life than to other competing rights and interests that are associated with and protected by the right to die. Of course, a morally pluralistic society cannot prima facie account for such a hierarchy unless other considerations support such a conclusion.

Regarding the critique from the perspective of rationality, people can, as studies show, make perfectly rational decisions to engage irrationally (even if only instrumentally and not necessarily telically),[50] to harm themselves, and to bring an end to their lives in accordance with their fundamental interests,[51] including what they project as their future

---

[49] Roy F. Baumeister, 'Suicide as Escape from Oneself' (1990) 97(1) *Psychological Review* 90; Thomas Joiner, *Why People Die by Suicide* (Harvard University Press, 2009).

[50] Michael Cholbi, 'What is Wrong with "What is Wrong with Rational Suicide"' (2012) 40 *Philosophia* 285–93.

[51] Margaret Battin, *The Death Debate: Ethical Issues in Suicide* (Prentice-Hall, 1995) p. 116.

ends.[52] Yet, the requirement of rationality is neither a necessary precondition to making suicidal decisions nor a conclusive element in realizing such decisions. Moreover, it could be argued that suicide tourism does not necessarily make suicidal decisions more rational as these are prone to 'market failures' deriving from the complexity associated with the decision to commit suicide as well as the emotional burden associated with such decisions.

With regard to Kant's argument concerning the human body, it should be emphasized that the moral duty towards one's body is dependent upon the functionality of the body or body part and its contribution to self-preservation. However, when the body or a body part becomes a threat to one's life, Kant would have regarded such a case as an exception to maintaining the duty not to mutilate itself. It follows that the moral case against suicide, based on Kant's conception of the human body, may not serve as an objection to suicide tourism when the body itself does not contribute in any way to one's preservation and realization of humanity.

Finally, the argument as to the nature of dying does not necessarily lead to invalidation of suicide tourism but, at most, can offer a new or revised way of understanding and conceptualizing the dying process. Instead, it may suggest a new form of tourism, to which Miller and Gonzalez refer as 'dark tourism', namely the 'travel to sites linked with death and tragedy or sites where death and suffering has occurred or been memorialized'.[53] Moreover, commercialization of death and dying is being observed not only with regard to suicide tourism but with other social phenomena whereby society enters a 'death-deriding' age, under which, as argued by Pagliari and Walter, death is mocked, commercialized, or sold for the sake of art or entertainment, and is being industrialized through businesses in various procedures, such as hardware, real estate, and funeral or cryogenic services.[54]

---

[52] Richard B. Brandt, 'The Morality and Rationality of Suicide' in *Morality, Utilitarianism and Rights* (Cambridge University Press, 1992) 315.

[53] DeMond S. Miller and Christopher Gonzalez, 'When Death is the Destination: The Business of Death Tourism—Despite Legal and Social Implications' (2013) 7(3) *International Journal of Culture, Tourism and Hospitality Research* 293, 294 (hereafter: 'Miller and Gonzalez, When Death is the Destination'). See generally, Philip R. Stone, *Death, Dying and Dark Tourism in Contemporary Society: A Theoretical and Empirical Analysis*, Doctoral Thesis (University of Central Lancashire, 2010) http://clok.uclan.ac.uk/1870/, accessed on 22 February 2018.

[54] Bob Pagliari, 'From a Death-Denying to a Death-Defying to a Death-Deriding Society' (*Catholic New York*, 31 March 2004) http://cny.org/stories/From-a-Death-Denying-to-a-Death-Defying-to-a-Death-Deriding-Society,450?content_source=&category_id=&search_

In addition, one can argue that in suicide tourism cases the commodification of death and dying involves the de-medicalization of assisted death, thus revealing the 'true' nature of the tourism experience. As Miller and Gonzalez highlight, 'the final days of life are not consumed with the life-extending medical equipment or the next medical appointment, but rather the tour event is a way to embrace life's finality and enhance the quality of life during the last days'.[55] It thus follows that there are good reasons to morally justify and protect a prima facie position in favour of the practice of suicide tourism. It is time now to examine the question of whether, despite it being morally permissible and—as argued in Chapter 2—legally valid, states should interfere with suicide tourism and, if so, what the philosophical justification for it is.

filter=pagliari+death-deriding&search_headline=&event_mode=&event_ts_from=&list_type=&order_by=&order_sort=&content_class=&sub_type=stories&town_id= accessed on 22 February 2018; Tony Walter, 'Ritualizing Death in a Consumer Society' (1996) 144(5468) *Royal Society for the Encouragement of Arts, Manufactures and Commerce* 32.

---

[55] Miller and Gonzalez, When Death is the Destination (n 53) at 295.

4

Political-Philosophical Analysis
of Suicide Tourism

Previous chapters of this book argue that suicide tourism is a legal practice enjoying a prima facie moral status. Its moral status, it is claimed, mostly derives from arguments that focus on the micro, namely the individuals who participate in or are affected by this practice. However, the philosophical analysis of suicide tourism would not be complete without referring to the macro, that is, the states where assisted suicide is prohibited yet whose residents or citizens participate in suicide tourism. This chapter, therefore, broadens the philosophical investigation of suicide tourism by examining the justifications for and against state intervention. Such justifications, stemming from moral or other considerations, could help politicians, policymakers, and ethicists to choose the manner and direction in which they respond to the evolving practice of suicide tourism.

In this book, the term *state intervention* refers to the ways in which a state can express its views and take action by limiting or prohibiting suicide tourism, as elaborated on in Chapter 2. For example, state intervention can include investigating and prosecuting those who assist in suicide tourism (such as friends and family who refer or accompany a person to the host country or support her request to travel); publishing coherent guidelines for the public (regarding suicide tourism in general, and criteria for prosecution in particular); reviewing and monitoring contracts with agencies and other participating parties that deal in suicide tourism; limiting the practice of suicide tourism to approved organizations or certain destinations or to being carried out in certain manners; publishing an opposing view while still allowing the practice; and prohibiting suicide tourism.[1]

---

[1] For exceptional intervention, through which the country of origin prohibits tourism to evade its local laws, see the Legislation Concerning Assisted Reproduction Treatment Practices and Centres in Turkey. Zeynep B. Gürtin, 'Banning Reproductive Travel: Turkey's ART

The methods chosen by a state dealing with and intervening in suicide tourism may be shaped by a variety of justifications. This chapter presents political-philosophical justifications, which can be divided into five main arguments: state sovereignty; global justice and moral particularism; cosmopolitanism and moral universalism; inter-state moral pluralism; and common ownership. The first two justifications support state intervention with regards to suicide tourism while the last three oppose substantial state intervention. Before discussing these macro justifications in more detail, this chapter addresses the idea of governability of death as reflected in the writings of political sociologists, especially Michel Foucault and Giorgio Agamben.

Governability of death

The practice of suicide tourism reflects an important aspect of the governability of death. It represents a void in countries of origin while attesting to a unique approach to such governability in the country to which people travel to die. Countries that criminalize assisted suicide leave their citizens with a very difficult decision. They can either wait until death occurs naturally, commit suicide (sometimes by painful means), or attempt to travel to another country where assisted suicide may be legal and not excluded from foreigners. While choosing this latter alternative, they must comply with the requirements of the other country, which—as illustrated in the next chapter—may not always be feasible given their medical condition and suffering; they must have the finances, knowledge, decision-making capacity, support system, and so forth to be able to take this path. As such, it is argued, they are subject to social power that infringes their basic liberties both inside and outside the juridical order controlling their

Legislation and Third-Party Assisted Reproduction' (2011) 23 *Reproductive Biomedicine Online* 555. In other contexts of tourism, state intervention can also include reimbursement or otherwise acknowledgement of practices which are considered illegal or unavailable in one's country of origin. One such example is the reimbursement of an anonymous sperm donation in Belgium offered to a Dutch couple while the Dutch law only allows identifiable donation. Wannes Van Hoof and Guido Pennings, 'Extraterritorial Laws for Cross-Border Reproductive Care: The Issue of Legal Diversity' (2012) 19 *European Journal of Health Law* 187 at 188–9 (hereafter: 'Van Hoof and Pennings, Extraterritorial Rules'). However, this may not apply to ethically controversial medical services, such as euthanasia (at 194).

life.[2] In this way, they are being dominated by prevailing beliefs which do not accommodate the other.

Suicide tourism thus reflects the way the state—individually and with other states—exercises its dominion and control, especially in life and death issues, where it matters most. It is the move from the power of deduction and seizure to what Foucault coined *the biopower*. Indeed, the biopower, which coincided with the emergence of clinical medicine and bio-medicine, is concerned with the generation of forces which purport to administer, optimize, and multiply life. It is the shift from the right to take life and let live (both of which are promoted by the practice of assisted suicide) to fostering life or disallowing it to the point of death.[3] Foucault emphasizes that while, from the point of view of life and death, the subject is neutral, it is thanks to the will of the sovereign that the subject has rights to be alive or dead. In Foucault's words,

> Now that power is decreasingly the power of the right to take life, and increasingly the right to intervene to make live ... death becomes, insofar as it is the end of life, the term, the limit, or the end of the power too. Death is outside of the power relationship. In the right of sovereignty, death was the moment of the most obvious and most spectacular manifestation of the absolute power of the sovereign; death now becomes, in contrast, the moment when the individual escapes all power, falls back on himself and retreats, so to speak, into his own privacy. Power no longer recognizes death. Power literally ignores death.[4]

The shift from the right to take life or let live to the power, or to the new right, to make life and let die occurred in the seventeenth and eighteenth centuries, where jurists and political philosophers argued that the sovereign's mandate—the very social contract that granted him the power to rule—was based on the very basic need to protect life or on the fear of

---

[2] Carl Shmitt, '*Political Theology: Four Chapters on the Concept of Sovereignty*' (Trans.: George Schwab) (MIT Press, 1985).

[3] Michel Foucault, *History of Sexuality, Volume 1: An Introduction* (Trans.: Robert Hurley) (Vintage Books, 1990).

[4] Michel Foucault, '*Society Must Be Defended': Lecturers at the College de France* (Trans.: David Macey) (Picador, 2003) p. 248.

pain and death. Life itself was, therefore, the foundation of the sovereign's rights and so had to remain outside the social contract. With the emergence of techniques of power centring on the individual body, the human body was reinvented and made separate in space from other bodies. It became visible, controlled, and punished if needed.

However, Foucault adds, from the second half of the eighteenth century the disciplinary technology integrated a new power. Unlike the disciplinary technology which applies to man-as-body and whose meaning is that the person is no more than her individual body, this new power applied to the living man, namely to the person seen as part of a global mass, affected by processes of birth, death, production, illness, and so forth. This massifying power is, thus, directed at man-as-species.[5]

This new biopolitics of the human race was measured and conceptualized by statistical terms such as birth and mortality rates, longevity, etc. It was also expressed by, for example, birth-control practices, natalist policies, and the evolvement of the field of endemics which regards illness as phenomena affecting a population. Mechanisms introduced by biopolitics do not modify any given practice as such but intervene at the level at which they are generated. Hence, for example, they seek to modify or lower mortality rates, increase life expectancy, or stimulate birth control to achieve 'overall states of equilibrium or regularity'. Under this conceptualization, death is no longer a sudden and unexpected event in life but something permanent and gradual that diminishes and weakens it.[6]

Along with this shift, writes Foucault, death ceased to be a spectacular ceremony in which individuals, families, and society at large took part. It has become something private and shameful to be hidden away. In ancient times, death represented a transition from the power of the sovereign of this world to that of the next world (or of another sovereign) and from the power of the dying to the power of those who survived him. However, with biopolitics and the power to make live and improve life, death was excluded from the power relationship. Death is the moment when the individual escapes all power and retreats.[7]

[5] Ibid. at pp. 241–3.
[6] Ibid. at pp. 244–7.
[7] Ibid. at p. 248.

Following Foucault, it is argued that the practice of suicide tourism represents the integration of two technologies of power. The first is a disciplinary technology focussing on the stories of those individuals who travel to another country, most notably Switzerland, to receive aid in dying. Those stories centre around the bodies and illnesses of the people wishing to die, with the aim of producing individualizing effects. These travelling bodies both manipulate and are manipulated. They represent and are the result of (mostly) a serious illness associated with some sort of disability, extensive pain, and suffering. On the other hand, they reveal a strong and impressive capacity to contemplate and survive the travel of, sometimes, long-distance journeys. Under such journeys these men-as-bodies are sources of force and power. Their stories are emotionally striking and compelling but, regardless of their publicity, they are still kept in private and—as this book shows (especially the next chapter)—do not succeed in making a regulatory change.

Along with the disciplinary technology, suicide tourism reflects the existence of a second technology that is centred on life instead of on the individual body. Such a technology protects the interests of the population in controlling the general events which take place in a living mass, including those of suicide tourism. Given that the practice of suicide tourism applies only to a few and that its purpose is to bring about death, thereby eliminating the overall power relationship between the sovereign and the individuals at stake, it is unsuccessful in changing the current equilibrium which protects society from the dangers that might have been associated with the practices of assisted suicide and euthanasia. Under this conceptualization, the bodies of the men-as-bodies, referring also to those who are unable or do not wish to travel to another country to receive aid in dying, are replaced and made subject to more general processes that affect society as a whole.

Under this perspective, sovereignty is being regarded as lying largely in the power and capacity to dictate who may live and who may die. Because of that, argues the political philosopher Achille Mbembe, to take life or let live serve as the limits of sovereignty.[8] This argument may explain the challenges raised by suicide tourism and the call to respond to it

---

[8] Achille Mbembe, 'Necropolitics' (2003) 15(1) *Public Culture* 11.

through policy and law. Moreover, and as the Italian philosopher Georgio Agamben argues, such a shift blurs the separation between the domain of natural life (*zoe*) and polis.[9]

The literature provides support to the complex relationship between life and death. Early in the twentieth century we are told by Freud in *Beyond the Pleasure Principle* that the fundamental principles of life derive from the individual's death drive, referring to her attempt to reach her own demise.[10] More recently, in his *Homo Sacer: Sovereign Power and Bare Life and State of Exception*, Georgio Agamben argues that humans have become 'sacred men' (in singular, 'homo sacer'). The life that faces the force of the sovereign is life that, as in Karen Quinlan's case or with regard to those who suffered in the Nazi extermination camps, is situated in a zone of indetermination between 'life' and 'death'. It is exposed to its own death (bare life); it is fully vulnerable and subject to a power which decides whether—and, I should add, how—it lives or dies. It is being operated by a survival principle, thereby reducing the human body to its most fragile state. Under such an understanding death is being degraded and no one is allowed to die.[11]

Drawing on Aristotle's distinction between bare life (*to zen*) and the good life (*to eu zen*), Agamben acknowledges that politics has always been concerned with something more than the perpetuation of biological life. As such, it must always enact its internal distinction—and negation—from bare life. This relationship of negation can always take the form of death. Moreover, politics represents both the passage from bare life to itself and what exists beyond this passage.[12]

Following Carl Schmitt's understanding of the sovereign, Agamben argues that the sovereign has the legal power to make exceptions, namely decide what should be removed from the purview of law. The sovereign is simultaneously inside and outside the juridical order.[13] As such, sovereignty symbolizes the law's threshold with the nonlegal. In other words, it

---

[9] Neerav Dwivedi, 'Politics of the Threshold: An Analysis of Bare Life and the State of Exception' (2015) 2(3) *New Man International Journal of Multidisciplinary Studies* 13.

[10] Tyson E. Lewis, 'A Genealogy of Life and Death: From Freud to Marcuse to Agamben' (2013) 16(1) *Radical Philosophy Review* 237.

[11] Ibid. at pp. 247–9.

[12] Andrew Norris, 'Giorgio Agamben and the Politics of the Living Dead' (2000) 30(4) *Diacritics* 38, at 42, 45 (hereafter: 'Norris, Politics of the Living Dead').

[13] Catherine Mills, *The Philosophy of Agamben* (Routledge, 2008) p. 61.

reflects the authoritative relations between the law and that which has no legal standing. He then argues as follows:

> The exception does not subtract itself from the rule; rather, the rule, suspending itself, gives rise to the exception and, maintaining itself in relation to the exception, first constitutes itself as a rule ... The sovereign decision of the exception is the originary juridico-political structure on the basis of which what is included in the juridical order and what is excluded from it acquire their meaning.[14]

The practice of suicide tourism reflects Agamben's concept of the sacred life. It is both excluded and included in the political order. It is inside the legal order in the sense that not only does such a practice not contradict the laws in countries of origin (there is no legal prohibition to travel and receive aid in dying elsewhere), but it also corresponds to the laws of the country[15] in which assisted suicide is being offered.

Moreover, countries which specifically allow assisted suicide but only to their residents—such as Oregon and other states in the US that followed its model—or to those contributing to local health plans—as in Canada—create a (legal) exception which purports to exclude suicide tourism from their dominion of control. However, suicide tourism is also outside the legal order in the sense that other than a symbolic investigation required by the laws of countries of origin which does not always take place, aid in dying offered in such cases does not result in criminalization and does not represent an act which is subject to the spheres of law. As argued by Norris, 'it is law (political life) that is not law (insofar as it steps outside of the structures and limitations of formal law) dealing with bare life (that is, nonpolitical life), and insofar as it does so that nonpolitical (bare) life it treats is political'.[16]

The analysis put forward in this section thus calls for the careful examination of the justifications for and against state intervention with regard to suicide tourism as it applies to its own residents. The next sections explore them in detail.

---

[14] Giorgio Agamben, *Homo Sacer: Sovereign Power and Bare Life* (1995) § 1.2.

[15] Norris, Politics of the Living Dead (n 12) at 47.

[16] Ibid.

Justifications for state intervention

This section refers to two major arguments that support, prima facie, justifications for state intervention with regards to suicide tourism: the argument from the sovereignty of the state, and the argument from global justice and moral particularism.

The argument from the sovereignty of the state

According to this justification, the state should maintain its moral sovereignty and enforce its morality upon its citizens, even when they are outside its borders. Therefore, because assisted suicide is illegal and presumably also immoral, the state must forbid its citizens from participating in suicide tourism, even in countries where such a practice is permitted. As state legislation represents the moral norms of its society, it should also apply extraterritorially. The idea is that if a certain act is prohibited by a state because of the harm it causes or the fundamental moral duties within society, then it should be considered equally forbidden and wrong even if conducted outside that country.[17]

Michael Walzer holds that a certain 'fit' exists between a community and its government, whereby the community is governed in accordance with its own traditions and values.[18] It can therefore be argued that the state has the moral right to maintain and put into effect a consistent approach, whether conducted inside or outside its geographical territory. This argument is especially true when dealing with a practice such as assisted suicide that may reflect and affect the national culture.[19] In other words, it may be legitimate for the state of origin to intervene in suicide tourism since this practice questions and challenges consensuses

---

[17] Wannes Van Hoof and Guido Pennings, 'Extraterritoriality for Cross-Border Reproductive Care: Should States Act Against Citizens Travelling Abroad for Illegal Infertility Treatment?' (2011) 23 *Reproductive Biomedicine Online* 546. As explained by these authors in another article: 'The act of crossing a border does not change the morality of an act fundamentally: if an act is wrong, it is wrong wherever it takes place. From an ethical point of view, extraterritoriality would be the rule' (Van Hoof and Pennings, Extraterritorial Rules (n 1)).

[18] Michael Walzer, 'The Moral Standing of States' (1980) 9 *Philosophy & Public Affairs* 209 at 212 (hereafter: 'Walzer, The Moral Standing').

[19] David Miller, *On Nationality* (Clarendon Press, 1995).

regarding the morality of assisted suicide and actions relating to end of life. As argued by Walzer,

> [I]t is not the sign of some collective derangement or radical incapacity for a political community to produce an authoritarian regime. Indeed, the history, culture, and religion of the community may be such that authoritarian regimes come, as it were, naturally, reflecting a widely shared world view or way of life.[20]

Along these lines, it can also be argued that deriving from a collective right of self-determination, or—as Christopher Wellman writes, from the state's right to freedom of association—countries of origin are justified in setting the terms of their common lives.[21] Following Oliviero Angeli, it is also argued that this deontological right to collective self-determination reflects important choices that affect the lives of members of the collective of which they are a part. In essence, this pertains to decisions that determine which group a certain person is a member of.[22] This substantial aspect of state sovereignty includes the articulation and enforcement of the fundamental moral principles and values pertaining to the practice of assisted suicide, most notably those concerning and shaping the notions of dignity in dying, quality of life, autonomy, and choice.

There is a mandate under this argument, deriving from the collective right of self-determination and state sovereignty of the country of origin, for extending the enforceability of the collectively reached balance between such values to beyond its territory. A correlated argument would therefore deny the Swiss the duty to provide assisted suicide services to non-residents, as argued in the previous chapter, as such a position affects the institutional structure of rights and liberties in Switzerland—specifically the stability and continuity of democratic self-government and its benefits to Swiss citizens and residents.[23]

---

[20] Walzer, The Moral Standing (n 18) at 224–5.

[21] Sarah Fine, 'The Ethics of Immigration: Self-Determination and the Right to Exclude' (2013) 8(3) Philosophy Compass 254; Michael Walzer, Spheres of Justice: A Defense of Pluralism and Equality (Basic Books, 1983) pp. 61–2.

[22] Oliviero Angeli, 'Taking Rights Territorially: On Territorial Rights and the Right to Exclude' (2008) European University Institute Working Papers SPS 2008/09.

[23] Rainer Bauböck, 'Global Justice, Freedom of movement and Democratic Citizenship' (2009) 50(1) European Journal of Sociology 1 at 13 (hereafter: 'Bauböck, Global Justice').

The collective right of self-determination constitutes the right to make decisions which will affect the state's major institutions. Following this argument, Ryan Pevnick argues that citizens enjoy their rights of ownership over their collective institutions derived from their labour and investment. Such rights include the right to decide which direction their institutions will take and who will make these decisions in the future.[24] It will also lead to their authority in establishing and controlling the terms of membership in these societies, in turn affecting, entering, and existing in it.[25] This may also include limiting one's capacity to evade local laws which represent social values within the context of dying, including those that support an opposing view on assisted suicide. Continuing this train of thought, it could also be argued that law-abiding individuals in the country of origin have an interest in not being forced into a situation whereby their state lacks the power to punish fellow citizens who travel to another country to be part of an act that is forbidden in the state of origin, such as suicide tourism. This kind of interest stems from the individuals' sense of dignity and security pertaining to their collective right and their stake in political institutions.[26]

The argument from global justice and moral particularism

In the broad sense of the term, global justice includes standards that govern the justification for and conduct of war and that define the most basic human rights. In the socio-economic context, global justice requires that while there is and should be a (moral) disagreement about the most effective methods for allocating resources to the public—so that systems can and should vary in their wealth and economic stability—there is nevertheless some minimal level of concern and some form of humane assistance provided by those who are well off for the benefit of those in extremis.[27]

---

[24] Ryan Pevnick, *Immigration and the Constraints of Justice: Between Open Borders and Absolute Sovereignty* (Cambridge University Press, 2011).

[25] Christopher H. Wellman, 'Immigration and Freedom of Association' (2008) 119(1) *Ethics* 109 at 115.

[26] Alejandro Chehtman, 'The Extraterritorial Scope of the Right to Punish' (2010) 29 *Law & Philosophy* 127 at 141.

[27] Thomas Nagel, 'The Problem of Global Justice' (2005) 33(2) *Philosophy & Public Affairs* 113 (hereafter: 'Nagel, The Problem of Global Justice').

This argument can be developed by referring to John Rawls' seminal work on social justice. Indeed, Rawls argued that the liberal requirements of justice refer mostly to equality among citizens. This is reflected in his greatest equal liberty principle, which he saw as the locus of political life and thus held that it could not be applied to people's personal and non-political choices, relations between societies, or relations between individual members of different societies. The principles of domestic justice are established beforehand, and are independent of the principles of global justice, thereby benefiting from lexical priority. According to Rawls, principles of global justice are either derivatives of or compatible with principles of domestic justice.[28]

Yet according to Rawls, duties that govern relations between people around the globe include not only non-aggression and fidelity towards treaties, but also some developmental assistance for 'peoples living under unfavourable conditions that prevent their having a just or decent political regime'.[29] Note that the focus in Rawls' theory is on guaranteeing the political regime, usually through the respect and promotion of basic rights and liberties.[30] Under a Rawlsian theory of global justice, liberal societies should be tolerant towards non-liberal states, providing they meet a minimum degree of decency, so that the foreign policy of liberal societies should not seek to move all other societies towards liberalism.

It seems remote to argue that not respecting one's right to die with dignity (through suicide tourism, for example) could lead to an unjust or inappropriate political regime—even if this can be classified as a human right, as discussed in the previous chapter. Justice is understood as a fair distribution of the benefits and burdens of social cooperation which can only be applied domestically and in a particular social setting.[31] As Alasdair MacIntyre argues,

---

[28] Andrew Kuper, 'Rawlsian Global Justice: Beyond The Law of Peoples to a Cosmopolitan Law of Persons' (2000) 28(5) *Political Theory* 640 at 641 (hereafter: 'Kuper, Rawlsian Global Justice').

[29] John Rawls, *The Law of Peoples* (Harvard University Press, 1999) p. 37.

[30] Rawls stipulates three characteristics for a decent society: 1) it is peaceful and non-expansionist; 2) it is guided by a common-good conception of justice that secures the human rights of all persons, including the right to life, to liberty, and to formal equality; and 3) it has a just and legitimate consultation hierarchy which represents each segment of the society. Ibid. at pp. 64–7, 75–8, 115.

[31] Charles R. Beitz, *Political Theory and International Relations* (Princeton University Press, 1999) p. 131.

Goods are never encountered except as thus particularised. Hence, the abstract general claim, that rules of a certain kind are justified by being productive of and constitutive of goods of a certain kind, is true only if these and these particular sets of rules incarnated in the practices of these and these and these particular communities are productive of or constitutive of these and these and these particular goods enjoyed at certain particular times and places by certain specifiable individuals.

It follows that *I* find *my* justification for allegiance to these rules of morality in *my* particular community; deprived of the life of that community, *I* would have no reason to be moral.[32]

Hence, to say and apprehend that 'assisted suicide' is wrong and should not be permitted, as well as to adhere to this moral percept, has its own roots in one's society and social context. The application of and justification for this percept do not cease to exist when people leave their country to seek legal assisted suicide elsewhere, since such a moral standing is relevant to citizens regardless of their place of residence. It also follows that such a holding cannot promote an action on behalf of countries that permit assisted suicide towards revisions of current laws in other countries, nor does it preclude non-permissive countries from interfering with suicide tourism, specifically from taking action with regard to its citizens who participate in such a practice.

Additional support for this line of argument can be found by referring to Thomas Nagel's idea of minimal humanitarian morality (MHM). Nagel follows a Hobbesian view according to which, although we can discover true principles of justice by moral reasoning alone, actual justice cannot be achieved other than within a sovereign state. In his view, justice only applies to a form of organization that claims political legitimacy in imposing 'the right' decisions. This centralized system of authority provides the rules but also secures individuals' assurance that conforming to these rules is part of a reliable and effective system. Under such a view, justice requires government and the political sphere as an enabling condition.[33]

---

[32] Alasdair MacIntyre, 'Is Patriotism a Virtue?' (26 March 1984) The Lindley Lecture, Department of Philosophy, University of Kansas at 9–10 https://mirror.explodie.org/Is%20 Patriotism%20a%20Virtue-1984.pdf, accessed on 8 March 2018.

[33] Thomas Nagel, *Secular Philosophy and the Religious Temperament* (Oxford University Press, 2010) p. 62 (hereafter: 'Nagel, Secular Philosophy'). In fact, Nagel goes on to argue that without the operation of this collective system, individuals would not have been able to pursue justice

Since the idea of government in the global context is lacking, Nagel focuses on MHM demands which he distinguishes from the demands of justice. Such demands refer to the provision of some form of human assistance by those who are well off to those in extremis,[34] and they contain a normative force of the most basic human rights against violence, enslavement, and coercion, and of the most basic humanitarian duties of rescue from immediate danger.[35] Nagel writes,

> The minimal humanitarian morality governs our relation to all other persons. It does not require us to make their ends our own, but it does require us to pursue our ends within boundaries that leave them free to pursue theirs, and to relieve them from extreme threats and obstacles to such freedom if we can do so without serious sacrifice of our own ends.[36]

The MHM view may apply to a person's wish to end her life through assisted dying with the help of another person living outside her own country. However, as with Rawls, it may be difficult to apply this view to the case of suicide tourism in terms of requesting that a duty be performed by a more permissive state and its citizens in order to assist residents of a less permissive state so as to realize MHM in an end-of-life context. Under a Hohefeldian taxonomy of rights, permissive states have the liberty not to assist less permissive states, who have neither the right nor the liberty to manage such assistance. Therefore, this calls for a neutral view with regard to state intervention in suicide tourism, specifically with citizens who choose to travel to other nations to receive assisted dying. It follows that Rawls' and Nagel's respective theories of global justice and MHM do not preclude a state of origin from interfering in a practice of suicide tourism in which their citizens take part.

Furthermore, it is argued that the opportunity for patients to go abroad for treatment (or otherwise to access human-based services or goods,

---

by themselves or judge what is just or unjust. They would only fall under what he calls 'a pure aspiration for justice' but with no practical expression. Nagel, The Problem of Global Justice (n 27) at 116.

---

[34] Nagel, Secular Philosophy (n 33) pp. 65–6.
[35] Ibid. p. 76.
[36] Nagel, The Problem of Global Justice (n 27) at 131.

such as assisted suicide or reproductive procedures) is tempered by organized resistance to the law in the country of origin and allows or otherwise encourages governments to pass stricter legislation than it might do
otherwise. As Robert Storrow explains,

> We may for this reason characterize cross-border travel as a safety valve,
> but the valve does not promote or sustain moral pluralism—it merely
> removes pressure from lawmakers. Those who desire a procedure, if
> they possess the means to travel, may be less concerned about whether a
> prohibition of it is enshrined in legislation. Those who wish to prohibit
> the procedure may feel justified in assuming a stricter position than
> they otherwise might, knowing the cross-border reproductive travel
> will function to quell organized resistance. Under these conditions,
> government has an incentive, or at the very least an opportunity, to as-
> sume stricter and perhaps more symbolic positions on volatile issues
> than it might otherwise. Thus, cross-border reproductive care's func-
> tion as a safety valve against organized resistance at home is precisely
> what can trigger restrictive reproductive policies and permit them to
> flourish. Its availability eliminates the opportunity for dispassionate di-
> alogue that is the hallmark of moral pluralism and in its place creates
> the illusion of benign acceptance.[37]

This argument is strongly demonstrated in the interviews that were conducted for this book and is discussed in detail in Chapter 5. It is also argued in the literature that cross-border travel has been shown to have
harmful extraterritorial effects that violate the spirit behind the law in
the country of origin, create a burden in the host country, and are associated with the needs of the travelling patient. This may also be accompanied by financial exploitation, lack of informed consent, and at times
even criminal activity.[38] When combined with the concept of state sovereignty, the collective right of self-determination, and the argument of
global justice and moral particularism, these arguments provide prima
facie justifications for the country of origin to interfere in the practice

---

[37] Robert F. Storrow, 'The Pluralism Problem in Cross-Border Reproductive Care' (2010)
25(12) *Human Reprod* 2939 at 2941.
[38] Ibid.

of suicide tourism in which their citizens participate and to take measures for enforcing the moral and legal position against assisted suicide elsewhere.

Arguments against state intervention

This section refers to three major arguments against state intervention in suicide tourism, placing political authorities, governments, and prosecutors in a position of non-interference: cosmopolitanism and moral universalism, inter-state moral pluralism, and common ownership.

The argument from cosmopolitanism and moral universalism

Unlike the view that justice and morality should apply within a social condition of cooperation, usually taking place within and not between states, it is argued here that all persons around the globe should be subject to the same fundamental moral values and principles and, as a result, to the same allocation of burdens and benefits. A softer version of this argument, according to which there is a minimum moral code that is valid for everyone (for example in the ruling out of killing, deception, and torture), was even shared by strong advocates of communitarianism, such as Michael Walzer.[39]

Under a cosmopolitan approach to justice, people should be treated equally unless differential treatment can be justified by reference to fundamental moral principles.[40] The moral basis for the requirements of justice is a concern for fairness of the terms under which people share the world with others.[41] Moral cosmopolitanism holds that every human being has a global stature as an ultimate unit of moral concern. Thus, this view regards people as standing in certain moral relations with one

---

[39] Charles Jones, *Global Justice: Defending Cosmopolitanism* (Oxford University Press, 1999) pp. 190–1.
[40] Thomas W. Pogge, *World Poverty and Human Rights: Cosmopolitan Responsibilities and Reforms* (Polity Press, 2002) (hereafter: 'Pogge, World Poverty').
[41] Nagel, The Problem of Global Justice (n 27) at 119.

another that evolve around the fundamental moral duty to respect each other's status and moral concerns.

Deriving from this moral duty is the limitation on government constructing and using their institutional schemes that would otherwise violate people's status and moral concern.[42] This view asks for a common system of institutions which will fulfil, or attempt to fulfil, the same standards of fairness or equal opportunity that one expects in her own country. Moreover, it calls for the promotion and protection of an interest in greater distributive justice worldwide.[43] It asks for governmental sovereignty that is both centralized and decentralized. In other words, people should be able to govern themselves through a varied number of political units, none of which are or may be dominant.[44]

Hence, moral cosmopolitanism stems from the notion that sovereignty can be understood not only vertically (within states) but also horizontally (between states). Under this view, the tasks of governments should be divided based on functional criteria and not (only) on territorial grounds. Choices that reflect respecting human dignity, such as ones pertaining to a person's wish to die and the manner in which this wish is expressed, may serve as grounds for plural sovereignty, resulting in respect for policies and legislation in host countries on the one hand, and in the tolerance of laws which criminalize assisted suicide on the other hand.

Indeed, cosmopolitanism does not necessarily imply a consistent moral order or a universal understanding on diverse ethical matters such as assisted suicide and euthanasia.[45] It is, however, involved in creating mechanisms for holding dialogue, dispute resolution, and problem solving, thereby reflecting an equal moral concern and collective agency.[46] This will allow us to provide a universalist account of global justice that avoids assuming territorial boundaries and yet takes into consideration important human practices and resources.[47]

---

[42] Thomas W. Pogge, 'Cosmopolitanism and Sovereignty' (1992) 103 *Ethics* 48 at 49.

[43] Thomas Pogge, 'Migration and Poverty' in Veit Bader (ed), *Citizenship and Exclusion* (Macmillan Press, 1997) pp. 12–27.

[44] Pogge, World Poverty (n 40) p. 58.

[45] David Held, *Cosmopolitanism: Ideals, Realities & Deficits* (Polity Press, 2010) p. 76.

[46] Daniel Bray, 'Pragmatic Ethics and the Will to Believe in Cosmopolitanism' (2013) 5(3) *International Theory* 446 at 458.

[47] Kuper, Rawlsian Global Justice (n 28) at 657.

The moral cosmopolitanist requirement may, however, be restricted to cases where offering such opportunities to non-residents may harm the residents of the permissive country or result in harm in the country of origin. An example of the former concerns the situation in which travel to another country to escape local laws limits or jeopardizes access to some services and goods in one's own country. This can be seen, for instance, in the case of oocyte donation. Because of the shortage in available oocytes for donation, limiting the waiting list by giving precedence to local residents may be justified.[48] In the case of suicide tourism, giving precedence to local residents may also be justified if, for example, few physicians in permissive countries are willing to prescribe lethal drugs (as is evident in Switzerland)[49] or if there is a considerable waiting time for national committees who approve requests for assisted suicide or euthanasia (as is evident in the Netherlands and Belgium).

In terms of how respect for moral cosmopolitanism may also cause harm within the country of origin, in cases of transplant tourism or cross-border reproductive care, for example, people who obtain risky medical services abroad may require extensive healthcare when they return home, thereby placing a strain on national health services.[50] Unsuccessful attempts to commit suicide abroad may also lead to some burdens upon returning to one's own country of residence. This may be a remote risk, though.

The argument from inter-state moral pluralism

Following Martin Benjamin's argument that 'some important values, principles, rights, duties, and conceptions of the good are incapable of being

---

[48] Guido Pennings, 'Reproductive Tourism as Moral Pluralism in Motion' (2002) 28 *JME* 337 at 339 (hereafter: 'Pennings, Reproductive Tourism').

[49] According to one interview conducted with a right-to-die organization in Switzerland, there are only about thirty-five physicians in the whole country who prescribe lethal drugs.

[50] Alastair Mckelvey et al., 'The Impact of Cross-Border Reproductive Care or "Fertility Tourism" on NHS Maternity Services' (2009) 116(11) *BJOG: An International Journal of Obstetrics & Gynaecology* 1520; Johanna Hanefeld, Richard Smith, Daniel Horsfall, and Neil Lunt, 'What Do We Know about Medical Tourism? A Review of the Literature with Discussion of Its Implications for the UK National Health Service as an Example of a Public Health Care System' (2014) 21(6) *Journal of Travel Medicine* 410; Daniel Sperling, 'Human Trafficking and Organ Trade: Does the Law Really Care for the Health of People?' (2014) 16 *Law and Global Health: Current Legal Issues* 193.

combined into a single, fully consistent, comprehensive moral frame-work,[51] Guido Pennings[52] and Richard Huxtable apply the moral plu-ralism view to reproductive tourism and suicide tourism (respectively).[53] Under this view, the state demonstrates and should demonstrate a certain degree of tolerance towards the dissenting agents who violate local rules. Moreover, the state approves and should approve this violation, despite its discontentment with the tourists' conduct and its alleged power to stop or punish those tourists.[54] Pragmatically, this may involve internal tolerance, namely that the state allows the violation of its law within its territory by not punishing offenders and/or external tolerance so that people are not stopped or punished when travelling outside the state's territory.[55]

Such state tolerance—based on inter-state moral pluralism—not only demonstrates respect towards people who, according to some empirical data, leave their country of origin feeling under exile,[56] but also prevents clashes between the majority who impose their views on the country of origin (through legislation prohibiting the desired practice) and the mi-nority who claim to have a moral right to some medical or other human rights-based services or goods. As such, this represents a healthy level of moral relativism.[57]

International moral pluralism is, in fact, an application of the idea that the law must not reflect the substantive moral position of only one group at the inter-state level. If one acknowledges that respect for the moral au-tonomy of the citizens of one's state means that one must not imply only one alternative by law, then one must also accept this idea in the global context, thereby allowing much diversity across laws of different countries.[58] Such an argument relates to the more general liberal argument for free movement, according to which being able to move from one place to another is in-strumentally important in enabling people to determine for themselves, as

---

[51] Martin Benjamin, 'Conflict, Compromise, and Moral Integrity' in Courtney S. Campbell and Andrew B. Lustig (eds), *Duties to Others* (Kluwer Academic Publishers, 1994) pp. 261–78.

[52] Pennings, Reproductive Tourism (n 48).

[53] Richard Huxtable, 'The Suicide Tourist Trap: Compromise Across Boundaries' (2009) 6 *Bioethical Inquiry* 327 at 334 (hereafter: 'Huxtable, The Suicide Tourist Trap').

[54] Pennings, Reproductive Tourism (n 48) at 340.

[55] Ibid.

[56] Marcia Inhorn and Pasquale Patrizio, 'Rethinking Reproductive "Tourism" as Reproductive "Exile"' (2009) 92(3) *Fertility & Sterility* 904.

[57] Pennings, Reproductive Tourism (n 48); Guido Pennings, 'Legal Harmonization and Reproductive Tourism in Europe' (2004) 19 *Hum Reprod* 2689.

[58] Ibid. at 338.

much as possible, the circumstances of their lives. It also stems from the idea that freedom of movement fulfils the intrinsic value of autonomy, not only its instrumental value. Under this view, allowing people to travel in order to seek assisted suicide elsewhere is justified because it provides opportunities that would otherwise be missed by not being able to travel because of local laws; it is also justified since confinement to local regulations regarding assisted suicide lead to substantial constraints on freedom itself.[59]

The idea of moral pluralism is supported by the value of legal diversity and can be seen, for example, in the concept of a 'margin of appreciation' in implementing the European Convention on Human Rights. This concepts calls for the acceptance of variable interpretations of the stated human rights in different European countries. The extent to which a state may limit the ability to determine the time, manner, and place of one's death is no exception to this doctrine, as was ruled in *Haas v. Switzerland,*

> ... The research conducted by the Court enables it to conclude that the member States of the Council of Europe are far from having reached a consensus with regard to an individual's right to decide how and when his or her life should end. In Switzerland, pursuant to Article 115 of the Criminal Code, inciting and assisting suicide are punishable only where the perpetrator of such acts is driven to commit them by 'selfish motives'. By way of comparison, the Benelux countries in particular have decriminalised the act of assisting suicide, but only in very specific circumstances. Lastly, certain other countries accept only acts of 'passive' assistance. It should be noted that the vast majority of member States seem to attach more weight to the protection of the individual's life than to his or her right to terminate it. It follows that the States enjoy a considerable margin of appreciation in this area.[60]

According to the moral pluralism approach, no one can claim the right to have the last word with regard to the prohibition or permission of assisted suicide. Instead, efforts should be usefully directed to splitting the difference between the two, for example by eschewing talk of justification and replacing it with the language of excuse.[61] In practice, this could

---

[59] Bauböck, Global Justice (n 23).
[60] *Haas v. Switzerland* (Application no. 31322/07) § 55.
[61] Huxtable, The Suicide Tourist Trap (n 53).

mean marking the practice criminal but not ranking it as murder, or alternatively administering it as a punitive action. In the context of suicide tourism, this entails non-interference by the state of origin, namely ensuring 'that there is sufficient protection in place for travelling citizens'.[62]

However, it is important to emphasize that this reaction does not necessarily mark the first step towards legalizing assisted suicide in the country of origin. It also does not necessarily imply that this position is or cannot be subject to revision. Nonetheless, it does suggest that out of respect to the moral debate that exists among societies and the position held by other countries in support of assisted suicide, the country of origin opts for and chooses not to interfere and coerce its moral viewpoint against assisted suicide upon its citizens who choose to leave the country for this purpose.

Although moral pluralism calls for non-interference on behalf of the country of origin, one can rightly argue that a decision not to take steps against travelling citizens and impose the state's moral view on the subject is one form of interference in the practice of suicide tourism. Yet in practice, this leads to maximum freedom for citizens embarking on journeys to places like Switzerland to fulfil their wish to die.

The argument from common ownership

Another argument that can be made against intervention by the country of origin follows a Kantian notion that the global earth is collectively owned by all human beings. This concept refers to 'universal hospitability', whereby humans have the right to be mobile, safe, and treated without hostility while in foreign territories. Although political communities—most notably countries and their legislators—are justified in their right to regulate access to the part of the earth that they occupy, this does not offer them the same justification to interfere in similar matters that involve *other* territories.

In his essay 'Perpetual Peace', Kant argues that human beings enjoy a universal right of humanity based on the idea that they should be regarded as citizens of a universal state of mankind (*ius*

---

[62] Ibid. at 335.

cosmopoliticum).[63] Subjecting people to a particular rule of law should therefore be subject to this universal right of humanity that must be respected within one's country and between countries. As Kant writes,

> For morality, with regard to its principles of public right (hence in rela-
> tion to a political code which can be known *a priori*), has the peculiar
> feature that the less it makes its conduct depend upon the end it envis-
> ages (whether this be a physical or moral advantage), the more it will
> in general harmonise with this end. And the reason for this is that it is
> precisely the general will as it is given *a priori*, within a single people or
> in the mutual relationships of various peoples, which alone determines
> what is right among men.[64]

It follows that the global ownership given by nature allows and promotes a deontological conception of morality and the right to humanity. State interference with practices such as suicide tourism, premised on the de-sire to enforce the moral values of a particular society, impedes this pro-cess of acting in accordance with a unified concept of morality. This view may justify the duty of non-interference that, following a moral 'invisible hand', will realize the goals of morality itself, whether it defends or op-poses assisted suicide.

Conclusion

This chapter discusses the sociological concept of governability of death and its application to suicide tourism. Following such a discussion it analyses some of the major political-philosophical justifications for and against state interference in suicide tourism. These refer to five main ar-guments from the perspective of the state in which assisted suicide is illegal: the argument from state sovereignty; the argument from global justice and moral particularism; the argument from cosmopolitanism and moral universalism; the argument from inter-state moral pluralism;

---

[63] Immanuel Kant, 'Perpetual Peace: A Philosophical Sketch' in Hans Reiss (ed), *Kant: Political Writings*, (2nd edn, Cambridge University Press, 1991) p. 108.
[64] Ibid. at p. 123.

and the argument from common ownership. While these arguments do not necessarily rely on the morality of suicide tourism, as elaborated on in Chapter 3, their overall evaluation reveals that there are prima facie good reasons against state intervention or that support the exercising of a neutral view on behalf of permissive countries.

It seems that the arguments relating to the collective right to self-determination and state sovereignty have little convincing power when applied to cases of assisted suicide. People who travel to another country for assisted suicide do not challenge state sovereignty. After all, the first and foremost purpose of assisted suicide is to promote an aspect of people's well-being and autonomy concerning the way they choose to die; they do not need an ulterior motive. They are not asking to challenge the collective's will nor are they seeking to evade the law. Although in applying Rawls' theory of justice and Nagel's theory of minimal humanitarian morality to suicide tourism some justifications for state interference are achieved, they deliver a weak defence of a country's legal right to object to and forbid suicide tourism.

However, the arguments presented in respect of the individual's interests at stake enhance why countries of origin should avoid interfering in suicide tourism, namely, in order to respect human dignity and in turn promote—rather than undermine—(plural) sovereignty. Under Kantian ethics, the allowing of greater moral space to be exercised between societies and countries, such as suicide tourism, constitutes the required process of acting in accordance with a unified concept of morality. In turn, this leads to the 'right' and 'only' moral obligation and truth, pertaining to choices to end one's own life through the assistance of a third party.

It follows, therefore, that although there are relatively weak justifications for state intervention in suicide tourism, there are strong justifications for non-intervention. This conclusion receives even more validity when coupled with the strong justifications supporting the morality of suicide tourism, as argued for in the previous chapter. This also adequately represents the way in which countries of origin, from where people leave for a different country in pursuit of fulfilling their wish to die, regard this practice de facto and treat their citizens who participate in suicide tourism accordingly—as discussed extensively in Chapter 2.

Chapter 5 demonstrates how, in principle, de facto suicide tourism reduces pressure on the need to liberalize laws regarding assisted suicide.

However, it can be argued that allowing people to travel freely to seek assisted suicide with minimal (if any) state intervention may serve as a trigger for changing and revising local laws. Following the extension of Albert Hirschman's theory of exit and voice, it can be argued that voice can be exercised from outside or within one's country after exiting it, in a way that improves the performance of organizations and governments.[65] In other words, if one holds that assisted suicide is permitted, then allowing suicide tourism, with minimal or no intervention, may also pave the way for a shift towards a specific moral and legal position that supports this practice.

---

[65] Bauböck, Global Justice (n 23) at 8.

PART III

SOCIOLOGICAL AND CULTURAL ASPECTS OF SUICIDE TOURISM

5

Empirical Analysis of Suicide Tourism

The previous chapters analysed the phenomenon of suicide tourism from a philosophical, political, and social perspective. It is now time to complement these discussions with facts and experiences as they evolve from the key players in this field. This chapter is based on findings obtained from literature and policy reviews as well as on in-depth interviews—with policymakers, social activists, academics, and other key players in the field of assisted suicide—that I conducted in Switzerland, Germany, France, Italy, and the UK between 2015 and 2017, and on other communications with important figures in this practice from various countries. Each interview lasted between 1 and 6 hours. Interviewees gave informed consent following the review of an information sheet detailing the research programme as well as the possible risks and benefits associated with participation in the research. All interviews were tape-recorded and interview transcripts have been produced. Responses were strictly confidential and kept secret by the researcher. The ethics committee at Yezreel Valley Academic College approved the research plan. A complete list of the interviewees can be found in the Appendix.

The research findings described in this chapter are organized into three areas of inquiry. The first addresses general findings and observations pertaining to the practice of suicide tourism and its relation to local laws; the second area explores the social attitude towards suicide tourism from the perspective of participants living in Switzerland; and the third area addresses the effects of suicide tourism on legislation on assisted suicide in countries of origin. All three areas will help the reader better understand and evaluate the theoretical arguments put forward in the previous chapters and establish a comprehensive conceptualization of suicide tourism and its potential and actual consequences.

Suicide Tourism. First Edition. Daniel Sperling. © Daniel Sperling 2019. Published 2019 by Oxford University Press.

Findings and observations on local laws
and suicide tourism

Belgium and the Netherlands

The law in Belgium and in the Netherlands does not formally require a person requesting physician-assisted suicide to hold local residency. Although the law does require the physician to know the patient, have several discussions with her regarding her (repeated) wish to die, and confirm that such wish is persistent and not the result of external pressure, suicide tourism to these destinations cannot be ruled out.

While, in some of the interviews conducted in Switzerland, it was claimed that there are a few cases of suicide tourism to Belgium, especially from France, there is no formal data from the Federal Euthanasia Committee to support this. Moreover, there is no organization which actively facilitates or organizes suicide or euthanasia tourism to Belgium. Correspondence with prominent figures in the field of end-of-life care in Belgium shows no clear evidence of it either; as one figure mentioned to me, 'euthanasia tourism in Belgium is a black box as it has not been properly studied or reported'.

However, assisted suicide and euthanasia for foreigners may be offered in the country because of language similarities between South Belgium and France and due to a more lenient procedure associated with such requests. It may also be facilitated due to the way euthanasia and assisted suicide cases in Belgium are reported to the supervising committee. Interviews reveal that every such case is being reported in a large sealed envelope which contains another, smaller envelope. The large envelope includes general information about the case, the medical condition at stake, and circumstances relating to the legal requirements. The small envelope contains identifying information about the patient and the participating physician. Only if the committee suspects that the general legal requirements have not been met does it open the small envelope.

Hence, under the current practice, the committee is usually not exposed to identifying information about the patient, including her residency. According to one interviewee, the rationale for keeping the identifying information apart from the committee was to allow the committee to objectively evaluate the cases and avoid any prejudice or bias in judging acts performed by specific physicians.

Furthermore, interviews suggest that the committee in Belgium sits for twelve meetings per year, reviewing hundreds of requests per meeting. The time spent on each case does not allow the committee a thorough examination of the cases and much respect is given to the report provided by the physician concerning the non-identifying circumstances of each case.

In the absence of a positive requirement concerning the patient's residency—either by law or by practice—suicide tourism to Belgium can easily take place. Thus, media reports suggest that Italian, British, German, American, and mainly French people are coming to Belgium for aid in dying while assistance is provided for some. Most of these requests concern foreign people with psychiatric diseases, including depression. Help is primarily offered to terminal patients that are physically able to travel. A Minister of Public Health, Maggie De Block, confirmed in the media that there are dozens of foreign euthanasia cases each year in Belgium.[1]

As to the Netherlands, my communications with prominent figures specializing in end-of-life care there do not refer to cases of suicide tourism in the Netherlands. I was told by people who are familiar with the work of the supervising euthanasia committee that it closely examines whether physicians performing euthanasia (usually the attending physicians) have informed themselves thoroughly of the patient's condition.

In the Netherlands, physicians must also personally determine whether all due care criteria have been met. Therefore, only physicians who have known their patients for some time can base this conclusion on their knowledge of the patients. This provision is very much supported by the Dutch culture of the Dutch medical community that favours long-standing relationships between physician and patients.[2] A terminal non-resident patient building a long-lasting relationship with a physician may be less practical and/or would require several trips to the country. This view is also reflected in a statement by the Dutch Ministry of Health,

---

[1] Farid El Manrouk, '"Doodstoerisme" Naar Ons Land in de Lift', *Nieuws* (21 August 2016) http://www.nieuwsblad.be/cnt/dmf20160820_02432555, accessed on 22 June 2017.

[2] Alexander R. Safyan, 'A Call for International Regulation of the Thriving "Industry" of Death Tourism' (2011) 33 *Loy. L.A. Int'l & Comp. L. Rev.* 287 at 308.

Welfare, and Sport ruling out the possibility of assisted suicide tourism to the Netherlands because of the requirement of a close physician–patient relationship.[3]

In principle, a physician other than the attending physician can perform euthanasia as per the patient's request. However, she must clearly demonstrate that she took sufficient time to evaluate the patient's situation and acted in accordance with the safeguards specified by law. In such cases, it is important that she indicate in her report to the supervising committee how often and in how much detail she discussed with the patient her wish to die. From the evidence gathered so far, the Royal Dutch Medical Association has also not experienced assisted suicide tourism.

However, in a few of my interviews in Germany, the travelling of Germans to the Netherlands for assisted suicide (especially from western Germany) was confirmed, the Netherlands being preferred to Switzerland due to geographical proximity.

In recent years, amendments to Dutch law have included the Caribbean jurisdictions of Bonaire, Saint Eustatius, and Saba[4] acquiring a new status and becoming part of the Netherlands. There are no indications as to whether these places will become new destinations for assisted suicide or euthanasia but it may be that in the coming years the application of the Dutch law on these matters will make this possible.

Germany

Until 2015, there was no criminal prohibition on assisted suicide in Germany. In 2014, an attempt to legalize assisted suicide in Germany was carried out by a few politicians representing various political and social parties. Four different bills were introduced. In November 2015, Germany passed a new revision to the criminal code (§ 217 StGB) prohibiting organizations and individuals from assisting others to commit

---

[3] Ministry of Health, Welfare, and Sport, 'Euthanasia: The Netherland's New Rules 1' (2002), mentioned in Rohith Srinivas, 'Exploring the Potential for American Death Tourism' (2009) 13 *Mich St. J. Med & Law* 91 at 104.

[4] Government of the Netherlands, 'Bonaire, St Eustatius and Saba' https://www.government.nl/topics/caribbean-parts-of-the-kingdom/bonaire-st-eustatius-and-saba, accessed on 9 May 2018.

suicide on a regular, repetitive basis, including not-for-profit offers of such aid.

Interviews with German organizations, professionals, and scholars reveal that the new law on assisted suicide was driven by the Christian Democratic Union (CDU)'s desire to outlaw the society *Sterbehilfe Deutschland* (Assisted Suicide Germany), founded in 2009 by Roger Kusch, a former Minister of Justice in the state of Hamburg. This organization attracted much criticism from CDU which was itself encouraged by the two big churches in Germany. The interviews reveal that lawmaking in Germany is greatly influenced by religion as many politicians are associated with the main churches.

The general understanding of the new law on assisted suicide is that physicians are at risk of criminalization because it can be the case that they provide assistance with suicide more than once. Some interviewees claimed that the new law has worsened the situation of those who would have been able to travel to Switzerland before its enactment, as it is now more difficult to work with collaborating medical doctors to obtain medical reports, let alone obtaining general information from or making referrals to Dignitas. Since Dignitas closed its branch in Hanover, reliance on collaborating physicians has increased but has become riskier. Yet, this situation may change in the near future if the petitions against the law submitted to the Bundesverfassungsgericht, the German Constitutional Court, are accepted.

Other interviews, especially with Swiss right-to-die organizations, attest to the fact that there is still 'plenty of work with Germans, both advisory work and preparation of "emergency exits"'. It is reported that there are hardly any cases of family members worrying about what would happen if they helped a loved one to make it to Switzerland. Interviews also reveal that many people in Germany are not aware of § 217 or do not know what it means. This has to do with the lack of decent media coverage prior to the vote in the Deutscher Bundestag, accompanied by incorrect press coverage, for example holding that § 217 prohibits 'commercial' assisted dying.

In Germany, interviews with academics reveal that suicide tourism is used by people who oppose the new law, saying it is regrettable that people are forced to leave the country. However, according to one interviewee, suicide tourism 'is not seen an annoyance, so to speak ... they say that it's regrettable these poor people cannot receive the help they need in Germany but going to Switzerland is something that everybody can openly confess to in Germany without stimulating negative responses'.

France

In France, a law from 2005 allows the limitation or discontinuation of treatment and sedation until death.[5] Following an extensive public debate and parliamentary commission discussing issues relating to end-of-life care, a recent amendment to the Public Health Act (effective as of February 2016) acknowledges an explicit right to deep and continuous sedation for terminally ill patients.[6] Palliative sedation applies in two situations: when the patient is a victim of refractory symptoms and when she decides to discontinue vital treatment. The law requires that sedation will normally be accompanied by withholding life-sustaining treatment including artificial nutrition and hydration.[7]

Under the law, it is not required that the patient concerned would experience severe or unbearable suffering without it. Although such a practice is not identical to euthanasia or physician-assisted suicide it may be regarded similar to them.[8] It is also argued in the literature that continuous deep sedation was legalized to avoid having to decriminalize physician-assisted suicide, thereby detracting from the debates on euthanasia and physician-assisted suicide more generally.[9]

---

[5] LOI n° 2005-370 du 22 avril 2005 relative aux droits des malades et à la fin de vie 23 April 2005 https://www.legifrance.gouv.fr/eli/loi/2005/4/22/SANX0407815L/jo/texte, accessed on 27 June 2017.

[6] LOI n° 2016-87 du 2 février 2016 créant de nouveaux droits en faveur des malades et des personnes en fin de vie 2 February 2016 https://www.legifrance.gouv.fr/eli/loi/2016/2/2/AFSX1507642L/jo/texte, accessed on 27 June 2017. Sedation in this context may be defined as 'the use of a pharmacological agent(s) to induce unconsciousness for treatment of truly distressing and refractory symptoms in the terminally ill'. While causing death is not intended, it is implicit that it may not be possible to achieve adequate symptom control except at risk of shortening life. John D. Cowan and Declan Walsh, 'Terminal Sedation in Palliative Medicine: Definition and Review of the Literature' (2001) 9 *Supportive Care in Cancer* 403 at 403–4.

[7] Alexandre de Nonneville et al., 'End-of-Life Practices in France under the Claeys-Leonetti Law: Report of Three Cases in the Oncology Unit' (2016) 9(3) *Case Rep Oncol* 650.

[8] Henk Ten Have and Jos V.M. Welie, 'Palliative Sedation Versus Euthanasia: An Ethical Assessment' (2014) 47(1) *Journal of Pain and Symptom Management* 123.

[9] Kasper Raus, Kenneth Chambaere, and Sigrid Streckx, 'Controversies Surrounding Continuous Deep Sedation at the End of Life: The Parliamentary and Societal Debates in

According to some interviews, the new law resulted from a spectacular and dramatic affair, the Vincent Lambert affair, which had nothing to do with assisted suicide but with the question of under what conditions is it justifiable to stop treatment which keep a person in a chronic vegetative state alive. It was also initiated by physicians following some unsuccessful and painful sedation cases where the dying process was emotionally disturbing.

In France, suicide tourism did not receive much attention in the political and ethical debates on assisted suicide. It was not discussed by the Sicard committee on end of life and it served merely as part of the background situation in the national ethics committee. As one of the French interviewees mentioned, 'suicide tourism itself was only information for us: it showed a reality that we could not ignore. But it has not served as an argument in our debates and has been little discussed'.

Italy

Along with the rare case of the prosecution of Marco Cappato, discussed in Chapter 2, the lower house of the Italian Parliament raised, for the first time, a bill to decriminalize assisted suicide in Italy in 2016. However, no progress with this bill has been observed. Recently, following a 4-year debate, Italy passed a law acknowledging the right to refuse medical treatment, mandating the right to receive treatment which may alleviate pain at end of life, and also establishing the legal mechanism for advance directives and planned treatment.

Interviews reveal that suicide tourism is rarely discussed in Italy. Apart from the case of DJ Fabio, the media does not cover stories of people going to Switzerland for assisted suicide, although an Italian agency offering help with this was in place in Switzerland for a few years. Italy is being portrayed as a country 'in which no one had ever talked about end-of-life matters'. Medical practitioners are also being described as narrow-minded about these problems. The prevailing view is paternalistic,

France' (2016) 17 *BMC Medical Ethics* 36; Kasper Raus, Sigrid Streckx, and Freddy Mortier, 'Is Continuous Sedation at the End of Life an Ethically Preferable Alternative to Physician-Assisted Suicide?' (2011) 11(6) *AJOB* 32.

viewing the patient as a weak person who does not really know what is good for her. It is said that in Italy there are no more than four or five medical doctors who have expressed their support for assisted suicide. In addition, the political debate is concentrated more on what should be permitted in Italy than on what is allowed in Switzerland or travel to Switzerland. It is told that even those politicians who are strongly against euthanasia or assisted suicide are not impeding people from going to Switzerland.

If regarded at all, suicide tourism is regarded as being immoral twice over, first because of the very act of assisted suicide and second because it represents an intention to avoid the local law, like not paying taxes—an analogy made in one interview. In another interview, suicide tourism was referred to as exile, expressing the serious deficiencies existing under the current law.

Canada

Fear of Canada becoming a destination for suicide tourism served as one of the arguments supporting a residency requirement for medical assistance in dying (MAID) under the recent legislation. In the report of the special joint committee on physician-assisted dying issued by the Canadian Parliament it was specifically stated that 'MAID should occur in the context of a patient–physician relationship and the Committee does not want Canada to become a destination for people seeking MAID'. For this reason, the committee recommended that 'medical assistance in dying be available to insured persons eligible for publicly funded health-care services in Canada'.

The committee did not follow the recommendation of Prof. Carolyn Ells, which is mentioned in the report, according to which eligibility for MAID would be based on eligibility for publicly funded healthcare services *in the province or territory where the request is made*. If accepted, such a recommendation would have also prevented suicide tourism within Canada.[10]

---

[10] Parliament of Canada, *Medical Assistance in Dying: A Patient-Centered Approach—Report of the Special Joint Committee on Physician-Assisted Dying (Chairs: Kelvin Kenneth Ogilvie and*

The Canadian Senate report followed another report written by a provincial-territorial expert advisory group on physician-assisted dying. In this report the residency requirement was more broadly explained:

> In addition to the criteria set out in the Supreme Court's decision in *Carter*, we believe that only patients who are eligible for publicly-funded health services should be considered eligible for physician-assisted dying. The *Carter* decision does not include citizenship, residency, or status as an insured person as an eligibility criterion for access to physician-assisted dying, but almost all jurisdictions where physician-assisted dying is legal limit access to the service in this manner. Although imposing a Canadian residency requirement would prevent residents of foreign countries from visiting Canada to receive physician-assisted dying, imposing limits based on citizenship or permanent residency status could also create a barrier to access for some in Canada. As a result, we recommend that all—and only—those eligible for publicly-funded health services also qualify for physician-assisted dying.[11]

Given that physician-assisted suicide was intended to be publicly funded, in explaining its recommendation that physician-assisted suicide should not serve as an exception to interprovincial reciprocal billing, the expert group explains that such recommendations 'would mitigate concerns about international medical tourism within Canada, while still recognizing that some Canadian communities may not have the capacity to offer physician-assisted dying to their own residents, and that some patients may wish to move elsewhere within Canada towards the end of their lives.'[12]

In Canada, there is one reported case of suicide tourism from one province (Ontario) to another (British Columbia) involving the request of Adam Maier-Clayton, a 27-year-old who was diagnosed with somatic

---

Robert Oliphant) (Parliament of Canada, 2016) p. 24 http://www.parl.ca/Content/Committee/421/PDAM/Reports/RP8120006/pdamrp01/pdamrp01-e.pdf, accessed on 6 July 2017.

---

[11] Ontario Ministry of Health, *Provincial-Territorial Expert Advisory Group on Physician-Assisted Dying: Final Report (Chairs: Jennifer Gibson and Maureen Taylor)* (Ontario Ministry of Health, 2015) p. 37 http://www.health.gov.on.ca/en/news/bulletin/2015/docs/eagreport_20151214_en.pdf, accessed on 6 July 2017.

[12] Ibid. at p. 25.

symptom disorder (a psychiatric condition), to end his life. Maier-Clayton had difficulty obtaining a lethal drug for his condition, but in the end he succeeded in this journey and died by suicide in April 2017.[13]

Social attitudes within Switzerland towards suicide tourism

As discussed in Chapter 1, Switzerland is the only place where the regulation of assisted suicide does not exclude non-residents. This is not the deliberate result of a thorough process of regulation. Instead, it is a historical reality stemming from the fact that the law in Switzerland was enacted in the criminal code with no aims to expand into organized assisted suicide, extensively applied to terminal and non-terminal individuals alike.[14] The original intention behind this legislation was to allow (by decriminalizing) assistance in dying as offered by a close relative or a friend, when dying usually takes place at home. The drafters of this law did not anticipate that the law would be used to provide such services for non-residents as well.

Because of this unique legal situation, and given the significant rise in the number of people travelling to Switzerland from other countries for assisted suicide in recent years, it is important to reflect on the social attitudes pertaining to suicide tourism from the perspective of the peoples who live in Switzerland. Interestingly, there are very few studies or surveys examining social attitudes on suicide tourism, or even on assisted suicide, in Switzerland.

One of the few surveys that does exist is a Swiss public poll, conducted in 2010 by a group of researchers at the University of Zurich. This poll examined the views and attitudes of about 1,500 Swiss residents with regard to assisted suicide. While a majority of respondents supported

---

[13] Lisa Xing, '27-year-old Maier Clayton Took His Own Life After a Long Struggle with OCD, Anxiety, Depression' (*CBC News*, 21 April 2017), http://www.cbc.ca/news/canada/windsor/adam-maier-claytons-father-takes-on-assisted-dying-advocacy-1.4080553, accessed on 10 May 2018; Stuart Hughes, 'Adam Maier-Clayton's Controversial Right-To-Die Campaign' (*BBC News*, 19 July 2017), http://www.bbc.com/news/world-us-canada-40546632, accessed on 10 May 2018.

[14] Olivier Guildo and Aline Schmidt, 'Assisted Suicide under Swiss Law' (2005) 12(1) *European Journal of Health Law* 25.

assisted suicide for Swiss residents, 66 per cent of them fully or to some extent objected to the provision of assisted suicide in Switzerland for non-residents.[15]

The study above, showing a relatively large portion of the Swiss public opposing suicide tourism, is different to a previous study undertaken in the French-speaking area of Switzerland, which suggested similar rates of support for the practice of assisted suicide whether offered to Swiss or non-Swiss residents.[16] It may be the fact that the vast majority of foreigners travel to the canton of Zurich (where most of Dignitas' activities take place) that can explain the different social attitudes between cantons.

Nevertheless, such a comparison may also indicate a change in the attitudes of Swiss people over time, towards less tolerance for such a practice as it expands and grows both in its absolute numbers and in terms of the size and number of the organizations offering assisted suicide services. It is important in this discussion to mention the bill that was proposed in the canton of Zurich to ban assisted suicide for non-residents. As discussed in Chapter 1, although the bill did not pass, it represents some uneasiness with suicide tourism, at least in the German-speaking area of Switzerland.

This feeling of uneasiness towards suicide tourism can also be detected in an interview with a staff member at one of the assisted dying organizations I spoke with, referring to repeated feelings of threat, risk, and harassment by the police and the government. This person cites the prosecutor of the canton of Zurich (within which the organization's activities take place) saying that 'he [the prosecutor] does not want Switzerland to become Mecca for suicides'. This person explained her feelings of being discriminated against by the government and the police merely because she brings individuals from other countries to commit suicide in Switzerland.

Yet, it follows from the interview that these feelings of being subjected to threats and discrimination do not apply to the relationship between

---

[15] Christian Schwarzenegger, Patrik Manzoni, David Studer, and Catia Leanza, 'Was die Schweizer Bevölkerung von Sterbehilfe und Suizidbeihilfe häl' (*Jusletter*, 13 September 2010) at 14 (in German)(copy with author); Isobel Leybold-Johnson, 'Swiss Want a Say on How to End Their Lives' (*SWI*, 2 September 2010) https://www.swissinfo.ch/eng/swiss-want-a-say-on-how-to-end-their-lives/28250486, accessed on 27 April 2018.

[16] The published results of this study could not be found. This statement is based on an interview with a Swiss professor.

Exit and the police, given the agreement that the prosecutor of Zurich signed with this organization. This agreement established conditions which allow the police to work in this field with almost no risk or concern to Exit. Although the agreement was invalidated by the Swiss High Court, my interviews reveal that in practice it resulted in a more lenient approach towards the investigation of unnatural deaths reported by Exit, only 1.25 per cent of the members of which (according to data supplied by it) live outside Switzerland while the remaining members are all Swiss residents. No similar arrangement with organizations helping non-residents has been suggested. Such an observation was also confirmed in an interview with an Exit staff member:

> We have an agreement in Switzerland, especially in Geneva, between police, public lawyer, minister public, legal medicine and us. They trust us and we trust them. They know that we work very well with respect of the law ... we say 24 hours before the suicide that some people probably committing suicide; 'probably' because they can change their mind till the last minute. But we phone to the police, they know the name, the address and they say 'you call us when it's over' ... when it's over we phone them. They wait for about one hour intentionally before coming because it's more easy for the medical legist (the) doctor of law, to see that death is certain ... that the person is not sleeping, they come with the agreement without any uniform, no weapon, no blue siren, very discreetly, so people in the house or the hospital don't know that it's a police ... they have external examination of the dead. No autopsy. They see we are working well.

Reports from right-do-die organizations in Switzerland also reveal that most doctors who practice assisted suicide work for Exit and they feel it is much more dangerous to work for Dignitas or Lifecircle.

My stay and the interviews I undertook in Switzerland show that suicide tourism is of some concern to the Swiss public, but mostly constitutes a challenge for the government. The main concern with the fact that people from all over the world come to Switzerland to be assisted in their dying relates to the potential harm caused to Switzerland, especially to its image and reputation. As one Swiss professor has indicated,

I think that foreign people is not an issue. But it became an issue when they—we call it in French 'tourism de la mort' ... lot of people come here to escape their legislation from Germany, from England and it's not good that we offer ... so we attract these people by our practice ... the problem is not stranger or not ... death has a strong symbolic emotive power... so it'ss not like abortion, I think... not perceived the same ... we have seen a TV programme and seen these people were burned in Zurich and after their ashes were thrown to the lake. It shocked people that they come from England to be burned here. So the symbolic effect of coming here to die is, I think, probably the image of Switzerland having something else to offer to the other place to die ... because we think we are a nice place with mountains and chocolate and happy life and people come here to die, it shock ... so we are become perceived as die providers... it's not good publicity.

Another interview with a Swiss professor reflecting on this subject describes a more complex public attitude towards suicide tourism and the people who come to Switzerland for assisted suicide. According to this view, Switzerland is a liberal country in some respects. Given that these right-to-die organizations are already in place, with more than 100,000 members, the 'Swiss people don't want to step back. If it were 30 years ago, we might have succeeded in ruling out assisted suicide for foreigners and outlawing these organizations. In general, the Swiss people are welcoming to tourists but don't want to know about people coming here to die ... they don't want to know, like the Germans in the 30s and 40s refused to know much ...'.

Moreover, it is claimed, if suicide tourism is raised as an issue in public debate, it will make people confront the meaning of assisted suicide and its practice in Switzerland. These would be questions that nobody wants to answer.

An additional concern in this direction is reflected in an interview with another professor where it is claimed that Swiss politicians visit their colleagues all over the world and they have to provide an explanation in response to questions of 'what is going on with you', in reference to suicide tourism. Few politicians are ready to admit in the press that they are worried about the reputation that suicide tourism brings to the country.

They express the view that they 'do not want Switzerland to be a destination for tourism for suicide'.[17]

Another explanation for some of the criticism of suicide tourism in Switzerland, although less prevalent in the discussion and interviews, relates to the social expenses associated with the public cost of investigations of unnatural deaths taking place in this country. Under some estimates, every such an investigation costs around 5,000 Swiss Francs. It is argued in some of the interviews that it is unfair that the Swiss public has to pay for these costs, at least where they relate to investigations of assisted suicide cases performed by non-residents. It is therefore suggested that suicide tourism be restricted, or that these costs be borne by countries of origin or the persons seeking assisted suicide.

Other general concerns with suicide tourism, raised in some interviews, are that this practice is unfair to Swiss society, principally on two grounds. The first has to do with the more general question of why Swiss society has to be responsible for and take care of people who want to commit suicide. The other refers to the idea that if other countries, specifically countries of origin, do not take care of their own residents, this is not Switzerland's problem. As a Swiss professor mentions, these queries reflect 'a sense of disappointment that others don't do it and don't give it a priority. Because these people are vulnerable, very sick, and so forth, it seems as something we need to do, but [it] is a burden'.

Along these lines, another professor admits that she heard the following argument a lot, speaking with professionals and representatives of the Swiss public: 'there is a perception that in a sense some countries do not take responsibilities over the situation and why they are coming here. It should be regulated in their own country … it's comfortable for the other country to have Switzerland, not to deal with this issue'.

Indeed, in Switzerland there have been some attempts to regulate suicide tourism and limit its scope. As already mentioned, the canton of Zurich introduced a bill to ban assisted suicide for non-residents. The bill has not passed and scholars doubt whether the canton of Zurich would have been able to introduce it in any case, mainly because the principal

---

[17] 'Dignitas: Swiss Suicide Helpers' (*BBC News*, 30 January 2003) (citing Beatrice Werli from the Swiss Christian Democrats) http://news.bbc.co.uk/2/hi/europe/2676837.stm, accessed on 11 May 2018.

provision regarding assisted suicide rests within the authority of the Federal government and not with the cantons.[18] No other canton has introduced such a ban, not only because of the lack of authority but perhaps also because, as one professor indicates, there is not much reason to remove non-residents from the application of the criminal law. If Switzerland decides assisted suicide is legal when it meets the required conditions, then it seems incoherent to exclude this from non-residents.

More generally, it was claimed in an interview with a senior representative of the government that the Swiss criminal code does not distinguish between residents and non-residents, and there is no need to do this in the case of assisted suicide either. This latter reflection may be regarded bureaucratic and too formal as one can argue that if the government wanted to regulate suicide tourism, it could do so by introducing a complementary law that was not under the criminal law.

The social attitude towards suicide tourism in Switzerland is reflected by the different attitudes that exist towards Exit and Dignitas. As one Swiss interviewee explained:

> Exit is more respected. They are not fanatic as others. Dignitas is the most radical organization. For Dignitas, you go there and they kill you. It's almost guaranteed that they will help you. [Minelli,] He's fanatic.

Another explanation for the difference in attitudes relates to the manner in which these different organizations work. This was articulated in another interview:

> I think it's because the way they (Dignitas) do it. They make ... they want to do it really for the foreigners and they ... they get money for it, and.. yeh ... they go outside Switzerland and say, oh come to Switzerland, and they ... you can do here your suicide ... there's an homepage a German homepage Dignitas Germany or Dignitas International, I think, and it's somehow like an ad ... so they induce... Yeh ... may be. More than Exit does.

---

[18] Some support for this argument can be seen in the invalidation of an agreement signed by the prosecutor of Zurich with EXIT DS, initiated by EXIT, which would have provided EXIT some immunity under the criminal code by the Swiss Federal Court.

Support for this theme can be found in another interview with a senior Swiss public official who expressed very strong words against these activities:

> When people kill others for money, especially sick, lonely people, this exploitation of the needy is a scandal. It is a scandal if you're doing it for free. It is much worse if you do it for money. You judge society in the way it treats the poor and the sick ... I think these people are Nazis.

According to this view, in principle,

> there is no difference between Exit and Dignitas. The difference between them is like between Reinhard Heydrich and Heinrich Himmler. Exit is more sophisticated. It is better with its public relations, with reaching to the majority of the Swiss population. In a way, I prefer Dignitas because they do not pretend. Exit is worse since they kill more people.

It is also suggested in the interviews that people from Dignitas exert a lot of pressure on politicians and through public campaigns to influence, deter, and frighten policymakers, so as to stop them changing the current law. Hence, as explained by one Swiss interviewee, those at Exit are regarded as 'the good guys' and are contrasted with 'the bad guys' represented by Dignitas. Exit is believed to be more open and transparent and to better reflect the values of the Swiss public.

According to an interview with a prominent public figure in Switzerland, the difference between these two organizations is ideological. In his view,

> Exit is an organization with many people ... they are open. They are very accepted in the society and Minelli he wants only one thing that is at the end of the life you can decide yourself ... how do you say? self-determination is the only thing. And for me, there is another article in the constitution, also in the European Constitution, that state has to provide life ... if you see the people in the end of the life, even if they're ill, they need some help. There could be pressure on them. In Switzerland, you pay 10,000 Francs in normal home for elderly

people for difficult case. There could be money pressure for relatives also. There are cases where family doesn't agree and in Switzerland, tourism ... most people of the big cities of urban areas not of the landscape, you know, the doctors who follow them, they don't make all you can ... there are very not much doctors who are making the prescription ... cause Minelli has to go for the same (doctors), because those people are not connected with their doctor in Switzerland, you know, for the tourism, So Minelli works with a very small doctors. In reality, most of them are quite old ...

Interviews conducted with Swiss practitioners involved in requests for assisted suicide on the criteria for assisted suicide, and with a Swiss sociologist on the need for strict regulation, reveal that most of them admit more regulation is needed with regard to suicide tourism as opposed to Swiss people seeking assisted suicide. The prevailing view of these professionals is that by suicide tourism 'anyone can come, and it's enough to have money, in a sense. That's the image that they have ... The perception is that there could be mishandling of the situation. I think there are some questions about how these people are assessed, how long and by whom, and what's going on with these people coming here'.

The emphasis on the ideological differences between Exit and Dignitas is also echoed in interviews with right-to-die organizations in Switzerland. According to one such interview,

Much of the criticism on Dignitas is false, but it's sometimes homemade. We made mistakes in terms of public relations ... But on the other hand ... Minelli, he doesn't care about money, he's not interested in money at all and he doesn't care about power ... All that he's interested in is freedom of choice, and he doesn't care about public opinion, he does not care about what politicians or anyone else think of him ... he says 'look, they can think I am a total asshole ... I am independent, I am retired, and I work with the law, within the law, with the law and with court case and that's all what counts' ... It is a strength and an independence to say we don't care about public opinion, we don't care about politics. Some people will say it's arrogant. I don't think I am arrogant ... It's just about when you are personally fully independent ... then you are free to say I take the risk being frowned upon.

Interestingly, part of the social attitude and opposition to Dignitas is explained in terms of power relations between the state—represented by the prosecutor of the canton of Zurich, where most requests for assisted suicide for non-residents take place—and Dignitas. As evidenced in an interview with a member of staff at Dignitas:

> A lot of opposition to Dignitas, from my personal point of view, has to do with we discuss this, and we attack the establishment, we criticize the establishment ... that is a power question. Brunner (the former chief prosecutor in the canton of Zurich) always thought I am in a stronger position because I am chief prosecutor of the canton of Zurich and you're just a little lawyer. And I say, yeah, I am just a little lawyer, but I am not giving in to your threat, I am not giving in to your attempt to narrow freedom of choice, and we won.

A more general explanation to the opposition towards Dignitas is offered in the following citation:

> The Swiss public, especially the media, they like to have a 'bad guy' which they can point at. And Minelli had played this role perfectly ... ... The media was always focussing on him as a 'one man show', but behind him there was always a group of people which supported his work, which did part of the work, but the public like to see one person whom they can spit at ...

Following that line, a Swiss professor admits,

> Dignitas' rhetoric is always or very often pushing the button of the victim saying 'we are discriminated, we are not treated the same way as the other, we are more' ... this is part of their rhetoric over the years. But this is also right that they did some things, even though that the law is not against that. They did not respect the criteria they set, for example, or they did not do it properly in a sense.

Hence, the favouritism towards Exit and the criticism of Dignitas is 'the result of history and of some situations which were problematic independently from the fact that they were dealing with strangers'.

As such, a Swiss professor admits, 'it is well known that Swiss people go to Exit and not to Dignitas'. The division between right-to-die organizations that offer assisted suicide services either to Swiss or to non-Swiss residents, and their 'specialization' in this regard, is something which is consciously created and defended. As expressed by one staff member at a Swiss right-to-die organization:

> We prefer not to accept non-residents ... we are not accustomed for such cases. We have no legal counsel for that ... our president does not wish ... there are ... there is ... how do you say ... periodic television radio is very often speaking about Dignitas about Life Spirit and Exit International and there are polemic about death tourism and we prefer not to enter into this polemic even if it's possible to have some foreigner people.

The different attitudes towards these organizations is also reflected in the high number of members at Exit as opposed to Dignitas. In Switzerland, so it was described in one of the interviews, membership of Exit is regarded as a way of insuring against being dependent on an institutionalized death. It is something that Swiss residents do 'just in case', without knowing if they will *in fact* make use of it in the future. It represents a 'fear from being the object and not the subject of medical care'.

The strict divide and contrast between Dignitas and Exit has also led to miscommunication between the two organizations for 10 years. It came out from my discussions with these organizations that some people from Exit had expressed views against Dignitas in public, thereby supporting and strengthening an opposing attitude against this organization in Switzerland. Only when a few staff members at Exit had been replaced, did Exit and Dignitas rebuild their relationship as two organizations that supported and promoted freedom of choice at end of life.

In recent years, as Lifecircle-Eternal Spirit became another organization to offer assisted suicide for non-residents, some criticism was targeted towards this new organization as well. As one Swiss professor describes, while referring to a case in which the organization helped an elderly Italian person to commit suicide in the absence of any illness:

Erika Preisig (the Vice-president of Lifecircle) is foolish. The things she makes are outside of what is acceptable... She doesn't accept a second opinion. That's a scandal ... horrible, because she do not like to accept the guidelines by the academy. She do not accept second opinion by a colleague... In some cases, she did all by herself, alone, with a patient, and that's not serious, not acceptable ... without waiting to see if the wish to die is stable. She went by car to Zurich to buy the pentobarbital, which she could not get in Basel, only in Zurich, to get back the same day she helped the patient to die. On the same day! Do you see my problem? Exit would never make such nonsense and Dignitas too because people are looking at them. But Erika Preisig—she makes what she want without any ... people speak to her but she do not accept any critique.

Despite the relatively negative social attitude towards organizations that offer assisted suicide for non-residents, interviews reveal that the public attitude towards Dignitas may have changed during recent years. Moreover, according to one interview with a Dignitas member of staff, while such a change has only been observed recently, this attitude had in fact existed for many years:

It has changed ... despite all the difficulties and controversy we had ten years ago, already ten years ago we had delegation of the UK House of Lords visiting us. So, maybe in public they were frowning upon us, but behind the scene they were visiting us. All thirteen Lords and Ladies and Archbishops and their assistants (laughing) were sitting in the living room of Mr. Minelli's private house, I was there together with him and had a lot of questions. So, behind the scene already we were somewhat respected ... and the Commission on Assisted Dying, and then a delegation of the Australian Parliament, then Canadian ... There seems to be some respect and understanding to what we do, which is something that as a politician you would not necessarily say publicly. It's delicate to say 'I like Dignitas'.

Interestingly, suicide tourism is portrayed in Switzerland as the story of individuals and not as a social practice. Moreover, according to one interview, there is a difference in the way the public regards suicide tourism in the French- and German-speaking areas. Hence,

> In the French-speaking area, suicide tourism is not so . . . is not perceived as a big problem, because it's not very frequent . . . at least not very public or accepted as in German speaking area. This is because French Exit- they rarely accept people . . . they usually say that . . . in their rules say you have to live in Switzerland, to be a member for certain amount of time. This is one of their criterion of eligibility. There have been cases where they accepted . . . it's not evidenced, it's less frequent . . . one of their key points, when they were campaigning for the law in the canton of Vaud, was saying we don't have the same rules for this kind of assistance with strangers... They distinguished themselves from (Dignitas D.S.), at least in the newspapers and political and public debate proceedings.

Another important finding is that, in Switzerland, there are hardly any academic discussions, let alone publicly funded academic research, pertaining to social attitudes towards suicide tourism. This is reflected in the fact that research grants offered by the Swiss National Science Foundation (SNSF), although recently supporting research on assisted suicide, rarely funds social science research on this issue. This is borne out by the unexplained rejection of a research proposal for this book by SNSF, as well as by the Brocher Foundation, despite support for it from distinguished professors in Switzerland and abroad.

Avoidance of social science research on suicide tourism is also evidenced by the fact that in the interviews conducted for this research, Swiss participants refer almost automatically and exclusively to Schwarzenegger and colleagues' short survey (mentioned above) as a source for the social view on suicide tourism. However, this survey does not necessarily represent the whole population, not to mention the way such a view was measured.

One explanation for the lack of public debate on the social aspects of suicide tourism, admits a Swiss sociologist, stems from the general taboo existing around assisted suicide in the country more generally and the relative non-attractiveness to academics for developing this field through research. Another explanation offered in the interviews points to the fact that Switzerland is a liberal country, consisting of twenty-six cantons, four main languages, and very different cultures, making it difficult to explore the social view on this particular delicate issue.

The effect of suicide tourism on legislation on assisted suicide in countries of origin

The extensive empirical work I have undertaken over the last few years leads me to argue that suicide tourism has played only a small and insignificant role in legal proceedings in many of the countries from which people travel for suicide tourism and did not serve as a trigger to legalize assisted suicide in these countries, having instead negatively contributed to such an option. This section brings together empirical data, mainly from the UK, France, and Germany. Due to space limitations, I will elaborate the discussion of my argument on the British case only. However, because similar findings are ascribed to the French and German cases, I will suggest more general explanations to answer the question of why suicide tourism played such an insignificant role in the legalization of assisted suicide in all of these countries.

The UK

In Chapter 1, the various legal attempts to change the law in the UK were discussed at length. In the following section it is argued that while some reference to suicide tourism was made in a few of the proceedings, as well as in the public debate on assisted suicide in the UK, this practice did not serve as a powerful trigger for the legalization of assisted suicide. The section begins by referring to the Commission on Assisted Dying (chaired by Lord Falconer). This public commission, which was called to examine whether assisted suicide should be decriminalized or not, concluded that the current law in the UK is insufficient and incoherent. The commission laid out a proposal for assisted dying. A few of the witness statements submitted to this commission refer to suicide tourism. For example, a statement submitted by Dignity in Dying, a very active right-to-die organization in the UK, held that by removing the option of professional assistance in the UK, the legal system was relying on Switzerland to fill this gap:

> Therefore, the policy could be seen as discriminatory towards those who cannot afford, or who are not physically able to get to Switzerland, by leaving them facing the prospect of a more uncertain and painful suicide, and by continuing to deny them clarity in how the law will treat their loved ones.[19]

The commission discussed the disadvantages of travelling abroad to receive assisted suicide. It referred to the financial barrier associated with such travel (evidence by Pauline Smith/NHS and Debbie Purdy) and to the fact that travelling abroad may compel the person to make the decision to die earlier on, when they are still physically able to travel (anonymous written evidence from a retired doctor).

Some witnessed as to the financial burden and stress associated with the fees required for such a request:

> He [Raymond] was very ill travelling out. Dr Michael Irwin, who I assume that you are aware of, helped us to pay for the fee for Dignitas because both of us were claiming benefits, we had no money, no savings; we had no money to pay for the fee, which at the time was £2,200. And Dr Irwin's charity gave us £1,500 and then after Dr Irwin spoke to Mr Minelli [founder of Dignitas]. He said that he would accept a token amount from us so we actually paid £300. And without their help we couldn't have gone.[20]

The financial burden continued as the relative of the person who received assisted dying in Switzerland appealed for a funeral grant:

> [I had] various problems with some government departments regarding the funeral grant that I was entitled to because—I actually attended a tribunal twice. I appealed against their decision because they

---

[19] The Commission on Assisted Dying, *Final Report* (Demos, 2011) p. 99 https://www.demos.co.uk/files/476_CoAD_FinalReport_158x240_I_web_single-NEW_.pdf?1328113363, accessed on 14 May 2018 (hereafter: 'Commission Report').

[20] Witness from Alan Cutkelvin Rees, Commission Report (n 19) p. 101.

refused to give me the money on the grounds that his funeral was in Switzerland according to them, when it wasn't. It was in the UK. I eventually won the second tribunal.[21]

A representative from the British Association of Social Workers gave her witness to the commission and suggested that 'as a country, we don't believe that we should say to people, "well, you've got to travel the world if you want to be assisted in dying". Instead, we need to make provision within the UK for that to happen.'[22]

One of the witnesses to the commission was Dignitas. In its written evidence it stated:

No one should be forced to leave his or her home in order to make use of the basic human right of deciding on the time and manner of the end of his or her life. In this context it should be pointed out that only individuals with at least a minimum of financial resources—a right denied to many in the U.K.—can afford to travel abroad as a 'suicide tourist' in order to make use of the option of a self-determined end in life, a further unacceptable discrimination. The present legal situation in the U.K. (and other countries) is a disgrace. It shows the disrespect law-makers have towards public opinion which is in favour of freedom of choice in these 'last issues'. DIGNITAS strongly supports the notion that the U.K. and other countries should adopt a legal scheme similar to Switzerland which, and this in fact is the long term aim of DIGNITAS, would make DIGNITAS obsolete.[23]

In July 2014 the House of Lords held an extensive debate on the Assisted Dying Bill which was introduced by Lord Falconer. One year later, on 11 September 2015, the House of Commons held a debate on the Assisted Dying (No. 2) Bill which was introduced by Rob Marris MP. The bill was

---

[21] Ibid.

[22] Witness from Bridget Robb, Commission Report (n 19) p. 102.

[23] Dignitas, *Call for evidence by the Commission on Assisted Dying: Submission by 'DIGNITAS– to Live with Dignity–to Die with Dignity'*, Forch, Switzerland (2 May 2011) http://www. dignitas.ch/images/stories/pdf/diginpublic/stellungnahme-submission-by-dignitas-to-the-commission-on-assisted-dying-05052011.pdf, accessed on 18 May 2018.

rejected by 330 to 118 votes. In a note following this parliamentary process, Dignitas stated:

> Dignitas is very disappointed that UK residents are still forced to travel to Dignitas. The 330 MPs who voted against the Assisted Dying Bill should be ashamed for their disgraceful ignorance towards the clear public opinion which is pro-choice in 'last matters', and even more so for forcing the people who elect them and pay taxes for them to go abroad when all they want is to have the basic human right of a self-determined, accompanied by loved ones and safe end of suffering.[24]

Reviewing discussions in the UK Parliament from recent years reveals the different roles that suicide tourism has played in the attempt to legalize assisted suicide. These roles are summarized below:

1) Suicide tourism attests to the disadvantages of the current legal position:

> The context is that the current law does not meet the needs of the terminally ill, does not meet the needs of their loved ones and, in some ways, does not meet the needs of the medical profession. We have amateur suicides and what is technically illegal assistance going on, and those who have the means to do so are going off to Dignitas in Switzerland. In the Tony Nicklinson case, the Supreme Court recognized that there is a problem that needs to be addressed by Parliament (Rob Marris, House of Commons, 11 September 2015).[25]

> Are the Government not ashamed that so many British citizens feel compelled to travel to Switzerland because their own country refuses them a dignified death? I like to think that they do feel a little shame because they turn a blind eye to a public prosecutor who is not prepared to prosecute those family members assisting their ill relations

---

[24] Dignitas, 'Politics Worldwide' http://www.dignitas.ch/index.php?option=com_content&view=article&id=55&Itemid=89&lang=en, accessed on 18 May 2018.

[25] House of Commons, 'Assisted Dying (No. 2) Bill' second reading debate, *Official Report* vol. 599, col. 656 (UK Parliament, 11 September 2015) https://hansard.parliament.uk/Commons/2015-09 11/debates/15091126000003/AssistedDying(No2)Bill?highlight=%22assisted%20suicide%22%20Switzerland#contribution-15091126000576, accessed on 28 June 2017 (hereafter 'House of Commons, Assisted Dying (No. 2)').

to get to Dignitas, and thus blatantly flouting the law. The law badly needs to be changed to allow choice at the end of life and immunity to those who assist in this regard (The Earl of Glasgow, House of Lords, 5 December 2013).[26]

For me, it is a continuing matter of shame that our fellow countrymen and women still have to go to Switzerland to avail themselves of what should be possible in this country. I feel that we as politicians should apologise to those who might continue to suffer, for some time to come, until legislation with full safeguards can be passed (Viscount Craigavon, House of Lords, 5 March 2014).[27]

2) Suicide tourism serves as a bad alternative to existing law as it is not available for everyone, mainly because of its cost, and it is undesirable since people want to die at home. As such, it calls for a legal change or at least its discussion:[28]

---

[26] House of Lords, 'Assisted Dying: Legislation' question for short debate, *Official Report* vol. 750, col. 52 (UK Parliament, 5 December 2013) https://hansard.parliament.uk/Lords/2013-12-05/debates/13120556000119/AssistedDyingLegislation?highlight=%22assisted%20suicide%22%20Switzerland#contribution-13120556000065, accessed on 28 June 2017 (hereafter: 'House of Lords, Assisted Dying: Legislation').

[27] House of Lords, 'Assisted Suicide' question for short debate, *Official Report* vol. 752, col. 1425 (UK Parliament, 5 March 2014) https://hansard.parliament.uk/Lords/2014-03-05/debates/140305104000256/AssistedSuicide?highlight=%22assisted%20suicide%22%20Switzerland#contribution-140305104000105, accessed on 28 June 2017.

[28] In addition to the citations in the text see also: House of Commons, Assisted Dying (No. 2) (n 25), Jim Fitzpatrick, Kit Malthouse, Norman Lamb, and Andy Slaughter at cols 667, 717, 685, and 722 respectively; House of Lords, 'Assisted Dying Bill [HL]' second reading debate, *Official Report* vol. 755, col. 866 (UK Parliament, 18 July 2014) https://hansard.parliament.uk/Lords/2014-07-18/debates/14071854000545/AssistedDyingBill(HL)?highlight=%22assisted%20suicide%22%20Switzerland#contribution-14071857000186, accessed on 28 June 2017 (Lord Wigley and Lord Haskel at cols 787 and 891 respectively) (hereafter: 'House of Lords, Assisted Dying Bill [HL]'); House of Commons, 'Assisted Suicide', *Official Report* vol. 542, col. 1364 (UK Parliament, 27 March 2012) https://hansard.parliament.uk/Commons/2012-03-27/debates/12032752000001/AssistedSuicide?highlight=%22assisted%20suicide%22%20Switzerland#contribution-12032752000402, accessed on 28 June 2017 (David Winnick and Ian Swales at cols 1372 and 1409 respectively) (hereafter: 'House of Commons, Assisted Suicide'); House of Lords, 'Health: End of Life' motion to take note, *Official Report* vol. 750, col. 916 (UK Parliament, 12 December 2013) https://hansard.parliament.uk/Lords/2013-12-12/debates/13121261000539/HealthEndOfLife?highlight=%22assisted%20suicide%22%20Switzerland#contribution-13121261000086, accessed on 28 June 2017 (Lord Beecham at col. 949) (hereafter: 'House of Lords, Health'); House of Lords, 'Assisted Dying' question for short debate, *Official Report* vol. 735, col. 624 (UK Parliament, 13 February 2012) https://hansard.parliament.uk/Lords/2012-02-13/debates/12021316000099/AssistedDying?highlight=%22assisted%20suicide%22%20Switzerland#contribution-12021316000034, accessed on 28 June 2017 (the Earl of Glasgow at col. 624) (hereafter: 'House of Lords, Assisted Dying'); House of Lords, Assisted Dying: Legislation (n 26), the Earl of Glasgow at col. 50.

Our purpose here is as legislators, and as such we cannot continue to turn a blind eye to a situation where people with financial resources can make a choice about how and when they die, and travel to Switzerland, while those without resources cannot... People who wish to choose the time of their death can do so now, but must rely on Switzerland to manage the consequences. It cannot be right that some of my constituents can afford to go to Switzerland, but the majority cannot. ...the Rubicon has been crossed, the train has already left the station and Parliament cannot keep turning a blind eye. Our purpose is to establish the principle that terminally ill people can be afforded choice and dignity (Karin Smyth, House of Commons, 11 September 2015).[29]

My Lords, despite the advances made by the DPP's guidance, the new status quo still leaves the dying and their families with three unsatisfactory choices: to soldier on with their suffering; to accept assistance but still with risk of prosecution; or to pay up and travel to Switzerland to die away from home and family. Parliament should no longer hide behind an official, however enlightened (Lord Turnbull, House of Lords, 13 February 2012).[30]

I am concerned that the present law affects people unequally, given that going to Dignitas costs about £5,000 and is only available to the well-off and those fit enough to travel, and there is no safe way of having assisted death at home without risk of prosecution for loved ones, which is an unfair burden for the dying person to contemplate (Baroness Hayter of Kentish Town, House of Lords, 13 February 2012).[31]

3) Suicide tourism presents a legitimate choice that people should be able to take within their own country:

One comes back to a simple issue which, I suggest, is at the heart of this entire debate: to whom does a person's life belong? I suggest that a person's life belongs to the individual themselves. It is for those who are not as lucky as I was to make their choices about how they live their

---

[29] House of Commons, Assisted Dying (No. 2) (n 25) at cols 716–7.
[30] House of Lords, Assisted Dying (n 28) at cols 626–7.
[31] Ibid. at cols 628–9.

lives. That somebody cannot take those choices does not mean that we in Parliament should deny them any choice. It upsets me tremendously that the state prescribes that it knows best. It cannot be right that individual members of the public are prevented from doing something in this country that they are able to go and do at Dignitas in Switzerland, where they can die in the manner of their choosing (Guy Opperman, House of Commons, 27 March 2012).[32]

4) Suicide tourism demonstrates the shortcomings of the proposed new law:

... People will still have to go to Switzerland if they feel that their life is intolerable, unless they are likely to die anyway within six months. People may also still die undignified and unfortunate deaths, regardless of their prior wishes, if they cannot display current mental capacity. Those would be the consequences of the Bill. Paradoxically, the more likely it is that someone's end would be undignified, the less likely it is that they will be judged to have the capacity to comply with the legislation. In reality, what this Bill permits is for a strictly limited number of people to have their suicides assisted, regardless of whether their anticipated end is painless or pain-free, dignified or not (John Pugh, House of Commons, 11 September 2015).[33]

5) Suicide tourism highlights the need and opportunity for a domestic system to introduce safeguards for guaranteeing free choice:[34]

There is a concern that the patient may not make a free choice but may somehow feel under pressure from those close to him or her, possibly not always from worthy motives—I have had that point put to me. However, it is only right to point out that there are no safeguards at all in going to Switzerland to have an assisted death provided that one can

---

[32] House of Commons, Assisted Suicide (n 28) at column 1432.

[33] House of Commons, Assisted Dying (No. 2) (n 25) at cols 696–7.

[34] In addition to the citations in the text see also House of Lords, Assisted Dying Bill [HL] (n 28) Baroness Young of Old Scone at col. 871.

afford the air fare, so my noble and learned friend's Bill would actually improve the situation significantly by having safeguards in the process (Lord Dubs, House of Lords, 12 December 2013).[35]

Of course there must be safeguards. Today, there are none. If you can afford a flight to Switzerland, there are no safeguards at all (Lord Dubs, House of Lords, 5 December 2013).[36]

6) Suicide tourism is not the best option as it puts people in a stressful dilemma concerning their ability to travel and the point at which they wish to die:[37]

Compare that with the position here, where people have to agonise over whether to make the journey to Switzerland before they are really ready in their own mind to end their life. Yet they worry that they may be too ill to make that journey. This seems to be an intolerable dilemma which we impose upon people (Lord Dubs, House of Lords, 12 December 2013).[38]

7) Suicide tourism includes cases of people who need not have died; this supports the 'slippery slope' arguments against legalization of assisted suicide in the home country:

If you only look at Dignitas and Exit in Switzerland, for example, about a third of the people they treat—and in the case of women nearly half, I understand—are not terminally ill at all but are merely feeling rather miserable and want something to be done to help them. I urge noble Lords not to go down this slippery slope and to recall quite seriously the early 1930s in Nazi Germany. It is all too close to home. (Baroness Nicholson of Winterbourne, House of Lords, 13 February 2012).[39]

---

[35] House of Lords, Health (n 28) at col. 912.

[36] House of Lords, Assisted Dying: Legislation (n 26) at col. 54.

[37] In addition to the citations in the text see also House of Lords, Assisted Dying Bill [HL] (n 28) Lord Dubs and Baroness Morgan of Huyton at cols 779 and 911 respectively.

[38] House of Lords, Assisted Dying Bill [HL] (n 28) at column 914.

[39] House of Lords, Assisted Dying (n 28) at col. 628.

The citations above reflect the role that suicide tourism has played in discussions about a new law in the UK; many speakers in parliament referred to suicide tourism, raising it in various contexts. The vast majority of the references to suicide tourism in these discussions were made by supporters of the various bills. Suicide tourism was criticized mainly because of its high costs and the fact that it is not accessible to all Britons, such criticism being used to establish the need for legalization of assisted suicide in the UK. It was also emphasized that the state cannot ignore the limitations of suicide tourism and it must act to provide a dignified death for all with proper safeguards in place. Despite these relatively varied arguments concerning the relationship between suicide tourism and the bills under debate, the points raised about the ongoing practice were not sufficiently convincing, in combination with other arguments supporting the bills, to lead to legalization of assisted suicide in the UK.

Germany

As mentioned above, there was no criminal prohibition on assisted suicide in Germany until, in November 2015, it passed a new revision to the criminal code (§ 217 StGB) prohibiting organizations and individuals from assisting others to commit suicide on a regular, repetitive basis, including the not-for-profit offer of such aid.

Locally, while the law does not criminalize assisted suicide provided on a non-regular, non-repetitive basis, for example by a relative or a close friend, it does not allow for the provision of lethal drugs (as access to such drugs would have required a prescription by a medical doctor), thereby making it more difficult for these parties to assist their beloved ones at end of life.

Since physicians are no longer able to provide medical reports attesting to patients' conditions if they know that such reports will be used by organizations such as Dignitas or Lifecircle, patients will now have to either not share with their physicians the true purpose of the proposed document or submit an official report, for example from their hospital admission. However, the latter alternative will not be available for patients who have not been recently hospitalized, for example patients with ALS.

These patients will not be able to find a German doctor who can support their travel to Switzerland.

Moreover, with regard to patients who *have* been hospitalized shortly before their application to a Swiss aid-in-dying organization, patients with multiple sclerosis or patients suffering from cancer will usually also experience depression, sadness, and misery, which might also be diagnosed during hospitalization.[40] People travelling to Switzerland with a medical diagnosis of depression or similar will have to be referred to a psychiatrist who will, in most cases, not approve their request for assisted suicide. These patients will then have to return back to Germany.

Conversely to what one might expect, most of the interviewees confirmed that the practice of suicide tourism had played a role in drafting the new law criminalizing assisted suicide. While a few of the interviewees thought the number of people going to Switzerland would decrease in the near future, most of them anticipated it increasing. The former explained that the new law had hurt the legitimacy and attractiveness of assisted suicide as a practice and, as a result, would create a shift towards strengthening the legal and social mechanism of advance directives in Germany as a central solution to end-of-life issues.[41]

The latter group referred to the large amount of support for assisted suicide among the German public (estimated at 80%), arguing that the new law could not change such solid attitudes. According to this view, since the current legal situation makes it impossible to receive aid in dying from an expert, it should be expected that the number of people going to Switzerland to receive such aid will increase.

As one interviewee working for a right-to-die organization in Switzerland confirmed:

As this law is unconstitutional and completely against the German population's will (who favour assisted suicide with a record high of 90%) this law will be changed again, so far no influence anyway; no lawmaker can forbid people to die self-determinedly, right? There are many more

---

[40] Hospitals may also have a financial incentive to add a diagnosis of depression so as to receive more coverage, according to one interview.

[41] The legalization of advance directives in Germany took place in 2010.

means than just going to Switzerland, even a lot of German doctors help their patients without the authorities ever knowing it ...

France

As discussed above, following an extensive public debate and parliamentary commission discussing issues relating to end-of-life care (chaired by Didier Sicard), a recent amendment to the Public Health Act (effective as of February 2016) acknowledges an explicit right to deep and continuous sedation for terminally ill patients.

Interviews reveal that the new law passed because of a problematic practice by physicians concerning some unsuccessful and painful sedation cases:

> The law was particularly passed because those who wrote the law ... they really wanted to make sure ... because they don't trust French physicians ... there have been a few cases where physicians stopped active treatment like sustaining treatment ... and they didn't do it well, they didn't put in place alternative tracks that would alleviate, ease the patient's suffering ... there were few cases where patients have suffered or at least where the family has suffered a lot because they have seen the patient like moving and like not well treated and not well sedated ... Hence, the law reflects a medicalized approach to dying with a strong belief that medicine can offer sufficient solutions for many conditions.

Moreover, according to one interview the law also reflected an original and unique solution to end-of-life care that is different to the one that exists in other regimes. This was termed as a 'third way' or a 'French way' to die:

> It [the new law] was discussed as the third way or the French way ... they love to present things as the French way or the French solution to problems ... they tried to introduce something where they didn't have to call it euthanasia but they kind of found a back door to euthanasia and ... the provision of palliative sedation gives more possibility to the

doctor to make the decision to do this without the strict control as euthanasia is controlled in Belgium or the Netherlands.

Suicide tourism was negatively regarded by some professional bodies in France. Its expansion in recent years has led the Sicard committee to under-evaluate the current position in Switzerland, thereby strengthening the opposition to proposals to legalize assisted suicide in France. As a senior French figure admitted in one interview, 'suicide tourism does no credit to Switzerland's image and disturbs legal order in neighbouring countries'. Overall, suicide tourism has not played any special role in shaping the legal position at end of life. If anything, it supported and encouraged the disapproval of legalization of assisted suicide and paved the way for other alternatives.

In research presented by a Swiss team at the University of Zurich, Gauthier et al. argue that the very practice of suicide tourism caused Debbie Purdy to bring an action to clarify the position of the Director of Public Prosecutions (DPP) on prosecution in cases of assisted suicide. The revision of this position resulted in liberalization of the DPP guidelines and the prosecution practice and, in my view, will also lead to amendment of existing laws in this direction.[42]

To this claim one can add the recent litigation brought by a 50-year-old man suffering from locked in syndrome who challenged the General Medical Council (GMC) policy holding that doctors who give advice and supply the medical report required by Dignitas in connection with requests for assisted suicide may be liable to fitness-to-practice investigations and disciplinary action. It was claimed that the GMC should have followed the laxer and more compassionate DPP policy evolving from the same issue.

However, the High Court dismissed the claim and ruled that, in accordance with *R (Nicklinson) v. Ministry of Justice*, as the blanket ban on assisted suicide did not infringe Article 8 of the European Convention on Human Rights, any step taken to discourage a doctor from assisting a suicide would not infringe that Article either.

---

[42] S. Gauthier, J. Mausbach, T. Reisch, et al., 'Suicide Tourism: A Pilot Study on the Swiss Phenomenon' (2015) 41 *J Med Ethics* 611.

Moreover, the court ruled that the GMC guidelines could be justified by the need to protect vulnerable patients. It was also held that there is no reason why the analysis of the public interest in the context of public prosecution should dictate the way the GMC determines what was required to protect the reputation of the medical profession.[43]

From this perspective, one can argue that suicide tourism did not cause the Purdy litigation but served only as context to the English litigation which referred to the domestic situation. It is claimed that the prosecutorial policy did not change at all following this revised opinion as there were no cases of prosecution even before it.[44]

One would have thought that, as in abortion tourism, suicide tourism would have put much pressure on the public and politicians to change the law and legalize assisted suicide in countries of origin. However, as this chapter observes, despite a very long process of political debate taking place in recent years in Germany, France, and the UK, the legal position and public policy with regard to assisted suicide has not changed (the UK) or has even shifted to other or opposite directions (France and Germany). I would like to offer six groups of explanations for this practice based on the interviews I carried out in my research.

Explanations

Some explanations for the minimal role of suicide tourism in the legal and legislative proceedings carried out in countries of origin will now be offered.

The first and most obvious explanation concerns the relatively few cases that suicide tourism constitutes of all cases of assisted suicide and of all potential suicide cases. As suggested by one of the interviewees, 'possibly one explanation for not to consider those who leave the country, because you can forget them easier and they don't make a lot of noise in the country ... they are not those people who go to courts inside the country to claim their right to leave'.

---

[43] *R (on the application of AM) v. General Medical Council* [2015] P.T.S.R. D38.
[44] Charles Foster, 'Suicide Tourism May Change Attitudes to Assisted Suicide, but Not Through the Courts' (2014) 41(8) *J Med Ethics*.

With regard to the UK, one of the interviewees commented that suicide tourism and the DPP policy pertaining to it, given the small number of people who participate in such a practice, helped form the impression that the current prohibition on assisted suicide should persist:

> The proof that the current law is working, in a sense, is that there are, on the one hand, very few people attempting suicide, even going to Dignitas, and on the other hand, very few prosecutions ... we would say that's the best law to have: one that has an absolute prohibition on assisted suicide and gives discretion to judges and prosecutors to show mercy in hard cases.

Another explanation, pointing to the relative net benefit of suicide tourism as opposed to liberalization of the local law, can be attributed to Charles Foster. Foster argues that 'if Switzerland is happy to continue providing the facility then, however intellectually dishonest it may be to allow her to siphon off all our own English pain, fear, angst, and debate, it is likely to do less harm overall than introducing any conceivable assisted suicide law into England'.[45] Under such a consequential rationale, it may be beneficial that another country does the 'dirty work' of helping people to die.

A very common theme raised in the interviews analogized suicide tourism to the idea of a safety valve. According to one interview conducted in the UK,

> Politically, it functions in that way, it allows people on both sides to live with the present status quo, for the present status quo has all the exceptions which ... if you took it logically, would seem ought to be done here. Yes... The fact that you can't, you can't do it here still does allow for a status quo which could, is a bit messy ...is a bit more flexible for more people. So ... I do think it has some stabilizing function ... In practice, in a funny way, it acts as a safety valve and in that way reinforces the status quo.

---

[45] Ibid.

This line of thinking corresponds with the British Medical Association policy, mentioned in Chapter 1, holding that only a minority of people wish to die and the rules for the majority should not be changed to accommodate such a small group.

A third explanation for the minimal role of suicide tourism in the legal proceedings which would have resulted in a more liberalized law is that cases of suicide tourism not only fail to change attitudes towards a more liberal approach to the right to die with dignity but by perhaps misrepresenting reality they emphasize the ways in which safeguards to protect vulnerable people in cases of assisted suicide may be tricky, impracticable, and ineffective. Thus, suicide tourism may reflect a 'suicide factory' whose very existence represents a dangerous challenge to the principle of the sanctity of human life.[46]

Moreover, these cases explore the commercial interest associated with assisted suicide, thereby emphasizing not only discrimination and injustice but also the potential for abuse and disinterest. They are, once in a while, accompanied by stories demonstrating unacceptable practices, such as oxygen deprivation with a face mask as there were not many doctors willing to prescribe lethal drugs,[47] carrying out assisted deaths in a caravan,[48] or disposing of large amounts of urns in the nearby lake.[49]

In addition, interviews reveal that organizations specializing in suicide tourism (mostly Dignitas) do not look at the validity of medical reports but accept them as such. Some of these reports are written by physicians who are retired or by psychologists and not by medical doctors. A few of the interviews also refer to the selectiveness by which stories of suicide tourism are brought to the media, instrumentally serving right-to-die organizations in their campaigns to change public views and the law.

---

[46] John Bingham, 'Dignitas Clinic: Last Refuge or Suicide Factory?', *The Telegraph* (6 March 2009) http://www.telegraph.co.uk/news/uknews/4946290/Dignitas-clinic-last-refuge-or-suicide-factory.html.

[47] Russel D. Ogden, William K. Hamilton, and Charles Whitcher, 'Assisted Suicide by Oxygen Deprivation with Helium at a Swiss Right-to-Die Organisation' (2009) *J Med Ethics* http://dx.doi.org/10.1136/jme.2009.032490..

[48] Kate Connolly, 'Residents Call a Halt to Assisted Suicide in Swiss Housing Block', *The Guardian* (13 July 2007) https://www.theguardian.com/society/2007/jul/13/health.internationalnews, accessed on 24 May 2018.

[49] Alexandra Williams, '300 Urns with Human Ashes Dumped in Lake Zurich near Dignitas Clinic', *The Telegraph* (27 April 2010) http://www.telegraph.co.uk/news/worldnews/europe/switzerland/7641989/300-urns-with-human-ashes-dumped-in-Lake-Zurich-near-Dignitas-clinic.html, accessed on 24 May 2018.

Fourth, it also appears from the interviews that suicide tourism cases help change the discourse on assisted suicide from a moral, human rights-based debate to a more technical procedural discussion concerning safety and safeguards. As such, it helps create a larger consensus against the activities represented by it as it is no longer a moral or constitutional right-wing versus left-wing debate but a claim to protect the most vulnerable in the society, be it the poor (who are unable to pay for these organizations), the severely disabled (who are unable to travel), the mildly disabled (who may be subject to abuse and may be compelled to die sooner in the absence of proper safeguards), the mentally incapacitated, the elderly who have just 'had enough', or otherwise healthy spouses who wish to die with their partners.

As one of the interviewees claims, 'it demonstrates that the safeguards are not safeguards at all. They're just qualifying criteria ... you know a safeguard is something which holds the gate closed. Doesn't let it open too readily. Qualifying criteria are ... well... if you meet this, this, and this ... there you are! ... [They are] things that you can't really verify ... '.

A fifth explanation concerns the role that physicians play with regard to the practice of suicide tourism. My research demonstrates that physicians who are involved in this practice usually act in secret, and they rarely accompany patients. When confronted with this issue, one interviewee commented:

> I don't think there is a law in France that say you can't go to Switzerland and you can't follow the people that have decided to go to Switzerland for medical suicide..Perhaps because it would have been difficult for me, if I am honest, to be with the patient to cross the frontier and go with them ... because it make me ... there are a lot of questions for me about this medical suicide or euthanasia ... the law in France changed recently ... what is possible in France make me reflect a lot ... it's a big interrogation for me ... in fact, when you ask me this question, I never ask myself why can you go and I never, in fact, proposed to patient to go with them. That's right. That's the fact ... nobody asked me to go with him or her in Switzerland. Never.

Following this line, another attitude expressed by doctors in France regards suicide tourism as an ethical problem. This is because such a practice does not allow medical staff or family to accompany the person. Under this view, the criminality associated with assisting others in securing their trip to Switzerland makes the physician abandon the patient once she is provided with the required medical data. Hence, the doctor does not follow the patient or care for her during this journey.

It also follows that there are only a few physicians who collaborate with patients requesting aid in dying in their home country. These doctors are usually being tackled by the police. They receive no institutional support, especially by the medical profession. In the UK, they act under an existing policy issued by the GMC[50] which makes their actions liable and susceptible to disciplinary punishment. As expressed by one interviewee:

> The medical profession as a whole accepts ... accept is the right word? ... I mean ... the reality of the world is that people go to Switzerland ... the reality of the world is that people kill themselves ... the reality of the world is that there is torture and there are terrible things happening ... the question for the medical profession is what is the duty of the doctor toward the patient in front of him. And the medical profession as a majority do not view ending, the deliberate ending of, life earlier than it would have otherwise ended by being licensed to supply lethal drugs as part of their clinical and caring role.

The research reveals the difference between physicians' attitudes towards suicide tourism and that of the public and the way it is portrayed in the media. Policymakers and lawmakers may find it difficult to reconcile these differences:

> Doctors are well aware of the difference between accepting death which is inevitable for everybody and seeking death, but the public probably aren't really because there hasn't been enough debate over the way that clinical decisions happen ... the public tend to think that if death is the outcome then it doesn't matter always ... if the person is already going to die anyway then they think why won't we bring it forward ...

---

[50] General Medical Council, 'Guidance for the Investigation Committee and Case Examiners When Considering Allegations about a Doctor's Involvement in Encouraging or Assisting Suicide' http://www.gmc-uk.org/DC4317_Guidance_for_FTP_decision_makers_on_assisting_suicide_51026940.pdf, accessed on 24 May 2018.

Public coverage of stories of suicide tourism is, according to some interviews, being manipulated by right-to-die organizations to better effectuate their campaigns to change the law. As expressed by an English interviewee:

> A lot of the these people who are going to Dignitas are members of Dignity in Dying here as well ... and Dignity in Dying will say to them: 'well, we can't assist you but, if you are going to Switzerland, we can help you get your story into the media', and so that's what they do, and that will be accompanied by more changes or calls for the law, and often these suicides are very strategically timed in order to maximize their impact ... not only that they use these cases but they actually collaborate even to the extent of the timing of the announcement and the planning of death ... they see that suicide tourism is very powerful because it's all around story, testimony, stories in the media which will change public opinion and then on the back of it you can argue discrimination arguments ... without these cases we wouldn't have seen these laws at all and they wouldn't have had a campaign ... certainly not nearly as effective.

The same theme comes up with French interviewees. According to some interviews, most of the people in France, for example, think that people travel to Switzerland for euthanasia and not for assisted suicide because, as one French interviewee admits, 'media make point, insist about one or two points but they don't explain exactly what is possible or not. There are, of course, films or documentary which are very interesting or present the things as complete as possible but when you look at the TV... you have just a little bit of information... It's not complete. They don't insist present exactly what is possible especially in Switzerland'.

As a result, admits another French interviewee, 'the French do not appreciate that we do abroad what is not allowed in France. In addition, they feel social injustice because only those who can afford it can go to Switzerland or Belgium. But they are tolerant: they do not approve but they understand those who do'.

It also follows from the interviews that media coverage of suicide tourism has made a powerful impression on the public, though less so on policymakers and doctors, as this research shows:

I think there is a degree of suicide contagion, if you like, so that when people see high profile figures going to Dignitas and it's publicized either in drama or in news reporting or in BBC documentaries, it raises the whole profile and creates the impression that this is an acceptable solution to the problem.

A sixth explanation for the relatively minimal role and effect of suicide tourism is that although suicide tourism is an inter-state matter, involving the relationship between countries and residents of different countries, discussions of assisted suicide and end-of-life care usually focus on countries of origin which are also being regarded as holders of responsibility for such cases. As one interviewee commented on the French situation: 'The French debaters sufficiently focussed on what happens *inside* the country and what happened ... all the legal cases in the country were the cases that led to all the legal changes over the year ... All the legal changes that have been done were following a local case'.[51]

If assisted suicide is a local matter then it must be decided according to the norms of the states in question and, as ruled by the European Court of Human Rights in the *Diane Pretty* case, 'it is primarily for States to assess the risk and the likely incidence of abuse if the general prohibition on assisted suicides were relaxed or if exceptions were to be created'.[52] Under this rationale, suicide tourism and its universal effects as such could not prevail over a local consensus prohibiting aid in dying.

Conclusion

This chapter addressed general findings and observations pertaining to the practice of suicide tourism and to its relationship to local laws, discussed the social attitude towards suicide tourism from the perspective of

---

[51] Referring mostly to the case of Vincent Humbert, a paraplegic 22-year-old who died after his mother followed his wish to die and put an overdose of sedatives in his intravenous line, Craig S. Smith, 'Son's Wish to Die, and Mother's Help, Stir French Debate', *New York Times* (27 September 2003) but also to the national committees leading to the law in 2005. Other cases referred to include the case of Chantal Sebiré, a 52-year-old with a facial tumor that left her blind and disfigured. Sebiré asked the court to be allowed to receive aid in dying but was denied. Henry Samuel, 'Disfigured French woman Loses Euthanasia Bid', *The Telegraph* (18 March 2008).

[52] *Pretty v. United Kingdom* (2002) 35 EHRR 1 at para. 74.

participants living in Switzerland, and analysed the effects which suicide tourism might have had on legislation on assisted suicide in countries of origin.

The chapter explored the ambivalent way in which suicide tourism is perceived in the Swiss public sphere. While, in the media, such a practice is mostly portrayed as individual stories attracting empathy and tolerance, it raises strong feelings of uneasiness and discomfort—especially towards the organizations that promote it—among academics, medical doctors, and public officials. These strong feelings, which are exemplified by many citations from interviews with these players in Switzerland, are mostly based on the ease with which these organizations approve requests for assisted suicide by foreigners and the financial incentive they may have in doing so. Such feelings also result in different policies, for example the agreement signed between the prosecutor of Zurich and Exit and the legal attempt to restrict assisted suicide to residents only in that canton, as well as fierce comparisons of those organizations to the Nazis, thereby increasing the overall opposition to assisted suicide in Switzerland.

The chapter revealed that in many countries, including Germany, France, the UK, Italy, and Canada, there have been legal and/or public proceedings discussing end-of-life issues, specifically and most notably assisted suicide. These proceedings were accompanied by media coverage—varied in its extent—of stories of suicide tourism. In some of the cases, for example Canada, suicide tourism was a social practice which the legislator wanted to prevent while legalizing assisted suicide. In others, especially the UK and Germany, suicide tourism was referred to by opponents or supporters of proposed laws to legalize or criminalize assisted suicide.

Yet, despite these proceedings and the many arguments raised by campaigners to change existing prohibitions against assisted suicide in countries of origin, the law in these countries has not changed, and in some cases its position on assisted suicide has become more prohibitive.

In the UK it was mainly used as an argument by supporters of legalization of assisted suicide. The main arguments raised against it concerned its potential to discriminate and hasten death. Reference was made to the need to provide a local solution. These arguments were unsuccessful.

In Germany, suicide tourism was merely used by opponents of as-sisted suicide who supported the new law against such a practice. Suicide tourism triggered the need to stop the overall practice of assisted suicide in the country and the participation of doctors in it. It was also raised to some extent by supporters of such a practice but did not receive much political weight.

Finally, in France, suicide tourism was not referred to in the discus-sions on the new law. The law was dominated by the medical profession who wanted to secure its practice at end of life. It did not reflect choice or autonomy in end-of-life decisions. Hence, suicide tourism did not receive much weight in the political and ethical debates on assisted suicide in France.

Although, as the previous chapter demonstrated, suicide tourism cannot and should not have been prevented, these findings powerfully support Robert Storrow's claim that states may enact more restrictive laws than they would have done because they know that citizens can travel if they wish to opt for the more liberal option.[53]

Finally, the chapter offered possible explanations for these findings, supported by the interviews. These include the relatively little signifi-cance of suicide tourism; a consequential analysis supporting the claim that suicide tourism is more beneficial for countries of origin than le-galization of assisted suicide; the negative consequences implied by su-icide tourism on the practice of assisted suicide; the shift that suicide tourism caused towards a focus more on safeguards, along with the dif-ficulty of providing convincing reassurance that such safeguards could be easily and readily formed; the passive role of physicians participating in suicide tourism and the different attitudes towards assisted suicide and suicide tourism of doctors and the public; and, finally, the local context of suicide tourism.

It is believed that a combination of these explanations calls for concern or some comfort (depending on one's world view) on the positive and normative role that suicide tourism plays and should play in the regula-tion of death and dying in many countries, given its increasing prevalence and publicity.

---

[53] Robert Storrow, 'The Pluralism Problem in Cross-Border Reproductive Care' (2010) 25 *Hum. Reprod.* 2939.

Epilogue

It is now time to conclude the long journey pursued throughout this book. I begin by summarizing the main findings of each of the five chapters and then turn to discuss them more generally.

Major findings

This book looked at suicide tourism from different perspectives. The first chapter analysed legalization on assisted suicide around the globe. It showed assisted suicide is a practice that most physicians oppose, even when legalized. It is legally distinguished from euthanasia, usually attracts more legal recognition than the latter, and always includes safeguards to monitor the practice. These safeguards usually begin with a grave medical condition, suffering, and poor quality of life, and require ensuring the person's capacity and voluntary wish to receive assisted dying. In almost all countries where assisted suicide is legal, the person seeking it must be a resident of that country (several US states and Colombia), must benefit from and contribute to the public health system (Canada), or must hold a continuous relationship with the prescribing doctor (the Netherlands, Belgium, and Luxembourg). These countries make it very difficult for a non-resident to receive assisted dying in their respective territories.

Switzerland is an exception. As discussed in Chapter 1, Swiss law does not restrict access to assisted suicide by any of the above requirements. This is why Switzerland has become the main travel destination for assisted suicide.

Chapter 2 explored further why restrictions on a person's place of residency or the existence of a continuous relationship with the prescribing doctor attract criticism and cannot be justified. It also argued that, from a legal perspective, extraterritorial jurisdiction as to the criminality of assisted suicide and other international 'soft law' regulations

Suicide Tourism. First Edition. Daniel Sperling. © Daniel Sperling 2019. Published 2019 by Oxford University Press.

affecting the enforcement of the prohibition against assisted suicide if received abroad are doomed to fail. Analysis of case law and guidelines concerning the prosecution of accompanying family members and third parties—for example, doctors who provide information to facilitate travel for assisted suicide—reveals that these parties may not be at high risk of prosecution. Furthermore, any limitation of a person's right to travel to another country for assisted suicide prima facie violates the person's constitutional right to free movement and, if made on behalf of an incapacitated person, the guardian's decisional capacity to act in the best interests of that person. The phenomenon of suicide tourism, then, is not illegal in itself and does not allegedly endanger the people who participate in it legally.

Chapter 3 discussed the morality of suicide tourism. It argued that suicide tourism provides individuals with freedom and choice in exercising their right to die and promotes their moral right to free movement. The chapter also made the original argument that suicide tourism is supported by the moral duty to provide humanitarian aid to citizens of less permissive states suffering a social disaster, namely to people who live in countries where assisted suicide is illegal and who suffer from pain and a medical condition which significantly decreases their quality of life. In addition, the major moral arguments against suicide tourism were defeated. The chapter showed that not only did the consequential considerations against suicide tourism not prove true but, in some respects, reality showed the opposite. It contended that objecting to suicide tourism by reference to the immorality and irrationality of suicide is unsuccessful, especially in a morally pluralistic society and given the complexity and emotional burdens associated with the decision to commit suicide. It further showed that the moral argument against suicide tourism based on Kant's conception of the human body cannot serve as an objection when the body itself does not contribute in any way to one's preservation and realization of humanity. So, too, for the argument about the nature of dying; at most, it offered a new perspective on death and dying of which suicide tourism forms a part. This chapter concluded that there are good reasons to morally justify and protect a prima facie position in favour of suicide tourism.

Moving to the political level, Chapter 4 discussed the governability of death and its application to suicide tourism. Referring to the writings of

Foucault and Agamben, the chapter explored how suicide tourism reflects the way the state and states together exercise their dominion and control, especially in areas where they matter most: issues of life and death. It next argued that people who travel to another country for assisted suicide do not challenge state sovereignty or the collective will of their home country. It further demonstrated that the application of Rawls's theory of justice and Nagel's theory of minimal humanitarian morality to suicide tourism delivers a weak defence of a country's legal right to object to and forbid suicide tourism. The chapter concluded that countries of origin should avoid interfering in suicide tourism to respect human dignity and to promote plural sovereignty.

Chapter 5 discussed major findings by examining interviews with policymakers, social activists, academics, and other key players in the field of assisted suicide, which were conducted in France, Germany, Italy, Switzerland, and the UK between 2015 and 2017. The chapter describes the recent legal proceedings on assisted dying and end-of-life care in many of the countries from which people travel for assisted suicide, especially Germany, France, and the UK. It is evident that suicide tourism informed many of these proceedings, especially the creation of new laws on assisted suicide and/or end-of-life care. However, these proceedings tended to refer to suicide tourism inconsistently. In some countries, especially the UK, reference to suicide tourism was mostly made by those who sought the legalization of assisted suicide, criticizing the disadvantages of the current situation that involves the need to travel to another country to seek aid in dying. However, in other countries, those who objected to the practice of assisted suicide with the aim of criminalizing it (in Germany, for example) or allowing a different practice (such as palliative sedation in France) referred to suicide tourism as support for their argument.

Another empirical observation concerned the Swiss reaction to suicide tourism. This was of special interest since Switzerland is the only country in the world to respond institutionally to suicide tourism. The findings came from interviews with key players in Switzerland and found that, among academics, medical doctors, and public officials, suicide tourism raises strong feelings of uneasiness and discomfort, especially towards the organizations that facilitate it (Dignitas and Lifecircle). These attitudes come from the leniency with which these organizations approve requests for assisted suicide by foreigners, and the financial incentives associated with this. The different social attitudes to these organizations, as opposed to other right-to-die organizations offering aid in dying to Swiss residents in particular, most notably Exit, also results in attempts to create different policies.

A third important finding in the chapter relates to the limited role suicide tourism played in legal proceedings. Analysis of the efforts to change existing laws in the UK, France, and Germany reveals that despite these efforts and the many arguments raised by campaigners to change the current prohibition against assisted suicide in countries of origin, the law in these countries has not changed (for example, in the UK), and in some cases its position on assisted suicide became more prohibitive (most notably in Germany). A prevalent theme of the interviews sees suicide tourism as a 'safety valve' that on the one hand provides some sort of a solution to those few who seek assisted suicide, yet on the other hand perpetuates the existing prohibition on assisted suicide. The chapter offered six different groups of explanations for this finding, supported by the many interviews performed in these countries.

Discussion

The major findings above raise the following question: given its increasing prevalence and publicity, why is the practice of suicide tourism (and the organizations that institutionally support it) under-evaluated or socially ignored inside Switzerland and why is it regarded mainly as a 'safety valve' outside Switzerland (or within countries from which most people travel for assisted suicide)? This question is especially troubling given that suicide tourism is only available for those who are well informed about alternatives at the end of life, are physically able to travel, and, of course, have the financial means as well as the emotional strength to pursue such a journey. On the face of it, this question presents a puzzle. Allowing suicide tourism—which, as has been shown, is not an illegal practice and can be supported by moral arguments with minimal or no intervention—should have resulted in more support for the practice and in its receiving more weight in the consideration of new laws on assisted suicide in home countries. Why, then, does this research point the other way?

One possibility is that, as suicide tourism has become more popular and freely discussed in the media and in public policy circles, the coverage is not always presented in a positive light. Since such a practice is being exposed selectively, reference is made to two categories of cases. The first involves 'celebrities' or public figures, such as a famous 104-year-old scientist, a leading conductor, a renowned journalist, and a well-known rugby player. Reports on these people's journeys convey a perception that suicide tourism is something that they (and only they) can afford and that, in a way, it is all about a luxurious death—surely a concept of death inaccessible for most. Portrayed in this way, this message—when made constantly and steadily—creates a feeling of injustice and unfairness on the one hand and the conceptualization of commercialized death and medicine on the other.

The second category of cases includes unfamiliar 'ordinary' people who suffer from grave illnesses or experience exceptional states of affairs (such as being of a young age, having mild or serious psychiatric disorders, or suffering from a merely chronic disease or from multi-morbidity in old age). While in stories from the first category individuals are at the centre of discussion and death is only another 'service' or commodity they can 'buy' for themselves, in stories from the second category the focus is on death itself. In these cases, suicide tourism brings an end to the suffering or poor quality of life of these people. Suicide tourism is the means by which that most highly sought after end—death—is and can be achieved. As such, at the crux of suicide tourism is the strong desire to be extinguished. The condition described is so bad or the circumstances of the person seeking assisted suicide are so controversial that suicide tourism is associated with duress and exploitation (in the first case) or with nonexistent or weak safeguards to protect the person (in the second).

It follows that while suicide tourism enjoys increasing publicity and is present in public discourse and policy-making in many Western countries these days, reference to it damages its reputation and underlines a strong message that it is an unjust, expensive, eccentric practice that has the potential for much exploitation with minimal safeguards to protect the most vulnerable people in society, especially at times and in situations when they need such protection to the full.

There are strong arguments to justify suicide tourism morally; the challenge raised by this book is to address the political practices needed to support it institutionally. Chapter 4 argued that the call for state intervention in suicide tourism is difficult to justify from a political-philosophical perspective. But this conclusion is insufficient. A more immediate argument, raised in Chapter 5 and based on empirical findings from countries from which most people travel to Switzerland for assisted suicide, held that while political systems in these countries referred to suicide tourism (mainly in respect of its disadvantages for people who seek assisted suicide but also for society more generally) this has not resulted in the legalization of assisted suicide in these political systems. Rather, these references have worsened access to assisted suicide and to suicide tourism by, for example, introducing criminal risks and practical hurdles to supporting these requests, especially for medical experts.

In order to address this question, I would like to refer to Levinas' concept of the face and the Third and to his discussion on the relationship between ethics and politics. For Levinas, the face is the point that both symbolizes our meeting with the Other and determines our relation to her. But the relation with the Other is a non-totalizing relation, namely it does not involve ownership of the Other by, for example, thinking about, noticing, or seeing her. What allows for the social relationship with the Other is exactly that which cannot be reduced to perception.[1] Moreover, encountering the face represents the uncensored and 'nude' realization and recognition of mortality and vulnerability of the Other as well as a call from the Other to take responsibility for the Other, to respect and protect her, to be attentive to her call. The face-to-face relation entails infinite and immediate responsibility for the Other.

Yet, to address our responsibility to the Other—or as a way to complement it, under some interpretations—Levinas introduces the concept of the Third.[2] This concept is a representation of justice and politics that, under some readings of Levinas, does not constrain or otherwise interrupt one's ethical responsibility to the Other but is present in it. It is because of the effect of the one-to-one relation and responsibility to the Other on other Others, and the compromise of one's responsibility to the other Others deriving from her absolute responsibility to the first person,

---

[1] Emmanuel Levinas, *Totality and Infinity: An Essay on Exteriority* [1961] (Trans.: A. Lingis) (Duquesne University Press, 2005) p. 297.

[2] Madeleine Fagan, 'The Inseparability of Ethics and Politics: Rethinking the Third in Emmanuel Levinas' (2009) 8(1) *Contemporary Political Theory* 5.

that the Third is imbedded in the relationship to the Other. The Third does not limit one's responsibility to the Other, since such responsibility is infinite, but places more demands on her. Specifically, it makes her consider and negotiate between the Other and the Third, the latter of which represents one's duties to many Others. It holds an additional responsibility upon the moral agent to weigh, calculate, and choose between Others. It thus calls for some institutionalization of ethical guidelines and the making of political institutions and processes by which one is able to compete, mediate, and organize claims of the Other and the Third.[3]

The concept of the Third helps us understand that because there is always more than one Other, taking up responsibility towards one Other necessarily disregards one's duties towards the other Others and more generally to the rules and norms and the political institutions which are meant to adjudicate and balance between competing duties.

But here comes an important element in Levinas' work. Levinas does not require a *specific* response to the call of that which the Other is making upon us (represented by the idea of the face). The realization of our responsibility to the Other (in terms of obligation as opposed to responsible response) is dependent upon and conditioned by the Third and the contents that it represents.

Applying these notions to suicide tourism may be helpful to handle the challenges raised in this book. Individual cases of suicide tourism that include stories of people who travel to another country to seek assisted suicide out of despair, misery, suffering, and poor quality of life call upon us to acknowledge their vulnerability and wish to die. Moreover, they call for a responsible reaction to their state of affairs and for their decision to leave their country and die abroad. When taking up our responsibility towards these individuals we are confronted with our responsibility and obligations as set in our local laws and political institutions. When these include a legal prohibition on assisted suicide or a professional and ethical opinion opposing the collaboration of medical doctors in the practice (as is mostly evident in countries of origin), we are confronted with a dilemma: should we take up our responsibility to these individuals *qua* individuals and be attentive to their suffering and to the expression of their autonomy and let them die while also receiving aid from their families,

---

[3] Ibid. at 11.

friends, and practitioners who are subject to these laws and professional opinions, or should we enforce the law and interfere?

Although from an international law perspective there would be no strong justification for doing so, we are not obliged to refrain from prosecuting and enforcing our criminal laws and guidelines with regard to these people who allegedly violate accepted norms. We are not obliged to ignore our own norms which reflect society's preferences and moral values.

However, it will be argued that, under Levinas, responding responsively to these cases should entail an obligation always to reflect upon our laws and political institutions and reconsider them so that a new balance between competing values could be realized. Our responsibility to these individuals should make us aware and be alert to their cases. It should put us under a constant obligation to substantially refer to these cases and to this practice more generally so that it could have *some* (albeit not a particular) effect on our reconsideration of existing laws and institutions. The more ethical and social challenges the practice raises, the weightier our responsibility to these individuals will be, and the graver our obligation to refer to the practice in our continuous efforts to re-examine existing laws and policies.

The rise in ideas of death with dignity, choice in dying, and choice to die, as well as the proliferation of right-to-die organizations, was a response to concerns that medical technology and medical science more generally were being used inappropriately to prolong life at the cost of its quality.[4] As recent interviews with people who were actively planning to go to Switzerland for assisted suicide show, aid in dying in Switzerland is being portrayed as an idealized and aesthetic death: guaranteed, painless, giving the appearance of going to sleep, natural.[5]

Yet, this research shows that suicide tourism makes right-to-die organizations in Switzerland take on complex responsibilities and act in ways that may hurt this image. Paradoxically, these organizations declare

[4] Fran McInerney, ' "Requested Death": A New Social Movement' (2000) 50(1) *Social Science & Medicine* 137; Daniel Hillyard and John Dombrink, *Dying Right: The Death with Dignity Movement* (Routledge, 2001).

[5] Naomi Richards, 'Assisted Suicide as a Remedy for Suffering? The End-of-Life Preferences of British "Suicide Tourists" ' (2017) 36(4) *Medical Anthropology* 348.

that they advocate, educate on, and support suicide attempt prevention[6] or are committed to suicide prevention,[7] but on the other hand arrange accompanied deaths for considerable amounts of money and, as some interviews and media reports reveal, with few safeguards. Moreover, the association between money and one's universal (human) right to die with dignity is unclear, unconvincing, and, as this research shows, raises many concerns about the activities of these organizations. These activities, and especially the way in which they take place, are referred to by opponents of legalization of assisted suicide in countries of origin and are heavily criticized within Switzerland. If right-to-die organizations truly care for the 'dignity of mankind' and for people's rights of self-determination and decision-making at the end of life and if they are really committed to promoting legalization of assisted suicide worldwide, then they should also re-examine their actions and institutions. Under Levinas, they too are responsible for the individuals whom they serve; they are also accountable to Swiss society, and—as part of their global mission—to the international community more generally. Taking up this responsibility entails an obligation to look again, more carefully, at their activities.

Analysing cases of suicide tourism also raised some questions as to the relationship between palliative care and assisted suicide.[8] To some surprise, this research reveals that even though palliative care is well developed in some countries, especially the UK, people still seek assisted suicide in another country where it is legal and feasible. While a few interviewees make an argument that investing more resources in palliative care and shifting attention to such care may decrease suicide tourism, most interviewees impress that these are two separate end-of-life needs rather than equal alternatives. What is missing here is the voice and involvement of the palliative care providers: a more active role played by this community would help to change social perceptions on palliative care, thereby redefining end-of-life needs in a way in which palliative care could be sufficient.

---

[6] Dignitas, 'To Live with Dignity, To Die with Dignity' http://www.dignitas.ch/?lang=en, accessed on 15 June 2018.

[7] Lifecircle, 'The Association Lifecircle: Support and Promote Quality of Life' https://www.lifecircle.ch/?l=en, accessed on 15 June 2018.

[8] See for example Raphael Cohen-Almagor, 'Dutch Perspectives on Palliative Care in the Netherlands' (2002–3) 18(2) *Issues in L. & Med.* 111.

Finally, this book explores the fact that, contrary to conventional wisdom (as expressed in the interviews), people do not necessarily want to die in their home country surrounded by their loved ones if they cannot die with dignity in line with their personal wishes. It may even be easier for them to finalize their decision to kill themselves when this is done abroad, in an impersonal and bureaucratic way. Suicide tourism reflects more of what we already know: people want to be more involved in the process of their dying. They want to have a say on the means, place, timing, and circumstances of their death. Death is a personal, subjective matter. It is regarded as apolitical, not aimed at changing the law or making legal battles. Most of the cases represented by suicide tourism reflect private interactions. These are people who do not necessarily want to die as heroes, although they are sometimes perceived as extremely courageous and worthy of appreciation. They are the objects and the subjects of this book, and it is for them and for the just legal and political institutions that will follow from their cases that this book has been written.

List of Interviewees

Dr Christian Arnold, former medical practitioner (Urology), Germany.

Dr Regis Aubry, Médecin des Hôpitaux—Professeur Associé des Universités—HDR and member of the National Committee on Ethics, France.

Dr Pierre Beck, Exit ADMD, Switzerland.

Prof. Dr Dieter Birenbacher, President, the German Society for Human Dying (DGHS), Germany.

Mr Paul Bowen QC, Brick Court Chambers, UK.

Mr Andreas Brunner, Chief Prosecutor, canton of Zurich, Switzerland.

Baroness Jane Campbell, House of Lords, UK.

Mr Marco Cappato, treasurer of Associazione Luca Coscioni, Italy.

Dr Dolores Angela Castelli Dransart, Faculty of Social Work, University of Applied Sciences and Arts of Western Switzerland.

Prof. Thierry Collaud, Department of Moral Theology and Ethics, University of Fribourg, Switzerland.

Dr Emilio Coveri, President, Exit-Italia, Italy.

Prof. Baroness Finlay of Llandaff, House of Lords, UK.

Prof. Gherard Fiolka, Faculty of Law, University of Fribourg, Switzerland.

Prof. Dr Christopher Geth, Faculty of Law, University of Bern, Switzerland.

Prof. Dr Olivier Guillod, Faculty of Law, University of Neuchatel, Switzerland.

Ms Davina Hehir, Director of Policy and Legal Strategy, Dignity in Dying, UK.

Dr Ruth Horn, Ethox Centre, Department of Population Health, University of Oxford, UK.

Prof. Samia Hurst, Institute of Ethics, History, and Humanities, University of Geneva, Switzerland.

Dr Vincent Indirli, palliative doctor, Centre Hospitalier Annecy Genevois, France.

Dr Michael Irwin, former President of the World Federation of Right-to-Die Societies, founder of the Society for Old Age Rational Suicide, UK.

Prof. David A. Jones, Director, The Anscombe Bioethics Centre, Oxford, UK.

Prof. Dr Regina Kiener, Faculty of Law, University of Zurich, Switzerland.

Dr Mélanie Levy, Faculty of Law, University of Neuchatel, Switzerland and Edmond J. Safra Center for Ethics, Tel Aviv University, Israel.

Ms Pia Locatelli, Member of Parliament, The Socialist Party, Italy.

Mr Silvan Luley, Dignitas, Switzerland.

Prof. Dr Mona Martino, Faculty of Law, University of Bern, Switzerland.

Justice Eliyahu Matza, retired Supreme Court Justice and President, LILACH: the Israel society for the right to live and die with dignity, Israel.

Prof. Alex Mauron, Institute of Ethics, History, and Humanities, University of Geneva, Switzerland.

Dr Julian Mausbach, Faculty of Law, University of Zurich, Switzerland.

Prof. Dr Reinhard Merkel, Faculty of Law, University of Hamburg, Germany.

Prof. Maurizio Mori, Professor of Moral Philosophy and Bioethics, University of Turin and President, Consulta di Bioetica Onlus, Italy.

Prof. Baroness Onora O'Neill, House of Lords and Cambridge University, UK.

Ms Erika Preisig, President, Lifecircle, Switzerland.

Mr Robert Preston, House of Commons, UK.

Dr Kasper Raus, University of Gent, Belgium.

Dr Mario Riccio, physician, Italy.

Mr Yves Rossier, Secretary of State, Federal Department of Foreign Affairs, Switzerland (currently Ambassador of Switzerland to Russia).

Dr Peter Saunders, Campaign Director, Care Not Killing Alliance, UK.

Mr Bernardo Stadelmann, Vice Director, Federal Office of Justice, Switzerland.

Dr Anthony Stavrianakis, Centre National de la Recherche Scientifique, France.

Mr Bernhard Sutter, Exit DS, Switzerland.

Prof. Didier Truchet, Professor Emeritus of Public Health and Communication Law, University Panthéon-Assas (Paris II), Honorary President of the French Association of Health Law, and former member of the National Committee on Ethics, France.

Prof. Dr Urban Wiesing, Institute of Ethics and History of Medicine, University Hospital Tübingen, Germany.

Dr Herbert Winter, President, Jewish Federation, Switzerland.

Prof. Markus Zimmermann, Department of Moral Theology and Ethics, University of Fribourg, Switzerland.

Index

Note: *For the benefit of digital users, indexed terms that span two pages (e.g., 52–53) may, on occasion, appear on only one of those pages.*